The Percussionist's Art

Photograph of the author by Kevin Wilkes, 1996.

The Percussionist's Art
Same Bed, Different Dreams

Steven Schick

Foreword by Paul Griffiths

 University of Rochester Press

The publication of this volume was made possible, in part, through support from the Howard Hanson Institute for American Music at the Eastman School of Music of the University of Rochester.

First published 2006

University of Rochester Press
668 Mt. Hope Avenue, Rochester, NY 14620, USA
www.urpress.com
and Boydell & Brewer Limited
PO Box 9, Woodbridge, Suffolk IP12 3DF, UK
www.boydellandbrewer.com

ISBN: 1–58046–214–6

Library of Congress Cataloging-in-Publication Data

Schick, Steven.
 The percussionists art : same bed, different dreams / Steven Schick ;
foreword by Paul Griffiths.
     p. cm.
 Includes bibliographical references and index.
 ISBN 1-58046-214-6 (hardcover : alk. paper)
 1. Percussion music–Analysis, appreciation. 2. Percussion
instruments–Performance. I. Title.
 MT90.S286 2006
 786.8–dc22

                              2005034680

A catalogue record for this title is available from the British Library.

This publication is printed on acid-free paper.
Printed in the United States of America.

To
Maya, Rami, Dorian, and Aurielle

Contents

Figures

Compact Disc Contents

Steven Schick performing:

Track

1   Charles Wuorinen, *Janissary Music*, Part 1
     Unreleased private recording

2   David Lang, *The Anvil Chorus*
     From Bang on a Can, *Industry*, Originally released by SONY: SONY Classical SK66483.
     Rights currently held by Cantaloupe Music. Used by permission of Cantaloupe Music

3   Edgard Varèse, *Ionisation*
     Unreleased recording of a live performance by the percussion group "red fish blue fish,"
     at the University of California, San Diego, on May 18, 2005

4   Michael Gordon, *XY*
     Unreleased private recording. Reproduced by permission of the composer

5   John Luther Adams, "Wail" from *The Mathematics of Resonant Bodies*
     To be released in 2006 by Cantaloupe Music. Used by permission of Cantaloupe Music

6   Brian Ferneyhough, *Bone Alphabet*
     From the recording *Drumming in the Dark*, Neuma Records 450-100.
     Reproduced by permission

Foreword

His entire body seems to be gearing up to the actions the music demands, or relaxing after them. . . .

In Stockhausen's *Zyklus*, his marimba glissandos turned wood into water, and his volleys on unpitched instruments had fizz, crackle and shape. . . .

In Aperghis's *Le Corps à corps* hands at a drum suggested the noises of an unknown language. . . .

Feldman's *King of Denmark* he played like a cat, and its last sounds—a chord performed with fingers on the vibraphone and a soft stroke on an antique cymbal—were breathtaking.

—*New York Times*, November 6, 1998

Anyone who has seen Steven Schick perform, or even heard him on record, will have such indelible memories—memories of, to quote further from the same review, this extraordinary musician's "alacrity, intensity and grace."

Readers will find those qualities here. Schick writes as he plays: with spontaneity (the fruit of experience, care and preparation), fully and persuasively. He makes us listen.

His domain is fresh: percussion music. The most venerable work he considers has yet to reach its half-century. Virtuoso percussionists, such as he is, are new arrivals on the western scene.

At the same time, his is a very ancient world. People must have been drumming to each other, and to their gods, a thousand generations ago, when our species was young.

With this deep underpinning, Schick's repertory connects with the music of Asian, African and Latin American traditions; it connects also with jazz and rock.

Percussionists will be unable to ignore this book. But Schick has much to say also to performers of all kinds, and to anyone curious about the art of performance, or about what makes the music of our time—music rooted in pulse, gesture, action—tick.

Paul Griffiths

Preface

The Percussionist's Art: Same Bed, Different Dreams is a book about solo percussion music. Not long ago the very notion of a percussion soloist would have seemed ludicrous. Imagine a soloist taking the stage. However, instead of tuning a Stradivarius or dusting off the keyboard of a Steinway, a percussionist takes a bow and sits amid a junk heap of instruments often bought (or found) at auto salvage yards, kitchen supply and hardware stores, garden shops, and (a few) specialty percussion stores. A classical soloist performing with brake drums, mixing bowls, gongs, cymbals, xylophones, and flowerpots? Really? They write music for that?

Yes, Virginia, there is a repertoire for solo percussion. It is a growing and vital part of the larger percussion world. But solo music is only a small part of that large world. Therefore it is with some remorse that I concede here the absence of a lot of wonderful music: the vast world of percussion traditions from scores of musical cultures lies outside of the scope of this volume. Likewise I was not able to treat the vital and growing art of percussion improvisers, instrument builders, and technology-based musical practices. There will be readers who note with regret the omission of wonderful percussion parts by Mahler or Debussy or great percussion ensemble music by Harrison and Barraqué. Others will notice that there are no analyses of solos by Elvin Jones or Zakir Hussain. I myself wish I could have found the right spot to discuss the luminous music of Harry Partch. I can only say to those who note these gaps that you are right. In some cases because of the constraints of focus and space, and in other cases, frankly, because I understand my own limitations as a music historian and scholar, this book views the teeming world of percussion music through the narrow frame of contemporary solo playing.

In spite of these constraints, however, there are many avenues of access to solo percussion playing. *The Percussionist's Art: Same Bed, Different Dreams* consists of distinctly different parts with potentially distinct uses for a reader. Although it certainly not my intention to predetermine how a given reader will engage this book, I think some clarification of my intent may help a reader find passages that may be especially relevant to his or her interests.

The first two chapters, "Because the World Is Round" and "Loud Americans: American Percussion Music under Construction," constitute a rough history of percussion music in the nineteenth and twentieth centuries. I call it a rough history, because it was never my intention for these chapters to be catholic. Far from an all-inclusive historical survey of percussion music and ideas, the path through percussion history sketched in these chapters is a particular and personally relevant one. In this regard I am most interested in music that I feel created the basis for the development of solo percussion music in the mid- and late twentieth century. However, as piecemeal as my historical sense may be, I hope that these opening chapters will be valuable to a percussionist who seeks to frame contemporary solo percussion music in an evolving historical context, and to nonmusicians who have never thought much about how a rowdy gang of noise-making percussionists ever got through an artists' entrance to a concert hall.

The four chapters that follow—including a study of Brian Ferneyhough's *Bone Alphabet* ("Learning *Bone Alphabet*"), a look at the importance of memory in percussion performance ("The Affliction of Memory"), a view of the palpable role of gesture and theatricality in percussion music ("Face the Music: A Look at Percussion Playing"), and an examination of the fluid evolution of sonic material in percussion music ("This Is Not a Drum: Manipulating the Material of Percussion Music")—are not organized on a historical model. While I hope that each chapter succeeds in positing a consequential argument based on my understanding of particular issues and pieces, and might therefore be read from front to back as a narrative, I also hope that this series of chapters might also be used like a reference book. Discussion of individual pieces or sets of ideas are articulated by subchapter headings so that a reader will feel invited to pick and choose among topics if that suits the purpose at hand.

A final chapter, "Same Bed, Different Dreams: A Personal Epilogue," needs no clarification beyond the fact that music has often been the sharpest tool at my disposal to puncture the shallow habits of life and thereby to try to reach levels of greater intellectual and spiritual awareness. My thoughts on Steve Reich's masterpiece *Drumming* are therefore intended less in the manner of an analytical treatment and more as an allegorical representation of how I use the music I play to better understand the life I live.

I engaged in considerable internal debate about whether or not to include concrete performance advice including instrumental set-ups, mallet choices, and other issues of practical consequence. Friends and professional colleagues argued strongly for me to do so, and the conversations and correspondence I generally have with young percussionists are largely related to these important questions. This latter aspect was very persuasive to me, since offering some illumination about the percussion music that I love to young percussionists who are beginning their careers as performers or teachers was the overriding reason for writing this book in the first place. However, I have decided to minimize the "how-to" component of the book and deal in practical specifics only when they were the most sensible way to illustrate the world of ideas or emotions at the heart of a piece of music.

The dangers of offering a "User's Guide to Contemporary Solo Percussion Music" are clear. I am writing these paragraphs in early 2006, and any practical suggestions I may make to percussionists now will necessarily be based on the instruments, mallets, and types of heads, racks, and stands that are available today. This, of course, leaves untouched the much more volatile world of music technology and what it may or may not have to offer to us in the future. We smile at quaint, historically outdated performance indications such as Stravinsky's demand for a "cane-headed mallet" in *L'Histoire du Soldat*, for example, or Bartók's well-meaning advice that the pianists in his *Sonata for Two Pianos and Percussion* watch the percussionists carefully to be sure that they scrupulously follow the indications of the score. These are just two examples of the short shelf life of practical performance suggestions.

There a more ominous danger present in the rush to establish standardized performance approaches to major solo pieces. The very beauty of *Zyklus*, *Psappha*, and *The King of Denmark* is that they are not in fact fixed as unalterable performance practice. Any percussionist who learns this great music is invited to reinvent performance practice to suit the intellectual, emotional, and technical demands of his or her point of view. These demands reflect themselves in practical terms as questions about set-up mallet choice and sticking. I resist answering flat-footed practical questions when my students pose them, instead preferring to refer them to the scores and their own imperatives in interpretation. In the same vein I will resist offering answers that accelerate the rate at which the freely traded ideas of our newest music become the indelible traits of established musical practice. Instead, I extend the hope that these pages may help sharpen important questions for anyone who wishes to know this music.

So whether you are reading this as a percussion performer, a composer, a person with a more general interest in the arts, or someone who accidentally picked this book up thinking it is really about beds, I wish you well. And I wish us all a future that is rich with music.

Steven Schick
La Jolla
January 2006

Acknowledgments

As with any undertaking of this size and scope, there are many people to thank. I would like to start with Wendy Labinger, with whom I shared twenty-five years of life and who saw the birth of most of the ideas and pieces represented here. Her affirming presence in my life marks every page of this book. I would like to thank three valued friends and colleagues whose informed reading and constructive criticism of my manuscript proved to be invaluable. To Paul Griffiths, Roger Reynolds, and John Luther Adams, thank you for your intelligence and insight, but beyond that for your love of music, dedication to art, and generosity of spirit. Thanks also to Dixie Salazar, who read an early version of the first two chapters and, in what must have seemed like a long shot to her, urged me to continue. I am deeply grateful to my musical partners over the years: to Maya Beiser, James Avery, the percussion group "red fish blue fish," the musicians of the Centre International de Percussion de Genève, and the Bang on a Can All-Stars. It is no exaggeration to say that I learned how to play and think by making music with you. No words here can repay that. Many thanks to several generations of students—performers, composers, and scholars alike—at the University of California, San Diego; at California State University, Fresno; and at the Manhattan School of Music. Working with you, I have felt prodded and challenged as well as loved and supported. Thanks also to my colleagues at UCSD and many professional friends in the percussion world for your help, friendship, and, at times, forbearance. I am grateful for the support and guidance I received from Suzanne Guiod, Ralph Locke, and Louise Goldberg at the University of Rochester Press. To two great teachers—Thomas L. Davis of the University of Iowa and Bernhard Wulff of the Staatliche Hochschule für Musik in Freiburg, Germany—I continue to chip away at my immense debt to you by playing as well and thinking as clearly as I can. I will never break even. And on a personal note, to my family—Ed, Sarah, Dan, and Mary—as well as to Maya, Rami, Dorian, and Aurielle—for making me a part of their family. To Anna Fienberg for our long friendship and for urging me to write. To Brenda Brown for showing me new ways to look at and listen to the world. And finally to Wendy Sutter, whose friendship, warmth, and support were very important to me as I wrote this book. I thank you all from the bottom of my heart.

For permission to reprint materials in the music examples, I would like to thank the following: John Luther Adams; BMG Music Publishing NA; Carl Fischer, Inc., New York; Kirk Gaburo; Henmar Press; Hinrichsen Edition; Ione Press, a division of ECS Publishing, Boston; Hendon Music, Inc., a Boosey & Hawkes company; Henry Litolff's Verlag, Frankfurt; Merion Music; C. F. Peters, New York; Peters Edition Limited, London; Red Poppy; Frederic Rzewski; G. Schirmer, Inc.; Sonic Arts Editions and Smith Publications, 2617 Gwyndale Ave., Baltimore, MD 21207; Taiga Press; Universal Edition Ltd., London; Universal Edition A.G., Vienna; James Wood. Should any acknowledgments have been inadvertently omitted, we will be glad to include them in any future edition.

For permission to use the recordings on the compact disc, I would like to thank the following: Cantaloupe Music, Michael Gordon, Mode Records, and Neuma Records.

Because the World Is Round

". . . it turns me on"

—The Beatles, *Abbey Road*

In 1939 when John Cage formulated his famous dictum, "percussion music is revolution," I doubt he had my mother in mind.

Cage's ragtag percussion revolution punctuated the end of a decade of volatile change in contemporary music. Classical composers who had once written string quartets and piano sonatas now marched under the banner of brake drums, pod rattles, conch shells, and tin cans. Cage himself had been educated in the European tradition of Arnold Schoenberg, yet he looked at the effete complacency of European classical music and in his famously soft-spoken manner simply pronounced, "off with their heads." Of course Cage wasn't the first American musician to fall in love with percussion music. Beating him to the punch by decades, African American musicians had already upended popular music. The sedate, oleaginous *clip-clop* of high society dance music got its comeuppance under a brutal tattooing of noise and rhythm, the famous one-two punch of all great jazz drummers from Baby Dodds to Elvin Jones. The percussion revolution bridged style and ideology, class and race—as good revolutions will—and steamed noisily ahead.

Percussion music as we know it today is truly a child of the twentieth century. It took flight in a culture where velocity and cacophony were mirrored in a music founded upon striking and friction. But the twentieth century did not invent percussion. Percussion playing was alive and well at the time of Haydn and Mozart and indeed well before that. What separates that music from today's percussion music is not the amount of noise it made, but how that noise was used. In the orchestra for example, early percussion usage often simply meant doubling the bass instruments, and as such reinforcing their large-scale timekeeping functions of formal and harmonic demarcation. Since percussion music borrowed its utility from other instruments, its evolution was firmly tied to those instruments. Changes occurred, as we would then expect, gradually and intermittently, following the rough outlines of change within a global compositional vocabulary. As sonic tastes and compositional orientation among eighteenth- and nineteenth-century composers became incrementally more adventurous, so did the uses they found for percussion instruments. It was in music by composers like Beethoven and Berlioz that percussion music began its shift from evocative to provocative. This new and unfamiliar family of instruments, which had so often borrowed meaning from others, was beginning to earn its own place in a broader musical syntax. Change was still slow and subtle, but it was real. The percussionist's job description was changing. No longer shackled to the basic role of timekeeping, by the late nineteenth century percussionists had become sound effects artists often spinning out kaleidoscopic collages of unheard-of colors and textures. Composers were finding increasingly that percussion instruments were the musical and expressive equals of other instruments in the orchestra. Finally, after more than a hundred years of development, percussionists were standing near the front of the line for acknowledgement and respectability. Then Cage, Edgard Varèse, and Henry Cowell came along with their revolution and greeted this newfound respectability with a brick to the head. Color and texture became noise and rhythm.

Noise and Rhythm. Everywhere you looked in the early twentieth-century percussion music was erupting with noise and rhythm. Out from the back of the orchestra and down from the top risers of the dance band, noisy percussion elbowed its way into polite company. A gauntlet of cymbals, anvils, and cranked sirens in Varèse's electrifying *Ionisation* (1931)—composed for thirteen percussionists—pummeled audiences accustomed to the hushed and reassuring conventions of the concert hall. Or, if that weren't bad enough, listeners could wait until 1939 for the polyrhythmic discord of water gongs, oxen bells, and scraped piano strings in Cage's own *First Construction (in Metal)*.

Noise and Rhythm. The new percussion music was shocking. It rocked with the volcanic beginnings of a new experimentalism where the ear-splitting noises of an industrial age were fused in a New World crucible of dynamic optimism with the rhythms of Africa, Latin America, and Asia. This music reflected the noises of its day, but it also pointed ahead. Early works for percussion ensembles were much more than just music; they were also social phenomena rising from a growing fluidity of cultural boundaries and new models of immigration in the New World. Early experimental percussion music was already on top of much of our new-millennium *mishegas*. Cage and his fellow revolutionaries were voicing concerns that we think of today as globalism, futurism, and individualism in the guise of polycultural noise constructions as early as the 1930s.

Noise and rhythm. The intellectual gyroscope of the percussion revolutionaries pointed towards the clamor of early twentieth-century America under construction and the noisy "impoverished" sounds (to use Cage's word) of percussion that seemed to imitate it. The new was noisy, and percussion music was new. It was not the tired agent of European romanticism, nor was it an aging denizen of the *salon*. It was certainly not a bloodless artifact of the sacred European social order. Percussion music *was* impoverished of calcified and genteel traditions, of convention and cliché. Freed from the weight of all that history, the percussionist revolutionaries were busily scrubbing away the stain of the nineteenth century and starting afresh with vital and unpolluted sounds.

My mother enters the picture in 1962. On a form sent home with prospective music students at Wilson Elementary School in Mason City, Iowa, parents were asked to put a check beside the instrument their son or daughter wished to play. The instruments I found most interesting came toward the top of the list—the violin, trumpet, and French horn. (I remember the "French" part seeming particularly exotic in the context of northern Iowa.) At the very bottom of the page were "drums," with the notation that parents did not have to buy an actual drum, just the sticks. My mother was a frugal Iowa farm wife, and she thought of my four younger brothers and sisters and their future braces, ballet slippers, and ice skates. With the family finances in mind, she acted decisively. No instrument, just sticks: it would be drums for me. My mother, like John Cage, admired percussion for what it was *not*.

In fact, many people continue to think of percussion as what it is *not*. To many people, percussion is *not* capable of the melodic finesse of most other western instruments. Percussion is also not emblematic of most people's view of culture and art. To this day many music lovers are surprised that a sophisticated solo repertoire might be developed for an instrument known mostly for its noises and sound effects. And by choosing "no instrument, just sticks" my mother put her finger on the central tenet of Cage's polyglot percussion revolution: percussion is not even an instrument. It is not a single instrument anyway. The percussion family consists of thousands of instruments coming from dozens of world cultures. And, having a thousand instruments is very much like having no instrument at all. There is not *an* instrument that defines percussion playing in the same way that the piano, for example—the singular physical object of the piano, ubiquitous and universal—defines piano playing. A pianist never wonders what the piano *is*. Pianists look to the piano as the source of their identity. With its immediately recognizable shape, its standard configuration of keys, its dramatic profile on stage, the piano is *the* physical object of importance to a pianist. The instrument itself serves as a physical connection to its performance practice and as a link to a musical past shared by all of its practitioners. The piano as object is singular and totemic. It is the footprint of Chopin and Monk. It is what pianists put on their coffee cups. But what about the percussionists? Which of the thousands of instruments, from *anklung* (an Indonesian instrument consisting of tuned bamboo pieces mounted in a rack that allows them to be shaken) to triangle to xylophone, do we put on our coffee cups? A percussionist in search of self-definition is left with the sinking feeling that an instrumental category broad enough to include a bass drummer from a midwestern marching band, a *tabla* master, a ragtime xylophone specialist, and an Inuit drummer is probably too vague to be of much use as definition.

What is percussion then? What does it mean to be a percussionist? If such questions of identity were to occur to a pianist, cellist, or violinist—an extremely unlikely possibility since indeed the piano, cello, and violin *are* specific and singular objects—the brief moment of uncertainty could easily be answered by citing repertoire. The "Hammerklavier" Sonata of Beethoven, the Bach Cello Suites, the Brahms Violin Concerto. The piano, cello, and violin are the instruments used to play those pieces. Those instruments are bounded in a physical sense by their firmness as objects and in a metaphysical sense by the completeness of their musical language. However, understanding percussion by trying to understand its repertoire gives an incomplete picture at best. Even today the question of definition in percussion is confused by the small amount of important repertoire upon which meaningful discourse might be founded. In my first concerts of solo percussion music in the mid-1970s the situation was extreme. There were a half dozen or so major works in the solo repertoire. A single concert could include all of them. A listing of those early pieces would include Cage's *27'10.554"*, the first major work for percussion solo dating from 1956, as well as Karlheinz Stockhausen's *Zyklus* (1959), Morton Feldman's *The King of Denmark* (1964), *Interieur I* (1965) by Helmut Lachenmann, and Charles Wuorinen's *Janissary Music* (1966). This small number of pieces meant that a performance practice for thousands of instruments was defined, at least within the arena of contemporary solo percussion, by less than ninety minutes of music.

Composers who did write for the newly conceived medium of solo percussion naturally had a lot to say about its early development. That also meant that every new piece by a major composer added an important but potentially destabilizing weight to the rapidly growing sense of percussive definition. A new work like Iannis Xenakis's *Psappha* (1975) increased the size of the serious solo percussion repertoire by nearly 20 percent. There was no question that every serious percussionist would immediately learn *Psappha*. When Donald Knaack played one of the first American performances of *Psappha* in the Carnegie Recital Hall in 1977, it was amply reason enough for my first trip to New York City. I clearly remember seeing the room full of other percussionists who had also traveled to check it out. In 1977 many percussionists were looking for a new direction, but there was not much new percussion music to light the way. *Psappha* exerted an extraordinary musical and historical impact in large part because it was born into a relative vacuum.

With the ambiguity of percussion instruments as a family on one hand and the limited amount of music written for these instruments on the other, how can a percussionist effectively define his or her art? Components of definition come in the form of a small constellation of musical and social constructs. In some cases the ideas seem atomic and axiomatic and at other times part of a skein of interrelated cultural and critical concerns. In either event, fifty years after the composition of the first contemporary percussion solo, the encroaching middle age of the percussive art (and many of its practitioners) invites some illumination of the creation and practice of this vigorous music.

But what, finally, is percussion? Of course, we all know what percussion is. Percussion is that slightly dysfunctional family of struck sounds: a barroom brawl of noises, effects, and sonic events that can be created by striking, scraping, brushing, rubbing, whacking, or crashing any and practically every available object. The most succinct definition of percussion comes from the German, *Schlagzeug*; *Schlag* means "hit" and *Zeug* means "stuff." We percussionists are musicians who hit stuff. It is the quality of the hitting and the nature of the stuff that effectively define the basic substance of our art and apply focus to the music we make.

But the dialectic of *Schlag* and *Zeug* often seems awkward and unbalanced. *Zeug*, the stuff of percussion, is ill defined, consisting of an unwieldy confederation of instruments from *bonang* (a set of small knobbed gongs, which are placed horizontally) to glockenspiel—but, *Schlag*, the art of performance by striking, consists of just a few basic actions that are common to almost every percussionist in the world. Every drummer, for example, whether he or she plays *tabla* or *zarb* (a drum of Persia), whether as a professional musician with the New York Philharmonic or a real estate agent reliving a misspent youth by playing along with old "Kiss" records, engages percussion instruments with a remarkably similar set of actions. The instruments involved in various percussion traditions may be quite different from each other—in construction, in cultural origins, in historical lineage and musical vocabulary—but the basic action of performance, at the root of which is the stroke with its lift, quick descent, and contact, remains largely consistent.

There seem to be, in short, more differences among drums than among drummers. The notion that the percussion family is defined less by percussion instruments and their sounds than by how we make and use those sounds, seems to challenge the historically preeminent view that sound itself lies at the center of percussion as an art form. Certainly more than one author has described percussion in the twentieth century as one of the principal agents in the "liberation of sound," and indeed percussion instruments are an almost inexhaustible source of new and potent sounds and noises. However, sound is far too imprecise a guideline to serve as a definition for percussion. "A sound," or more accurately that sound's application to compositional practice as timbre, is difficult to measure and hard to remember, and it generally has been less central as a strategy of musical organization in western music than elements like melody and harmony have been. A performance of the *Grosse Fuge*, for example, where all of the pitches have been replaced by notes that are different but close, will not sound much like Beethoven, but replacing all timbres with sounds that are different but close in *Third Construction* will undoubtedly sound a lot like John Cage.

Sound as a quantifiable and memorable element among percussion instruments is made more problematic by the ambiguous sonic qualities of the instruments themselves. A composer calls for "medium gong," for example. It seems clear enough. However, a performer soon realizes that the number of objects qualifying under that description is horrifyingly large. There are gongs from Thailand, China, Korea, Java, and Bali, among others. They may be pitched or not, and, if they are pitched they may adhere to different tuning systems. They may be made of a variety of materials in differing thickness. Multiply these options by twenty or so possible mallets and the set of sounds corresponding to the indication "medium gong" quickly becomes unmanageably large. If this many sounds can be prompted by the simple indication of "medium gong," then clearly "sound" is a poor mechanism for definition.

Percussion as Tools in Action

The nature of percussion sounds may be difficult to specify—a direct result of the ambiguities of *Zeug*, as it were. But, I hasten to add that it would be wrong to assert that percussionists do not care about sounds. Percussionists spend their lives immersed in the details of sound. The difference between the way a tam-tam (a flat gong, which notably does not produce a specific pitch when struck) sounds when it is played at the center with a soft stick as opposed to being played near the edge with a slightly harder stick could easily be the difference between the success and failure of a performance. We are not just aware of sound, we are swimming in it. But as every practicing contemporary percussionist understands, there is a difference between sounds and instruments. An instrument is an object; a sound is a construction, an audible volition. Furthermore, what we are talking about here is not just sound, but the relevance of a sound or sounds to a moment in music. We are talking about impact. I am often disappointed when I hear new percussion music that is scored for brake drums, tin cans, and wood blocks, as I did in a recent concert. These are very worthy sounds, as Cage and Cowell proved sixty years ago. However, at that time they were the choices of active musical imaginations; now they are fixed instruments that one can buy from a catalog.

As an example of the problematic position of "the instrument" in contemporary percussion music, note that percussionists frequently do not have preferences for specific instruments. It would be rare for a contemporary percussionist to insist on a given and specific pair of bongos the way a violinist, for example, insists on playing a specific and personal violin, not just any violin of quality. He or she owns and travels with that particular instrument. (Imagine Gidon Kremer sending Carnegie Hall a tech rider calling for "one quality violin plus bow.") This personalized approach is largely true for other instrumentalists as well. After all, BB King doesn't play guitar; he plays "Lucille." But most percussionists are willing to play on any quality set of bongos. In fact, if no quality bongos are available at a given moment, a percussionist might improvise by using tightly tuned tom-toms or roto-toms as substitutions. (My tours in Eastern Europe in the late 1980s were often rescued by just this kind of inventiveness.) Most of the instruments in the arsenal of a contemporary solo percussionist, then, are interchangeable objects: musical value comes from their momentary utility in addressing specific musical problems. They are, in effect, more like tools than instruments.

As a child I watched my father work on our family's farm. When a repair called for a hammer, any hammer of good quality would suffice. My father's need for a hammer was really his need for "hammerness." For him a hammer was a tool: a generic and interchangeable object that was valuable only if it was useful. On the farm generic tools were wielded with sharply defined intent to address highly specific situations: a hammer could be used to fix a fence or a tractor, repair a feed trough, or open a bottle of beer. In short the tool was a necessary object, but it was effective only as an extension of action. Likewise, most percussionists do not need bongos they need "bongo-ness." Bongos are sonic tools; they are interchangeable objects that are wielded with precision to address a specific and momentary musical need.

In some cases—rare ones I think—percussionists play exclusively "instruments," that is to say they play specific and noninterchangeable objects. I am thinking of Fritz Hauser's custom-made mini–drum set or of an orchestral percussionist with an assortment of personal and prized snare drums, triangles or cymbals. In contemporary music, a performance of Karlheinz Stockhausen's *Mikrophonie* (1964) would typically be learned and performed on a specific tam-tam so that nuance of color could reliably be found. For the most part, however, contemporary percussionists mix instruments with tools. I travel with certain essential, irreplaceable instruments: the small set of pipes I use for *Psappha*, a special cowbell and opera gong I need for Brian Ferneyhough's *Bone Alphabet*, a very well-traveled whisky bottle for Roger Reynolds' *Watershed*. The irony of contemporary percussion is that these unique bits of junk are the real instruments; they are specific and personal. The most recognizable icons of percussion—the cymbals, bongos, bass drums, and triangles—are in fact just tools of the trade: generic, interchangeable, and nonspecific.

The fact that percussive tools may often be interchangeable and percussive sounds elusive may seem strange given the huge number of important sounds this instrumental family is capable of producing. Noisy, raspy, pure, calming, fricative, resonant, or irritating: there are literally tens of thousands of sounds in our repertoire. However many sounds we may have at our disposal, I am normally much less interested in a sound than I am in the *significance* of a sound—in the way that a sound generates impact as the sonic extension of meaningful thoughts and actions. Morton Feldman's advice to focus on "the sounds themselves" was not a call to minimize the role of the performer but, to the contrary, an admonition against squandering sound in sonically comatose performances. If we hear not just what a sound is, but what it does, we begin to approach the critical rapport between *Schlag* and *Zeug*, between the actions of performance and the sound or sounds that action produces. The central truth of percussion music is close to what American painter Philip Guston once called the action of painting.[1] Guston felt that action incited a critical moment where material—the formal and coloristic substance of painting—was united with the spontaneity and force of doing as different states of the same entity. It was there, he maintained, that art came to life as the permanence of material arrested in form by an eye-blink of action. This is a performer's view to be sure: percussion playing, for all of its potential for momentary vigor, is destined to be rootless—an imprecise drama of hitting things staged on a marshy terrain of uncertain sound—unless those sounds can be embodied with action and thought, and harnessed with purpose and significance. Then *Schlag* and *Zeug* might be united as *Schlagzeug*.

The percussion family, either as tools or instruments, differs fundamentally from other instruments in many important ways. A cellist, for example, must cope with a single complex instrument that is steeped in tradition. He or she must learn an involved set of performance techniques and engage a sophisticated and established performance practice. A contemporary percussionist is usually faced with a large set of uncomplicated objects, many of which have a short history as musical instruments. I clearly remember wandering the halls at the University of Iowa, where I was an undergraduate percussion student. I would listen for a while to the violists, pianists, or clarinetists playing their strains of Debussy or Janacek or Ellington and sigh wistfully about the absence of a venerable tradition in contemporary percussion music before I returned to my practice room to see whether or not I could bow a brake drum or play a cowbell under water. Furthermore, except for specialized techniques like conga slaps, a snare drum roll, or four-mallet marimba techniques, most percussion instruments are simple and relatively easy to play. Percussion instruments are, after all, simple objects: hit them and they will make a sound. Hit them harder and they will make a louder sound. As a questionable part of their ongoing "percussion-is-as-good-as-any-other-instrument" campaign, the academic

1. *Philip Guston, Peintures 1947–79*, Exhibition Catalogue, Centre Georges Pompidou, October, 2000 (Paris: Centre Pompidou, 2000).

percussion establishment has argued to the contrary: percussion instruments are as worthy as any other instrument. Therefore they are as difficult to master. Understandably percussionists feel entitled to the same level of respect that other instrumentalists and vocalists command. And, clearly a pristine performance of the Bartók *Sonata for Two Pianos and Percussion* or Lachenmann's *Interieurs I* is a feat of considerable difficulty. But making a decent sound on nearly any percussion instrument is not. A cymbal, a gong, and a drum: these are simple objects and that's a good thing. With simplicity comes intimacy, and with intimacy the strong sense of shared musical experience that many listeners feel when they hear percussion music.

To the Earth (1985)

Frederic Rzewski

Among the most intimate and approachable works in the solo percussion repertoire is Frederic Rzewski's simple *To the Earth* (see figure 1.1). Rzewski scores his piece for four terra-cotta flowerpots and asks a solo percussionist to play them while reciting the text of a Homeric Hymn in honor of the earth. For years I performed *To the Earth* on "outreach" concerts sponsored by the New York based agency Affiliate Artists. I played in schools, Kiwanis Clubs, hospitals, and jails; at construction sites, fruit packing plants, shopping malls, and mental hospitals. I was touring a full repertoire of hard-hitting percussion music. (I played Karlheinz Stockhausen's *Zyklus* more than a hundred times in and around Wenatchee, Washington, for example.) I was carrying a load of exotic instruments from log drums to automobile brake drums, but none of the instruments received as much comment as the four flowerpots in Rzewski's piece. Most of the listeners, including school children, construction workers, and retirees, had never heard a live concert of "classical" music before. They never would have dared to come on stage to try out a viola after a string quartet performance. Yet, they did come onto the stage to examine and play the flowerpots.

These new listeners understood the Homeric text of *To the Earth* as a kind of Whitmanesque populism. That is to say that they were attracted to its simple sentiment and clear voice. The aristocracy of trained instrumentalists plays no role here, because in *To the Earth* flowerpots are not instruments. To make a beautiful sound on a flowerpot one need not spend years of study in a conservatory; one needs only a flowerpot and something to hit it with. *To the Earth* points again to Cage's notion of the "impoverishment" of percussion. Rzewski's pots, as the universal and transparent agents of a true *musica povera*, can be owned by anybody and therefore are *owned* by everyone. Even the score of *To the Earth*, while clear and specific, is neither elevated nor remote. Rzewski told me in conversation that the pitches he indicated for the flowerpots—one of the few

Figure 1.1. Frederic Rzewski, *To the Earth*, for four flowerpots and speaking percussionist, bars 1-32. Used by permission.

truly "musical" elements in the piece—are not sacred. Change them if you like, he said. Moreover the pots should be of local origin and not be too expensive. Just choose nice ordinary flowerpots.[2] The gap between artist and amateur; performer and listener; percussionist and gardener, all but disappears.

In his coaching of my performance in preparation for a 1994 recording of the work, Rzewski pushed me towards a performance of the piece as common and accessible rather than exalted and artistic. He asked repeatedly for a flexible reading of the text, suggesting an incantatory stance, as one might imagine the text to have been read in ancient Greece. But he also asked for interpretive dryness and a distinctly humble and nondramatic performance. An experience of the piece should be common—that is to say available and approachable.

2. I use terra-cotta flowerpots that are readily available at local garden shops. They produce strongly focused pitches when struck on the open side with small lightweight sticks.

To the Earth questions the differentiation of role between the expertise of performers and the passivity of listeners that has long been central to the psychology of performance in western music. If you doubt the firmness of the boundary between performers and listeners, try joining the New York Philharmonic on stage the next time the spirit of Mahler moves you to play along. However, in *To the Earth* there is no expert on stage, and as a result a listeners feel invited to come closer. They think, "*I could do that.*" And they could.

Indeed, by any standard *To the Earth* is not difficult music to perform. The flowerpot music is rarely demanding and the text is meant as a simple homage to the earth. Where difficulty occurs it is found in the competing demands of playing and speaking at the same time. In some cases difficulty ensues from the simple acoustical differences between the suppleness of the voice and the less mutable sonorities of the pots. The goal in *To the Earth* lies in finding a flexible linkage between flowerpots and voice: the goal is two lines in dynamic rapport, neither one is shackled to nor estranged from the other one. This balance is critical. If the flowerpots pull the text too far in the direction of their flatness, words become wooden and a prayerful text sounds like an empty recitation. The sense of a "common" aesthetic experience becomes merely ordinary. If the reverse situation occurs and the voice pulls the flowerpots towards oratory, then their presence in the piece becomes artificial, and both simplicity and universality are lost.

On one level, the issue of interpretation in *To the Earth* is simple. The performer is simply a person who reflects aloud on the beauty of the earth. As a hymn, *To the Earth* shows the closeness of the flowerpots, which speak for the earth, with the voice of its human inhabitants. The intertwined vocal and flowerpot lines convey the intimacy of our alliance with the planet. But follow this approach too far and the interpretation will fail to establish two distinct and distanced points of view. An interpretation that posits no friction between the voice and the pots ignores an essential layer of dissent in the music: we are not the world. In fact we very often live at cross-purposes with the earth. Imagine a performance where the vocal layer is given greater emotional or rhythmic flexibility so that it seems to shift over a sense of stillness in the flowerpot music. Perhaps this might serve to reveal a critical friction.

I have found that listeners are very sensitive to the relationship between the human performer and the flowerpots. Audiences often adopt a sense of guardianship towards the pots. People often say that the pots sound and look beautiful; people are sometimes afraid the pots might crack. In fact concern over the fragility of the flowerpots often seems to border on tenderness. In essence audiences seem to identify with the flowerpots to a much greater extent than they identify with the human performer who ostensibly speaks for them. (None of the several dozen of people who have expressed concern that I might break a flowerpot ever worried that I would cut myself on it!) This heightened awareness of fragility—the way the breakable flowerpots echo the impermanence of the earth and the life it sustains—made for one of the most memorable concert experiences I have ever had. My final performance as a member of the Affiliate Artists roster took place in Wilmington, North Carolina, in October of 1987. Immediately after I finished that performance I was to leave North Carolina and fly back to Iowa to be with my mother in the last weeks of her life. On that night I cracked the highest pot about a minute into the ten-minute-long piece. Under more ordinary circumstances, I might have played the rest of the piece on the three remaining good pots or simply stopped the performance altogether and gone to the car where I had a spare flowerpot. But I kept playing the piece as written, without changing the cadence or nuance of my voice, without working around the broken pot but also without leveraging it as an unexpected source of drama to be explored. Where there was once a high pure tone, there was now, suddenly and without warning, a dull, dead sound. When I first played the dead flowerpot the audience shifted uncomfortably, but as the piece went on and the broken sound became a part of their experience of it, people settled. Over the last several minutes of *To the Earth* the room went meaningfully still. No one wanted to talk about it later. I simply played. And they got it.

To the Earth

To the Earth, Mother of all,
I will sing, the well established, the oldest,
Who nourishes on her surface everything that lives.
Those things that walk upon the holy ground,
And those that swim in the sea,
And those that fly in the air,
All these are nourished by your abundance.

It is thanks to you if we humans have healthy children,
And rich harvests.
Great Earth, you have the power to give life to,
And to take it away from creatures who must die.
Happy are the ones whom you honor with your kindness and gifts. What they
    have built will not vanish.

Their fields are fertile. Their herds prosper,
And their houses are full of good things.

Their cities are governed with just laws.
Their women are beautiful,
Good fortune and wealth follow them.
Their children are radiant with the joy of youth.
The young women play in the flowery meadows,
Dancing with happiness in their hearts.

Holy Earth, undying Spirit,
So it is with those whom you honor:
Hail to you, Mother of life,
You who are loved by the starry sky,
Be generous and give me a happy life in return for my song,
So that I can continue to praise you with my music.[3]

Radical Discontinuity

In *To the Earth* we find friction in the competing activities of speaking and playing; and of course friction is inevitable between the conflicting ancient and modern views of the rapport between humankind and the earth. In fact friction, at least in its manifestation as vivid and often noisy sounds, seems readily available in most percussion music. After all, percussion is almost always some kind of noise. And, historically, there has been friction as the noises of percussion have intruded upon the relatively euphonious sound world of classical and romantic orchestral music. There is even friction in noise itself: it is a bracing slap in the face that reminds us we are alive. (Has heaven ever been represented in music by an anvil or a snare drum?) The production and management of friction drives most interpretations of percussion music. Minimize friction and you curate similarity, allowing sonic and metaphorical elements to fold more easily together into a linear musical space. As disruption is reduced, the sense of continuous line, including the kind of line we call melody, is maximized. The reverse also applies. Polyphonic constructions need the friction of distinction in order to allow a listener to track the multiple trajectories of independent lines. As noise, percussion stands in opposition; it articulates; it marks and signals; it flavors, offsets, and shades the music around it.

---

3. Line breaks and stanza divisions are mine.

Percussion disrupts. The disruption might be minimal, consisting of highlighting the rhythmic group-ings in dance music. (See examples from the dance music of the Renaissance to the Chemical Brothers.) Accenting strong beats or highlighting syncopated rhythms spurs the music forward and lends a sense of rhythmic urgency and agogic vitality. In his Ninth Symphony, Beethoven doubled the advantage of percus-sion. He used it to create a vivid dance-like variation of the famous melody in the last movement. And fur-ther, by borrowing the perfumed percussion sounds of the cymbals, triangle, and bass drum from exotic Turkey, he managed to spice up an otherwise straightforward orchestration. Beethoven, not above dressing up yesterday's ideas with a splash of color, was a composer who knew how to accessorize.

In tonal orchestral music percussive disruption frequently operates on a profound level as a signifier of har-monic and formal articulation. Noise engages memory to mark important structural moments and flag them to be recalled at a later time. A cymbal crash at a critical harmonic juncture floods the senses and captures the musical moment. The message is: "This is important; you'll hear this again." Big moments are made memorable both by the imprudence of the disruptive noise and by the attention-getting gestures of performance. In other words the cymbal crash functions both as an acoustical event and, via the glint of the metal plates and the big waving motions of performance, as a kind of semaphore. In whatever ways percussion instruments manage to get our attention, they have acted historically as the medium of otherness. They counterpoise their disruptive agency against the primarily continuous discursive material of the orchestra or chamber ensemble.

Yet percussion instruments are not complete outsiders in the orchestra; they also act on music from within. Sometimes they disrupt as dissenting participants, double agents in a way that are both *a part of* and *apart from* the group. Social demarcations in the orchestra underscore this musical duality. Timpani are capable of producing every bit as much noise as gongs and drums; however they often act to outline har-mony and at times even play melodies. (See again under Beethoven: the thematic octaves in the Scherzo of his Ninth.) As a result, timpanists historically have been fully vested in the aristocracy of the orchestra, the peers of the cellos and double basses rather than of the ratchet and slapstick. Times may be changing, espe-cially in American orchestras, but it would still be unlikely for a timpanist to wander over in a spare moment and pick up a triangle to help out.

There are notable instances of thematic and melodic use of percussion instruments in the orchestra, usually in music played by timpani and keyboard percussion instruments, but percussion often weighs in on the side of what critic and author Paul Griffiths has called "radical discontinuity."[4] This radical discontinuity,

4. Paul Griffiths, Review in *The New York Times*, November 6, 1998.

the very foreignness of percussive noises, was needed for the percussion family to fulfill its dual imperative in tonal music: percussion marked time—as a mechanism on the small scale for the creation of rhythmic vitality and on a larger scale for formal demarcation; and percussion acted metaphorically—as a sonic representation of strong emotion or the power of nature. As the orchestra grew both in size and timbral vitality over the course of the nineteenth century, the needs for both temporal and emotional distinction and demarcation grew accordingly. The triangle may have sufficed as a noticeable noise in Beethoven, but in Hector Berlioz's mammoth *Requiem* an entire arsenal of disruptive percussion was required to make the same point. You can never go back. Percussive articulations had to be readable against the background of orchestral color, and as background colors became more vivid, the noises of disruption needed extra potency.

The twinned roles of formal demarcation and metaphorical punch went together well in tonal music since structurally memorable passages were also often ones colored by high emotion. As the nineteenth century fell increasingly in love with passionate, macabre and even devilish musical imagery, it also fell under the spell of the crashes and jolts of percussive attacks. Understandably a composer such as Johannes Brahms, whose music relied much less heavily on the sonic object as a perfected artifact that mirrored emotion, used percussion less often and in a less purely representative manner than did Hector Berlioz in his *Symphonie fantastique* with its "ladies and gentlemen" call of the snare drum roll just before the noose tightens in the "March to the Scaffold." A consistent line of compositional strategy was developing whereby percussion instruments emerged as prime signifiers of strong emotion. From the storm scenes of Beethoven, Berlioz, and Debussy (in the Sixth Symphony, *Symphonie fantastique*, and *La Mer* respectively), through the alpine nostalgia of cowbells in Mahler's Sixth Symphony and the pre-Hendrix psychedelia of Scriabin's *Prometheus*, percussive noise provided the metamusical jolt necessary for audiences to *feel* and not just understand the sense of the music.

In one important sense the dissolution of tonality in the early twentieth century led percussion to the verge of an identity crisis. Tonal harmony meant statement and recollection and in that context percussion noises had historically served as memorable markers within the event profile of a tonal piece. But, after all, if nothing is to be repeated in a post-tonal piece, then nothing needs to be marked as memorable enough to recall. In the turbulent wake left by the collapse of tonality, many composers leaped to embrace fully the collateral function of percussion instruments as emotional and metaphorical provocation. To these composers percussive noise became what color had meant in the late nineteenth century to *fauvist* painters: an untethered, nondoctrinaire, and utterly savage means of expression, often abstracted and distilled to nearly grotesque potency. In Alban Berg's *Wozzeck*, percussion sounds stood for emotional and psychological states too intense or lurid for the polite context of the concert hall. After the adulterous Marie is slashed and murdered (by Wozzeck just before his own death by drowning in what he imagines is a lake of blood) the percussive commentary is positively caustic—an indictment of timpani explosions and a massive gong, cymbal, and snare drum crescendo. To many composers and listeners percussion was quickly becoming symbolic of the "terrifying event." And truly, from the exorcisms of Igor Stravinsky's *Rite of Spring* through the exploding nebulae of Varèse's *Arcana*, the new percussion noises were indeed shocking and fearful. Many late twentieth century composers picked up this line of argument. John Luther Adams's boreal *Strange and Sacred Noise* (1991–97) and James Tenney's baptism by noise in *Having Never Written a Note for Percussion* (1971) continued the lineage by using the power of percussion to evoke massive and terrible landscapes that often seem to dwarf their human performers.

The early twentieth century turned to new compositions and a novel kind of musical intelligence as a way to make sense of the potent forces of percussion sounds. The stage was set for works such as Varèse's *Ionisation* or George Antheil's *Ballet mécanique* (1925/1953). Percussion was poised to compete (and win) against an entire chamber ensemble as the triumph of the devil in Stravinsky's *L'Histoire du soldat* or to outlast the pianos as the last word at the end of the Bartók *Sonata for Two Pianos and Percussion*. Ultimately though—and in my opinion this was the real impact of Cage's revolution on percussion music of the late twentieth century—the noises and sounds of percussion ceased needing a reason to exist. Since Cage and his confreres were no longer indebted to what they saw as antiquated forms and modes of expression, the sounds of percussion were simply let off the leash. The noise curtain had been razed and behind it the sounds were raw and elemental. Uncaged.

Percussion sounds didn't stay uncaged for long. Almost immediately a new process began of organizing them into meaningful components of a new musical language. In two very early examples, both *L'Histoire du soldat* and the Bartók *Sonata* featured a mode of organizing percussion as a "multiple instrument." A multiple percussion instrument consists of several individual instruments arranged so that one percussionist might play them as a single polyinstrumental unit. After 1956 most percussion solo and chamber works, with the exception of music for single solo instruments like the vibraphone or marimba, were composed for multiple percussion. The sonic impact of multiple percussion music is collective, the unified result of the accumulated sounds of single instruments.[5] The desire for a large and varied instrumentation means that the physical set-up for a multiple percussion piece might *look* like a utility closet,

5. In his wonderful book *Percussion et musique contemporaine* (Paris: Klincksieck, 1991), Jean-Charles François describes this phenomenon as "une organisation multiple de l'espace sonore."

a junk heap of unrelated objects, but it must *sound* singular and clearly focused. The notional equation is that quantity and diversity in the set of instruments provide sonic complexity, but the sounds must be focused by compositional imperative if they are to function coherently as musical language.

In the service of sonic diversity, instrumental set-ups in multiple percussion music quickly grew to almost unmanageable size. It is easy to imagine how this might happen. Start with a piece for wood block solo, for example. One sound, especially the sound of a wood block, is probably too restricted a palette of sonority for an entire composition. To achieve a sufficiency of color you add more instruments. Additional wood blocks might create a scale of similar sounds if linearity is a compositional goal. Contrasting sounds might be added to enable polyphonic structures. Entropy in the realm of musical color was the natural result of the sheer plenitude of the percussion family. And indeed early percussion concerts often featured a warren of exotic and complicated set-ups. Unfortunately the compositional language needed to make sense of the explosion of color and material developed more slowly than the instrumental resources did. One was very often more impressed with the sheer number and variety of instruments than one was with the music itself. Composers began to realize that the calculus of multiple percussion instruments described the need to balance sonic diversity with compositional limitation. Possibility and limitation, which are competing forces in any adolescence, were no less defining for percussion in its early development. Each percussion piece became a negotiation between the cosmology of infinite sonic possibilities on one hand and, on the other, the gravitational force of limitation that lies at the core of any coherent compositional syntax.

Composers did not need to look far to find a workable model for organizing the large number of new percussion sounds and uses. The orchestra—the very institution that contemporary composers for percussion had only recently rejected—became the principal archetype for a new means to organize thought. From ensembles of percussion instruments to the recently arrived domain of solo percussion music, composers began, again, to think in terms of sections of instruments. That is to say that they began to organize percussion instruments into groups with sonic and behavioral affinity with one another. From Stockhausen's use of wood, skin, and metal instruments in *Zyklus* to Wuorinen's dodecaphonic plan of instruments by the dozen in *Janissary Music*, tried and true methodologies of coherence and coexistence were borrowed from the orchestra. To the extent that it was possible, instruments of similar sound, material, and mode of performance were treated as a unit, allowing for the development of a strong sense of internal coherence among an otherwise disparate set of objects.

Many composers used the orchestral model effectively as a means of organizing a large and potentially unwieldy group of sounds. However, as you might imagine, a group of metallic percussion instruments is not as predictable and well behaved as a group of violas, for example. Oddities among the size, shape, resonance, and mode of performance within a group of percussion instruments meant that almost any subset of the family constituted a special case. Each early orchestral-based percussion piece therefore consisted of a unique set of instrumental objects and each piece necessitated a unique compositional solution often with a custom-made notational scheme. And by extension each multiple-percussion piece featured a unique physical arrangement of instruments. Imagine you are a pianist and in a Mozart concerto "middle C" is in the middle of the keyboard as usual, for the Brahms Quintet it is in the upper register and for *Pierrot Lunaire* in the bass. Replace "middle C" with the word gong or cymbal or marimba and you have an idea of the logistical problems facing a multiple percussionist. One might develop expertise on each of the basic individual instruments such as vibraphone, timpani, or snare drum, however percussion as a multiple-instrument is inevitably *sui generis*. The first step in learning a new percussion piece is always mastering a new multiple-instrument, and with it engaging the corollary concerns of notation and choreography.

The First Generation: An Orchestral Medium

Janissary Music (1966)

Charles Wuorinen

It follows then that early multiple percussion works were almost exclusively demanding works that were scored for very large group of instruments and marked by a similarly large set of unique problems in performance. These first pieces included, among others, John Cage's *27'10.554"* (1966) Stockhausen's *Zyklus* (1959) and Charles Wuorinen's composition from 1966, *Janissary Music* (see figure 1.2).

I first saw the score to *Janissary Music* when I was an undergraduate student at the University of Iowa. It was a time when I was frankly envious of my pianist and violinist classmates. They had, it seemed, all the great music, and we had mostly silly etudes. *Janissary Music* seemed like an answer to my prayers. It was by far the most intricate, the most difficult, and the most *serious* piece of percussion music I had ever encountered. William Parsons, who was the percussionist with the university's Center for New Music and occasionally my teacher at the time, threw the score across a marimba at me one day and said that here was a piece to rival the difficulty of any Beethoven Sonata. He was not wrong by much. *Janissary Music* is imposing. Its physical architecture is enormous: it is scored for marimba, vibraphone, twelve drums, twelve metal instruments, and a single timpano. In my set-up, the vibraphone and marimba are "stacked," one placed in

Figure 1.2. Charles Wuorinen, *Janissary Music*, bars 1–3. Copyright © 1967 by C. F. Peters Corporation, Inc., New York. All rights reserved. Used by permission.

front of the other, with the drums in a large semicircle behind me and the metal instruments suspended on a rack to my right. The distance across the set-up is very large, and the need to be able to reach all of those instruments in rapid succession demanded a level of virtuosity that I had never experienced before. But as great as its physical demands are, the real challenge of *Janissary Music* lies in anchoring its considerable difficulty to the structural architecture of its composition in a coherent way.

Like many composers of his generation, Charles Wuorinen was interested in extending the serial practices of twelve-tone music into the realm of rhythm and beyond. As early as 1960, Karlheinz Stockhausen rotated serial sets in *Kontakte*—his masterpiece for piano, percussion, and four-channel electronic tape—to produce transformations in a wide range of musical qualities from pitch to timbre to the movement of electronic sounds around a set of four loudspeakers. Wuorinen's interest was primarily in the serial organization of rhythm, a time-point system that tied the temporal distribution of notes to a master twelve-tone pitch system. Wuorinen's series in *Janissary Music* is based on a simple chromatic series of twelve pitches starting on the note F. In Wuorinen's system the F occurs on the downbeat of the bar, F sharp is on the second sixteenth note, G on the third sixteenth note, and so on until all of the twelve pitches are assigned to a specific point in the twelve sixteenth notes of a 3/4 bar. An equivalent assignment of twelve pitches can occupy the twelve eighth-note triplets of a 4/4 bar or the twelve eighth notes of a 12/8 measure. Since musical measures carry the notion not just of distribution of notes in time, but also of agogic import and meter—that is to say the relative importance and weight that one point in time in a measure of music has over another—F becomes the most important note in the series because it is consistently placed in the most metrically important position when the tone row is read in its most basic "prime" version. This created a dilemma. Twelve-tone music had started decades earlier as a system to exclude tonal hierarchy—no note in the series was to be any more important than any other note—but, by giving the first note of his series the metrically important function of "downbeat," Wuorinen effectively instituted a hierarchy and therefore a surrogate tonality. *Janissary Music* is "in F": it is the first note of the series, it is the beginning and ending notes of both movements, and it importantly occupies the most metrically privileged position in the piece.

Of course Wuorinen was not interested in consistently assigning the same note to the same point in time over the course of the entire piece. Predictability and boredom would soon set in. So by standard methods of twelve-tone manipulation—inversion, retrograde, and the rotation of subsets of the original twelve tones—the series is reordered, effectively transmuting both the pitch material and reorienting metrical hierarchy within the rhythmic material. In essence a sense of metrical weight is transposable in the same way pitch material is. Serial transposition in *Janissary Music* also involves reorchestration, since material heard in the pitched music of the vibraphone/marimba pair is often simply lifted off of the staff of pitches and overlaid onto the staff of drums to the set of twelve drums or twelve metallic instruments. The standard transposable equivalencies of Wuorinen's serial language—pitch, rhythm, and metrical placement—must be rendered clearly on a wide variety of sonorities.

Herein lies the principal interpretative difficulty of *Janissary Music*. Twelve-tone methodology relies on the capacity to mutate the order of the series at will: pitches are fundamentally equal and the series therefore fundamentally balanced and transposable. The first note of a twelve-tone set is not the most important pitch in the series; it simply appears first. In an interpretation of *Janissary Music* a performer must be able to articulate changes of meter, but because of Wuorinen's extension of the series into the domain of rhythm, these changes of meter are in fact also tied to permutations of the series. The problem surfaces when a performer is faced with the challenge of presenting the permutations of the series and meter on a large group of very different instruments. We have seen that Wuorinen divides the large instrumental arrangement of *Janissary Music* into families of pitched, skin, and metal instruments. This seems like a sensible division in the same way the division of the orchestra into sections of instruments is sensible. However, whereas any given section of the orchestra is relatively monochromatic, the sections of percussion instruments in *Janissary Music* very often are not. The arrangement of drums, for example, starting with two bass drums in the low register and working upwards through tom-toms and bongos, is fundamentally unequal and unbalanced. The bass drums through their weight and sound density, and the bongos because of their high register and penetrating attacks are more potent—therefore more memorable and more important—than is the less noticeable array of tom-toms in the middle of the scale. A set in which some elements are *de facto* more important than others poses serious problem for serial treatment. Will the bass drum or bongo always sound like a downbeat because of its loudness and acoustical presence? Can a performer effectively recalibrate weight and force to give a sufficient a sense of metrical importance to the middle drum voices when they in turn occupy downbeat functions?

The serial treatment of the metal instruments poses even more extreme problems. An important criterion in the manipulation of a pitch series lies in the equivalency among elements of the series. It is precisely this equivalency that allows for the transposition of order in the series. When the series is presented on pitched keyboard instruments, this equivalency among the elements is clear. The pitch E at the end of the first bar of the primary series is related as a member of the same sonic family to the F that begins the bar. In other words the E is a soprano version of the F: it is made from the same kind of material (thus creating a strong affinity between the two), but distinguished by pitch (thus allowing for a differentiated position in the series). One might also say, with slightly greater difficulty, that the bongo and bass drum are equivalent—that the bongo is a soprano version of the bass drum in other words. But a triangle, the highest metal sound, is certainly not a soprano version of the large tam-tam, the lowest of the metals. The absence of equivalency among the metal instruments fractures the internal coherence of this group and greatly impedes a performer's ability to present and a listener's ability to track the shifting syntax of pitch and metrical hierarchy that comprises the core set of musical values in *Janissary Music*.

It is here again that Wuorinen and any solo percussionist who plays *Janissary Music* butt heads with an unalterable truth: multiple percussion instruments are fundamentally unlike other instruments. Every sound made by an instrument—whether that instrument is the piano, the oboe, or the grand meta-instrument of the orchestra—is strongly related to every other sound produced by that instrument by means of the force of singularity that is exerted by the instrumental object itself. The resulting set of sounds with a large degree of affinity enables compositional strategies of statement, permutation, and transformation. On the other hand multiple percussion works are often collections of simple and disparate sonic objects. Coherence in percussion is therefore derived more from context—from the local application of the unifying forces of a given piece—than from naturally existing sonic affinity.

Timbral diversity among the members of the percussion family, initially a strong motivation for composers interested in engaging new sounds, in fact disenabled many conventional compositional practices.

Figure 1.3. Charles Wuorinen, *Percussion Duo*, bars 127–135. Copyright © 1979 by C. F. Peters Corporation, Inc., New York. All rights reserved. Used by permission.

In particular, orchestral strategies that rely on the capacity for transposition—the sure knowledge that similarity of musical function among instruments with different timbral qualities will allow for musical ideas to operate on the same plane—do not work with percussion. Radical discontinuity of tone color, the very element that provided the force of distinction and demarcation in nineteenth century tonal music, thwarts the attempt to universalize percussion instruments as a mini-orchestra in *Janissary Music*. Once again we are forced to confront what percussion is *not*.

Wuorinen rectified the disturbances in the timbral field of percussion instruments in his sonically unified *Percussion Duo*, the work for piano and percussion, a work that he wrote for pianist James Avery and me in 1979. In *Percussion Duo* the compatible sounds of a marimba and vibraphone pairing, played with a single set of four hard yarn mallets, allow for just the kind of transfer of material between piano and percussion that *Janissary Music* had been incapable of. Friction among the sonic resources of *Percussion Duo* was radically limited. Gone was the polarizing force of discontinuity. Gone the disruptions of percussive noise. And, gone as well was the heterogeneous sound world of the orchestra as a model for percussion compositions. Notice the great extent to which the two parts share similar melodic and rhythmic material in the excerpt from *Percussion Duo* in figure 1.3. Such highly integrated structures depend heavily on coloristic similarities between the keyboard percussion instruments and the piano.

The Second Generation: A Vocabulary of Limitation

First generation percussion music, like the orchestra it modeled itself on, was in many ways a product of a nineteenth-century aesthetic sensibility, which dictated that the chaos of possibility must be answered by the search for inclusion and interconnectivity. Every early percussion piece was a miniuniverse, a kind of percussive Noah's Ark featuring a representative spectrum of every possible kind of sound and performance skill, and the counterbalancing need to make sense of it all through a globalizing compositional scheme. The sheer number of instruments used in these early pieces was tiring. Often it takes longer to arrange the instruments for a piece like Luciano Berio's *Circles* (1960)—the composer's suggested set-up is shown in figure 1.4—than it takes to perform the piece. Every piece tried to do everything and ultimately the effect was numbing. In the movie *The Blues Brothers*, when Jake visits Elroy's apartment near the elevated trains in Chicago, he asks how often the trains pass by. The response, "so often you won't even notice," describes with equal accuracy the loss of sensitivity that attends musical saturation. Percussive color is easily exhausted as a musical commodity, and in the end the quest for plenty led to overstimulation and the concomitant absence of distinction. It became paralyzing.

In response, a generation of composers and percussionists who had steadily inhaled began to exhale. In the new music, a much sparer sonology reigned. As the poet James Merrill wrote about a failing love affair, the bald planet Ebb replaced the quest for the distant star Plenitude. By using much smaller set-ups, strategies

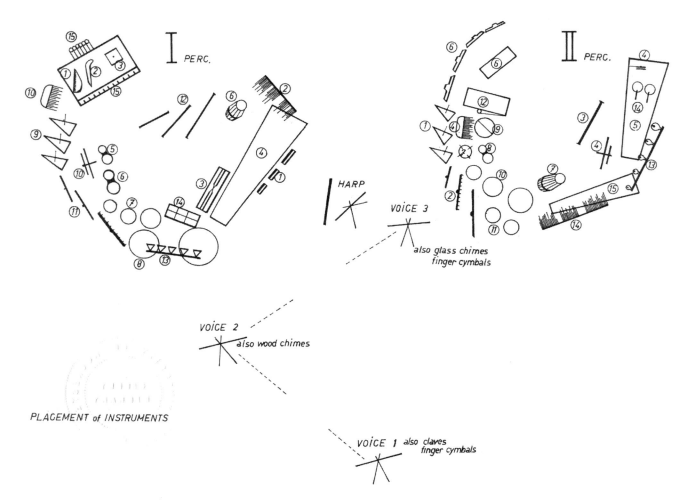

Figure 1.4. Luciano Berio, *Circles*, instrument diagram from score. London: Universal Edition Ltd., ©1961. Copyright renewed. All rights reserved. Used by permission of European American Music Distribution LLC, agent for Universal Edition (London) Ltd., London.

in the second generation of percussion works were less concerned with the *quantity* of sounds and more concerned with their *qualities*. Composers of the second generation posed two questions: Could a complex and satisfying music derive from a limited selection of instrumental sounds? And, since these composers rightly placed emphasis on the nature of the limitation, what was the relationship between initial qualities of musical color in a composition and the resulting complexity and expressivity in performance?

In one example, the strictly limited instrumentation of Brian Ferneyhough's skeletal *Bone Alphabet* controls not only surface qualities of color, but the deeper rhetoric of rhythm, texture, and dramatic force as well. The relationship between the bare bones of just seven dry sounds and the terrifying whirlwind of rhythmic layering is a kind of palindrome. The surface turbulence of extreme rhythmic complexity and density can be represented with clarity only by a small number of dry sounds, and, a small number of dry sounds needs activation by rhythmic complexity and density in order to thrive as a vital musical composition. Initial limitations of sonority in *Bone Alphabet* produce its musical essence, and ultimately its refinement as composition.

Severely limited instrumentation among many second-generation pieces leads us to the ultimate limitation of instrumentation: the large number of pieces for no fixed instrumentation at all. Many of the most important solo pieces are scored for some variation on the theme of "free instrumentation." These works cover the complete spectrum of stylistic difference and compositional approach. Michael Gordon's *XY*, Vinko Globokar's *Toucher*, David Lang's *The Anvil Chorus*, Brian Ferneyhough's *Bone Alphabet*, and Iannis Xenakis's *Psappha*, among others, are composed for instruments largely of the performer's choice. Sometimes the score offers some specific guidance in choosing the instruments; in most cases it does not. (In many ways, open scores for percussion solo also acknowledge that freedom of instrument choice is a part of *every* percussion piece. Even in a strictly determined instrumentation, a percussionist in search of just the right cymbal, wood block, or yarn mallet exerts a profound influence on the final sound of a percussion piece.)

The freedom of instrumentation exhibited in many percussion works of the second generation has a philosophical as well as musical angle. Most modern string and wind instruments and their performance practices came of age in the eighteenth and nineteenth centuries—precisely the moment when composers struck their most authoritarian and heroic postures. Recent solo music for percussion, to the contrary, was nurtured by the political discourse of the late 1960s where authority was suspect and individual freedom came to occupy prime philosophical and material concern. Nevertheless, in spite of its apparent liberty, this music was not anarchic and in many ways not even really free. The strategy of open instrumentation in much second-generation percussion music was simply another face of limitation. The instrumentation may have been open, but practical and aesthetic considerations in a score clearly favored some choices over others. In Xenakis's *Psappha*, for example, the instrumentation is largely free. However, a version for the resonant, spectrally complex sounds of ringing metal instruments would be completely unworkable. Xenakis's obsession with pulsed rhythmic cells in an interleaved presentation argues persuasively for dry, highly contrasted groups of instruments. In *Psappha* the particulars of an extreme and specific conceptual framework articulate an especially subtle form of compositional control. The illusion of freedom exists until you understand the piece.

The Anvil Chorus (1991)

David Lang

David Lang wrote *The Anvil Chorus* for me, and I premiered it in 1991 at the Bang on a Can Marathon. Bang on a Can, the renegade celebration of vital new music that Lang founded with fellow Yale composition alumni Julia Wolfe and Michael Gordon, was held that year at La Mama in New York City. As a reflection of David's music, the Bang on a Can aesthetic, and New York itself, *The Anvil Chorus* is a loud and raucous piece. The piece takes its point of departure from the blacksmith shop, which, in the preindustrial world, was also a very loud place. Beyond that it was a very rhythmical place. Several smiths might work simultaneously on particularly big jobs and to avoid whacking each other on the head they devised a system of counting. Ringing round a piece of metal, the blacksmiths hammered according to a commonly understood rhythmic plan. Each kept an internal pulse and struck on predetermined beats. *The Anvil Chorus* is a version of that idea where a single percussionist plays the part of many blacksmiths by performing several kinds of rhythmic material in several different speeds. The different rhythms and speeds create waves of pulsation: they cycle, overlap, and compete; the ebb and flow of these pulse cycles provides the genesis of large-scale sense in *The Anvil Chorus*. In Langian astrology, asynchronously cycling rhythms within sections eventually align themselves like so many planets to create an intricate and systematic structure. In the opening music of the piece a beat cycle performed on resonating metal instruments articulates a pattern of eight bars consisting, in order, of 8, 8, 7, 8, 8, 7, 7, 7 eighth notes (see figure 1.5). Every time this sequence of beats and bars is used, the resonant metals of the beginning are featured. Even as the basic sequence is permuted, the presence of the resonant sounds reminds us that the permutations are related to the music of the beginning.

In the second section of the piece, a syncopated wood block obbligato decorates regular pulses. Each of four semiresonant metal instruments is assigned a duration of 3, 4, 5, or 6 sixteenth notes in length (see figure 1.6). In the final section of the piece both systems of rhythmic cycling are combined (see figure 1.7), The description of rhythmic cycles in *The Anvil Chorus* does not need much elaboration. As creatively

Figure 1.5. David Lang, *The Anvil Chorus*, bars 1–26. Copyright © 1991 by Red Poppy (ASCAP). All rights administered by G. Schirmer, Inc. (ASCAP). International copyright secured. All rights reserved. Reprinted by permission.

interwoven as they are, the cycles are eminently audible. A performer should have little trouble understanding the rhythmic structure of the piece and an audience should have little trouble hearing it. *Should* have little trouble, that is. A potential problem lies in the instrumentation. The choice of instruments—free and open to the performer—must render the rhythmic and formal profile of the piece with clarity.

The set of instruments needed to represent this much independent rhythmic material is a percussive junk-heap, a mousetrap contraption featuring five foot-pedals and handfuls of noisy percussion instruments. The piece is scored for three major groups of metal percussion instruments as well as an additional pair of wood blocks and a kick drum. The score offers the following guidelines for choosing the three primary groups of metal instruments are as follows:

Group 1) three resonant instruments to be played with the hands;
Group 2) a group of four semiresonant metal instruments also to be played with the hands;
Group 3) a final group of four "junk metal" nonresonant instruments to be played by foot pedal.

Figure 1.6. David Lang, *The Anvil Chorus*, second section, 24 bars. Copyright © 1991 by Red Poppy (ASCAP). All rights administered by G. Schirmer, Inc. (ASCAP). International copyright secured. All rights reserved. Reprinted by permission.

David told me in conversation that he prefers that the performer stand while playing. Teetering on the pedals and reaching out for the array of brake drums, steel pipes, or frying pans is not a comfortable performing experience and undoubtedly not a graceful sight. But the necessity for the percussionist simultaneously to address each instrumental group with its distinct musical and choreographic particularities places the player (just as the blacksmiths put the piece of metal) uncomfortably at the center of the action. Musically, the percussionist must represent the diversity of sounds while urging them to merge as a single

Figure 1.7. David Lang, *The Anvil Chorus*, last section, final 18 bars. Copyright © 1991 by Red Poppy (ASCAP). All rights administered by G. Schirmer, Inc. (ASCAP). International copyright secured. All rights reserved. Reprinted by permission.

piece of music. Physically the goal is more basic: don't fall down. But in both cases the issue balance among instrumental groups is central.

It is the identity of the group, not of the individual instruments themselves, that serves as the primary unit of meaning in the piece. The rhythmic cycles in *The Anvil Chorus* are almost always contained within instrumental groups—material rarely wanders across the boundaries between groups. Note that the opening sequence of 8 and 7 eighth notes is played solely on the resonant metals. In the second section the regular pulsations of 6, 3, 5 and 4 sixteenth notes respectively are heard exclusively on the semiresonant instrumental group. Each of the four semiresonant instruments is assigned one of the four rhythmic values. To support these distinctions in performance, the instruments within groups should sound alike to curate maximum coherence, but each group must be unique to cultivate maximum differentiation among the groups. In my interpretation, the resonant music is played on three steel pipes of relatively pure pitch; for the semiresonant instruments I usually have used four brake drums, although recently I have started using sixxen bars (see chapter 6). The four foot-operated "junk" instruments consist of two large cowbells and two tam-tams. To preserve the integrity of the junk group it is important the sounds of the cowbells and tam-tams mix as well as possible. I try to make the tam-tams imitate the flat noise of the cowbells at a lower pitch by taping each of the tam-tams firmly to the heads of two bass drums. I can then easily play them with bass drum pedals that are attached, as usual, to the hoops of the bass drums. A wooden or hard plastic beater creates a persuasive industrial clanging sound. (I normally use a 20-inch tam-tam, which fits inside the hoop of a 22-inch kick drum, and for the lowest junk metal sound, I place a very large tam-tam inside the hoop of a concert bass drum.)

The stability of the instrument group allows the listener to track the formal development of the piece. If we clearly hear the music of the opening resonant group as being unified and different from other groups, then we will recognize its return at the end of the piece as a part of the formal strategy. And conversely, in those few instances where groups share rhythmic material, their momentary collusion is strongly marked by clearly interpenetrated colors. In the regular pulses of the second section, for example, a single foot-pedal note triggers the string of equal rhythmic values in the hand-played instruments. The pairings are static—each foot instrument is assigned a hand instrument and invariably triggers that and only that instrument. The hand and foot pairings become in effect a transitory, surrogate grouping that lends an attractive suppleness in the polyphonic design of the section.

There are also sculptural and choreographic considerations in the choice of instruments. Will the set-up convey an industrial metaphor—railroad ties and metal gas canisters might do the trick—or will it look like more like a standard percussion set-up? Why might a percussionist choose one design over another? The difficulty and interrelatedness of these concerns is enough to make you wish that the composer had simply written for a fixed choice of instruments.

Part of the reason that David did not make a piece for fixed instrumentation had something to do with our personal working relationship. David and I were classmates at the University of Iowa in the early 1980s, and we had worked together annually since 1988 in the context of the Bang on a Can Festival. We are friends. The first rehearsals of the piece took place over the phone; David was in New York, and I was working in my studio in San Diego. We began the rehearsal phase of *The Anvil Chorus* knowing that our friendship and the informality of our working relationship would allow us to develop the piece over time. The result of our collaboration was the development of an understanding about the piece that differs in many ways from the printed score. Over the course of the first several performances, we explored options of instrumentation, relative resonance and decay of instruments and mallet choice. A reasonably fixed version of *The Anvil Chorus* was finalized by the time the piece was first recorded in 1993. The *information* in the score—the notes, rhythms, tempi, and dynamics—did not change. But ideas of appropriate instrument choice and the resulting interpretive *spin* of the piece certainly did.

There are in essence two versions of the piece: one published and official and another as a part of an oral performance tradition. This is not that unusual in contemporary percussion music. Georges Aperghis's *Le Corps à Corps*, for example, is usually done with a glass of wine as the object of attention in the long pauses, exactly as Jean-Pierre Drouet, the brilliant French percussionist who championed it, has always done. The wine is a part of the piece but not a part of the score. Sylvio Gualda's contra-bass tom-toms in *Psappha* or James Wood's use of a quarter-tone pipe instead of triangle in his *Rogosanti* have also been encoded as part of an oral *urtext*. The oral guidelines to *The Anvil Chorus* originated through many conversations with the composer before and after the first several performances. They represent his now firmer ideas about sound and structure in the piece. However, they are not meant to supplant the written score. That is the nature of an oral tradition: it should remain a flexible confluence of collective experiences, a kind of group memory of how things are done or understood. It remains the task of future inventive performers of *The Anvil Chorus* to revise, add to, and indeed transcend its oral performance practice.

Issues surrounding the difficulty in choosing instruments for *The Anvil Chorus* were the initial sparks of in-depth conversations with David Lang. The score asks for resonant, semiresonant, and nonresonant metals, but I believe that resonance—in other words the length and nature of the decay of the instruments—was not precisely what David wished to specify. It is more accurate to say that he wanted to control the length of notes in combination with the relative sense of pitch of the instruments. By resonant, he means both sustaining instruments but also instruments of clearer and more appreciable pitch. By nonresonant he means dryer, but also noisier, junkier, and more jarring sounds. David uses the pitched "resonant" instruments to create an overall sense of the work as harmonically driven. The noisier "nonresonant" ones propel the work rhythmically and indeed even melodically. The ability to control resonance is central to developing a sense of melodic line within a diverse set of percussion instruments. Differences among noise instruments are audible only if the instruments are allowed to resonate. For example, a cymbal sounds nothing like a small tam-tam unless you choke it immediately. Then the similar noisiness of attack is more noticeable and the two instruments sound a great deal alike. The impression of melody and forward-moving narrative sense results naturally from similarity of noisy attacks.

No Instrument, Just Sticks

A fundamental similarity among noises is ultimately the key to coherence in *The Anvil Chorus*: however attractive or provocative its sound world may be at any moment, in the end the piece is about sound leveraged in the service of melodic sense and forward momentum. Part of the lesson is that melody derives from similarity of attack and color and not the "melodiousness" of any given attack or color. Melody does not result from sweetness but from sameness. The widely held view that percussion sounds are inherently nonmelodic because they are noisy is simply false. The noises of "nonpitched" percussion instruments can be vividly and persuasively melodic. The foot pedal part in *The Anvil Chorus* or the sweet "tune" of John Luther Adams's . . . *dust into dust* . . . for four snare drummers seems ample proof.

But by far the best example of the melodic potential of noise percussion instruments is right under our noses: the drum set. Listen to Max Roach for melodic elegance, to Elvin Jones for sailing melodic vectors and crosscurrents, or to Ringo Starr for perfectly crafted melodic countersubjects. To me, drum set playing is storytelling and at the root of this most rhythmic of instruments, it is pure melody. The shots, crashes and jolts are merely the consonants in a musical language—the necessary skeleton of an incantatory experience. By all accounts the drum set should sound like a mess. It was born out of a fit of efficiency that transformed the entire percussion section of a brass band into a contraption capable of being played by a single performer. (After all how would the New Orleans funeral procession have looked with a cornet, trombone, clarinet, and seven percussionists?) It seems plainly mysterious that a coherent musical instrument could possibly come out of the ragtag assortment of bass drum, snare drum, toms-toms, and cymbals of various sizes and sorts. Part of the secret unity of the drum set as an instrument has to do with the flow of cultural information. The components of the drum set—the individual instruments themselves—are of European heritage. However, the African American musicians who pioneered the drum set in the early twentieth century took their artistic point of departure from the aesthetic sensibility of West Africa, with its focus on a unified ensemble sound and its orientation toward communal music-making. The unifying force of art—the imperatives of synthesis and communality—came from Africa, the instruments by way of the European orchestra, and the clinical trials for the new African American instrument took place in the speakeasy laboratories of New Orleans, New York, and Chicago.

The acoustical reasons that the drum set functions as *an* instrument has less to do with the instruments than it does with the sticks. Imagine the sound of a Roy Haynes solo if all of the instruments were played with the optimal stick or mallet in order to cultivate the beautiful, "natural" sounds of the instruments. The snare drum would be played with snare sticks, but the cymbals should be played with soft yarn mallets to curate their spectral complexity. The bass drum would be treated with a very soft bass drum mallet to support its low fundamental tone, and the hi-hat cymbals as mini–crash cymbals played *a due* as in the orchestra. The potential of each instrument would be maximized; each would be beautiful and individual. And, there would be no chance that the entire assortment would blend together as a unit. The Roy Haynes drum solo sounds unified because the hard sticks with which he plays everything cultivate the noisy attack of each instrument's sound. It is the similarity of the noises rather than the insular beauty of the optimized sounds that creates the possibility for coherent melodic interplay among the instruments of the drum set. Sense comes not from the instruments, but from the sticks.

No instrument, just sticks. My mother was right: it is not the instruments, but the sticks that define percussion. Of course sticks are merely the mechanical extension of a player, the emblematic representation of the actions of playing. Sticks stand for the sweet kink of contact between a human performer and the expressive potential of a percussion instrument.

No instrument, just sticks. This phrase connects us to the mechanism for unity in the drum set. It connects us to the reason *The Anvil Chorus* is a plaintive melody and not an offensive noise. It reminds us that the simple actions of playing a drum or a gong or a bell are the same whether the percussionist is a member of the Korean group *Samul Nori* or the Berlin Philharmonic. It reminds us that in percussion music there resides a small but important model of the potential for connecting all human beings.

No instrument, just sticks. This phrase reminds us that percussion is the easiest instrument in the world to play and that playing itself is a thing common and basic to ordinary life. It was the reason a construction worker from Wilmington, North Carolina, and a school child from Evansville, Indiana, dared come on stage to make music on the clay flowerpots of Frederic Rzewski's *To the Earth*.

No instrument, just sticks. This phrase represents the source of our art as well as the root of our responsibility. By placing sticks before instruments I place the act of playing before the sounds of playing; I place the visceral, passionate, momentary connections to music before the historical weight of instrumental traditions or the dry rationale of performance practice; I place the human before the musical.

No instrument, just sticks. My mother's phrase has resonated with me like a mantra for forty years. Her decision to put sticks in my hands changed my life. And after all, isn't that the least we can expect of music, to change our lives?

Loud Americans
American Percussion Music under Construction

From Emerson to Ellis Island

Modern American percussion music arguably began when Edgard Varèse came to the United States and on the eve of American involvement in World War I conducted Hector Berlioz's mammoth *Requiem* in New York City. What a scene it must have been: the young Varèse, immigrant and father-to-be of American noise-art, amid the deafening swirl of antiphonal brass and twenty-some timpani while the culture of Beethoven and Berlioz was caught in a cross fire of European artillery. The moment that Varèse turned his back on Europe and looked towards his future as an American composer illuminated a critical juncture in the growth of American contemporary music and reflected the forces of redefinition in the ways America and Americans viewed art. Throughout most of the nineteenth century, cultured Americans saw themselves as guards stationed at the westernmost outpost of European art. To be "civilized" in America meant to embrace European artistic ideals. However, the early twentieth century saw a growing estrangement between European romanticism and a New World culture of noise and growth. Contradictions abounded in the crosscurrents of new American art. Landscape painters exchanged sunflower fields in Provence for the Brooklyn Bridge; there was Grand Opera on the Great Plains. The widening fissure between artistic meaning and perceptual context—the friction that comes from uncoupling of *what* from *where*—germinated in the early twentieth century as a critical quality of modernism in America.

America *was* different. Varèse could not have composed his early great works, *Amériques*, *Arcana*, and *Hyperprism* in Europe. *Ionisation*, the subject of these pages, is a quintessentially American piece. It was the first piece that Varèse began and finished after he bought his Sullivan Street apartment in New York in 1926;

it was the first piece that he began and finished after he became an American citizen in 1927. And although *Ionisation* was composed in Paris from 1929 to 1931 during a long return visit the composer made to Europe, it is first and foremost the music of New York City. *Ionisation* and its brand of vigorous experimentalism required an environment of reconsideration—the reexpression of inherited culture by means of new language—that New York in the 1920s offered in abundance. But he was certainly not the first American artist to have derived identity from the forces of place. Half a century earlier Walt Whitman's muscular verse celebrated the strength of the individual against the backdrop of vast, unexplored spaces. (If you're lucky enough to have a small print edition of *Leaves of Grass*, Whitman's lines span the page as his eye must have scanned the empty horizon where a "live oak glistens there in Louisiana, solitary in a wide flat space."[1])

By the turn of the twentieth century Frank Lloyd Wright, the *enfant terrible* of Louis Sullivan's "Chicago School" of architects, was busy constructing a new American monumentality. An organic American architecture, Wright held, was possible only through a "reverential recognition of the elements"[2] and would blossom as a regional form dependent on local materials, conditions of climate, and building methods. Many authors have noted that Wright's seminal Unity Temple, the culminating work of his "Prairie Period," lacks a steeple and with it the architect's foolproof device to direct the eyes heavenward. The newly constructed Eiffel Tower may have given French painters a dizzying vertical perspective, but for many Americans art was an expression of the horizontal. It was a phenomenon of *place* as filtered through the widely held perception that westward expansion and progress were manifest in the American personality.

In a musical version of Wright's "reverential recognition of new elements," sound itself became the *prima facie* determinant of new musical structures among young American composers. In search of new and vivid sounds, the bold music of Varèse, John Cage, and George Antheil leaned heavily on the raucous sounds of percussion. The appeal of percussion was twofold: percussion instruments could make hundreds of new sounds and they were largely untainted by inherited European traditions. After all, taken separately, the noises of percussion were constitutionally *unable* to represent the harmonic qualities of European musical language. In a particularly riotous example of percussive noise, Antheil's *Ballet mécanique* (1925) featured eight pianos, four xylophones, and a battery of percussion (the composer rescored the work in a

---

1. Walt Whitman, "I Saw in Louisiana a Live Oak Growing," in *Leaves of Grass* (Boston: Small, Maynard & Company, 1907).
2. Frank Lloyd Wright, *In the Cause of Architecture*, ed. F. Gultheim, reprint from *Architectural Record* (New York: McGraw-Hill, 1975), 53.

demi-orchestration for four pianos and two xylophones plus percussion in 1953). If that weren't cacophonous enough, Antheil added two electric buzzers and two airplane engines. The ensemble featured no actual airplane engines: Antheil's original solution called for "sound machines" that approximated propeller sounds by inserting thin wooden slats into the spinning leather straps that had been attached to the ends of fan blades. Later these sounds were generally played back via recording, but the specter of machines as musical instruments performing as soloists with an orchestra of percussion instruments, was enough to mark *Ballet Mécanique* with the scarlet letter of "S" for scandal.

New percussion sounds not only redefined the nature of musical material—and as a result, the nature of the compositional process—they also outlined a rapidly evolving social paradigm. In many ways the young composers who explored the *terra incognita* of percussion music fit neatly into traditional Emersonian views of American individuality and transcendence. Possibilities were meant to be explored; definitions of culture and society were meant to be inclusive and universalizing. (Cage returned frequently to Thoreau's view of humans as self-reliant creatures living in harmony with nature in pieces as widely variant as *Amores*, *Child of Tree*, and his *Imaginary Landscapes* series.) But America was moving rapidly towards a culturally diverse, polycentric society. An artistic representation of America and Americans as singular and monolithic was simply no longer possible.

As a reflection of changes in contemporary life, American percussion music developed along two intertwined paths. One path was "percussion as new sounds"—the historically preeminent view of percussion as an almost inexhaustible reservoir of varied and potent noises. The other path might be called "percussion as new culture"—the notion that western percussion practice was home to the instruments and sounds of *all* cultures. The American avant-garde in its infancy had to embrace both. On almost any given day a short walk from Edgard Varèse's Sullivan Street studio would take you by the metal-on-metal cacophony of New York City under construction. And on any given day you could also hear the sounds and music of immigrants from a dozen countries. Emerson was yielding to Ellis Island.

It would be difficult (and inaccurate) to portray Varèse and his contemporaries as "multiculturalists." But Varèse was nevertheless attracted to an enormous array of percussion instruments with roots in many world cultural traditions. Percussion music has been unique in its capacity to combine diverse cultural elements into a coherent whole. Composers of adventurous string music in the 1930s did not create ensemble combinations of cello, pipa, and koto. Yet we think nothing of hearing ensembles of xylophones, gongs, and temple blocks. This underscores the malleability of the percussion sonorities themselves—the ease with which one sound blends acoustically with another. But even more meaningful is the porous quality of cultural boundaries among percussion instruments. *Ionisation*, truly a percussive Tower of Babel, is the music of an immigrant culture. Its forty-one instruments comprise a veritable tour of world percussion traditions. The music of the maracas and bongos does not stray far from the short repeating cells of traditional Latin music. Chinese cymbals and gongs are used as timekeepers to mark big moments, reprising their structural role in Asian music. European and American marching traditions provide various sizes of snare and parade drums, and the sirens howl as they did nightly in the streets of New York.

As we listen to *Ionisation* today at the distance of more than seventy years from its creation, we must remind ourselves of the cultural charge these sounds once exerted on the piece. Years of listening to instruments like bongos, tambourines, and gongs in the context of dozens of pieces of contemporary music by Steve Reich to Iannis Xenakis, have numbed us to the vast range of highly individuated cultural origins and performance traditions found in *Ionisation*. However, in *Ionisation* and other works from the early percussion ensemble repertoire, a contemporary listener can still hear the polyglot struggle as the immigrant sounds of percussion instruments rub elbows. As a composer, Varèse navigated between the attractiveness of sonic, and therefore cultural diversity, and his need to smooth differences among the instruments into a common musical language. Again we find friction between *where* and *what*.

Ionisation (1931)

Edgard Varèse

Ionisation is only ninety-one measures long. No sound; no rhythmic, or timbral construction is extraneous. The piece may be only five minutes long, but it has prompted no small amount of written commentary. Nicholas Slonimsky's brief but well-known analysis declares, as the preface to the printed score, *Ionisation* to be a modified sonata form, with an introduction, statement of theme and countertheme, development, and, if not recapitulation, then at least apotheosis and coda. This squares the structure of the piece as a product of theme. In Slonimsky's view, themes consist of memorable instrumental colors, but the form of the piece ultimately conforms to classical-era practices where color was a provocative but secondary concern. In a much more sophisticated view, Varèse scholar and executor Chou Wen-Chung, himself a composer indebted to the subtleties of musical color, sees timbre as a paramount concern. In a lecture on *Ionisation* that Chou delivered at the University of California, San Diego, he observed that the structure of the piece is outlined by a dynamic and often oppositional correlation between subgroups of instruments. These groups are articulated by timbre and supported by theme and constitute powerfully distinguished, but essentially immutable blocks of sound.

Mr. Chou is certainly correct. *Ionisation* is fueled by interactions among groups of highly characterized, sonically distinct groups of instruments. By definition these groups demonstrate a high degree of coloristic affinity as Chou describes. But affinity is not limited to timbre alone. Timbre acts in combination with rhythmic, thematic, and cultural elements to define the identity of a given group. This creates instrumental "groups of affinity" that are distinguished from each other by a broad reading of timbre as *coloristic function*. I define a "group of affinity" as a subset of instruments with conspicuous similarities of timbre, which, importantly, function in conspicuously similar ways in the context of the composition. Affinity is therefore created not simply by how a group sounds but also by how it *behaves*.

Shared behavior is central to a group of affinity in *Ionisation*, but since behavior is by nature a momentary and fluidly evolving phenomenon, the membership of a group of affinity is changeable. An instrument with a rich harmonic spectrum or variability of attack—exhibiting flexible behavior, so to speak—may be a member of more than one group. A bass drum, for example, when it is played with vigor and rhythmic precision functions as a secco instrument. When in the very next bar it is rolled with soft mallets, it becomes a resonant instrument. Unusual combinations can result. At times seemingly dissimilar instruments function with affinity because they act in a similar fashion while at other times natural partnerships of sound are thwarted by antithetical behaviors. *Ionisation* is "charged" as a direct result of the complexities of musical behavior in flux. Groups coalesce, then disband; instruments rove and merge into new groups. Family resemblance and group identity become increasingly fluid as the blended groups develop new behaviors. The piece "ionizes" along physical models where charged elements bond to create new materials.

Groups of Affinity

Ionisation begins with an eight-bar introduction seen in figure 2.1. Here Varèse outlines his approach to two critical elements of compositional structure: sonic materials are parceled into functional groups of affinity, and compositional strategies are introduced that define the manner of interactions and evolution within and among groups of affinity. It follows then that from the outset timbre and process are twinned in *Ionisation*. Varèse quickly articulates three primary groups of affinity that I will refer to as *secco*, *resonant*, and *modified attack*. (See elaboration below.) Ultimately the goal of *Ionisation* is to use compositional strategies delineated in the beginning of the piece to effect a fundamental transformation of these initial groups. A group of affinity by definition requires that members of the group behave in consort. This does not mean, however,

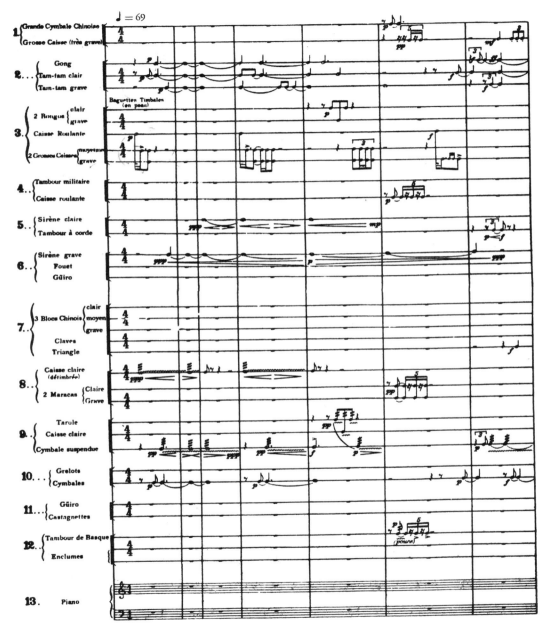

Figure 2.1. Edgard Varèse, *Ionisation*, opening. New York: Colfranc, © 1967. Used by permission.

that the behavioral rapport among the members of the group is frictionless. At the beginning of the work, groups of affinity feature persuasive sonic similarities but present important behavioral differences that are rooted in the multicultural sources of the instruments themselves. By the end of the piece new groups have emerged where deeply shared behavior—even among instruments of vastly different cultural sources—provides common cause that overwrites even striking coloristic dissimilarity. In short, groups characterized by a unified sonic world but which present complex culturally differentiated behaviors become groups of diverse sounds that act in consort. *Schlag* trumps *Zeug* again.

The three initial groups of affinity include:

1. *Secco*: Secco sounds include dry sonorities that are used primarily for the articulation of rhythm. In the introduction these sounds include bass and snare drums. In general, secco sounds provide a platform for the development of rhythmic ideas over the course of the piece. The bass drum part in Player 3, for example, begins with a 32nd-note rhythm, continues with sixteenth-note syncopated music throughout the passage and finishes with an eighth-note triplet just before the theme at rehearsal figure 1 in the score. This construction forms a broadening wedge of rhythmic values and cues Varèse's elaboration of temporal structures that will eventually result in the dramatic augmentation of these very rhythmic values in the coda of the piece. (See figure 2.8.)

2. *Resonant*: The introduction also features a set of resonant sounds including tam-tams, gong, low bass drum, and crash cymbals. Long phrases and mobile dynamic shapes result from the natural decay of these resonant instruments. Ringing sounds are cumbersome vehicles for the expression of rapid or highly articulated rhythms. Their music therefore lacks periodicity and lends a general non-rhythmic sensibility to this group. Just as the secco instruments form the basis for rhythmic elaboration in the piece, the resonant sonorities provide the crucible for the mixing of color. They prompt Varèse's plasmic embellishment of timbre seen in figure 2.9, for example, where anvils and rubbed cymbal plates (the composer's indication is *frottez*) boil over in a Promethean complex of resonant metallic sound.

3. *Modified Attack*: Each instrument in this group departs in some way from a straightforward stroke. There are two kinds of instruments in this group. The first consists of instruments that are not normally struck in performance: maracas are shaken, the guiro is scraped, and sirens along with the *tambour à corde* (lion's roar) are activated by friction. The second group consists of struck instruments whose color is permuted or extended by the modification of attack. A tremolo or grace notes can

modify a snare drum attack; gongs normally resonate freely, but can be choked after the attack. The instruments of modified attack are in fact chameleons—their principal attribute is textural and coloristic malleability. As such they conspire with both secco and resonant instruments to create an environment of evolution and serve to catalyze the process of ionization. A secco snare drum, when rolled, approaches the critical quality of sustain that is central to the resonant group; a dampened cowbell or cymbals can function as a secco rhythmic instrument as is shown in figure 2.7.

Formulation of Theme

The introduction of *Ionisation* shown in figure 2.1 is a statement of sonic and compositional ideas presented in miniature, as prototypes to be treated more completely in the body of the piece. Indeed the three groups of affinity do not function as complete entities until they are stated in three fully realized themes. It is ultimately behavior and not simple sound quality in which we are interested in *Ionisation*. The short fragments of material in the introduction are simply not long enough to manifest important behavioral traits. For that more fully fleshed-out themes are necessary. Three themes represent each of the three groups of affinity: The theme for the secco instruments—the music by which listeners most readily identify *Ionisation*—can be seen in figure 2.2. A resonant theme can be seen in figure 2.3. And the theme for instruments of modified attack is heard in the *grelots* (sleighbells), castanets, and *tambour de basque* (tambourine) music (see figure 2.4).

Predictably in each theme, its group of affinity assures a unified field of color as a consequence of timbral cohesiveness. In short, the sounds of the instruments are compatible enough to blend well. However, each theme also features the pairing of instruments of at least two cultures. The resulting friction among culturally distinguishable identities is amplified in the realm of musical action by means of differentiated rhythmic and textural behaviors. Therefore, instruments that sound alike bifurcate upon examination into culturally distinct subgroups of instruments that act differently.

The four-bar secco theme shown in figure 2.2 is a case in point: it is unified by dry, articulate sounds in all instruments, but is fractured by means of differences in rhythmic language into Latin and European subgroups. The Latin sounds of the bongos and maracas are phrased in three beats while the European agent, the snare drum, is phrased in four beats. (Note again the primacy of behavior: maracas and bongos may *sound* Latin, but they will *act* Latin only if they are given Latin-based music to play—here short repeating rhythmic cells.) After asserting differentiated behavior Varèse immediately builds two important links

Figure 2.2. Edgard Varèse, *Ionisation*, theme for secco instruments, beginning 1 bar before rehearsal number 1. New York: Colfranc, © 1967. Used by permission.

Figure 2.3. Edgard Varèse, *Ionisation*, theme for resonant instruments; 6 bars beginning at rehearsal number 2. New York: Colfranc, © 1967. Used by permission.

that narrow the gap between European and Latin instruments. By incorporating the European sound of the bass drum in the rhythmic language of the Latin instruments Varèse creates a timbral connection that bridges the distance between the two. To me the choice of cymbals and bass drum as agents of the non-European language seems especially appropriate. The bass drum and cymbals had already been thoroughly associated with African American music via the drum set and furthermore have close cousins with Latin percussion instruments such as the *bomba* (a low-pitched drum used in a Puerto Rican musical style of the same name). These very instruments were also famously associated with non-European influences in the Turkish-flavored music of Mozart and Beethoven.

A second strategy of rapprochement is purely rhythmic and seeks to unite the three-beat pattern with the four-beat pattern. The snare drum rhythm one bar at the end of the secco theme (figure 2.2) consists of a sixteenth-note triplet followed by 32nd notes on two halves of the same beat—effectively a rhythm of three *and* four. If one polyrhythmic beat seems like a small gesture towards unification, note the evolution of this idea in the massive commingling of triple and duple rhythms (and the resulting sharing of timbre) that follows at rehearsal figure 7 in the score (see figure 2.9) and at rehearsal figure 13 (see figure 2.8).

Resonant music follows a similar model (see figure 2.3). Traditional Asian instruments—two gongs and a tam-tam—resonate freely in a loosely decelerating rhythmic structure that presents a typical sustain/decay profile of metallic percussion instruments. They are attacked and gradually decay to silence. Instruments of modified attack—coming largely from the European and urban American traditions—invert those traditional shapes. The rolled suspended cymbal first crescendos then decays in unison with the gongs and tam-tam; two sirens support the cymbal shape with a similar crescendo/decrescendo figure.

As in the secco theme, the unifying force of timbral compatibility is counterpoised against a culturally differentiated group of instruments. Varèse's resonant instruments blend together readily, yet split into two culturally distinguished instrumental subgroups that trace quite different shapes of resonance and decay. Accordingly, Varèse's strategy for the unification of the two resonant subgroups relies on the merging of resonance and shape. Two paths diverge, and then meld together into an organic whole at the end of the phrase. A dissonance expressed as the divergence of shape is answered by the convergence of two lines as they decay into unity.

The instruments of modified attack, the tambourine, castanets and sleighbells, present a theme as seen in figure 2.4. With the instruments of modified attack we are less interested in the inherent sounds of the

Figure 2.4. Edgard Varèse, *Ionisation*, theme for instruments of modified attack; 2 bars. New York: Colfranc, © 1967. Used by permission.

instruments, but rather more in the large number of ways in which they can be activated. The techniques of tremolo, shaking, swirling, and friction outline the textural flexibility of this group, and by extension, the ways in which this group of instruments can amplify and extend the textures of the resonant and secco groups.

The instruments of modified attack are the diplomats of the piece—they seek alliance and compromise with the other groups. Their portfolio consists of a multiplicity of texture and wavering rhythmic structures. It is therefore not a surprise that their theme features a vivid portrayal of texture but cuts a less decisive rhythmic and cultural profile. A rhythmic structure in alternating duple and triple beats stutters forward through a thicket of grace notes and tremolos (note, two kinds of tremolo, the shaken sleighbells, and tambourine thumb roll). By toggling back and forth between duple and triple rhythmic contexts, the instruments of modified attack are stricken with a kind of rhythmic paralysis that mirrors the bifurcated duple/triple rhythmic language of the secco group. This polarity is answered firmly at the end of their phrase in figure 2.4 as the modified attack instruments reach their ultimate compromise in the only absolute unison of the passage, a single note played without any ornamentation. Its singularity connects clearly to the unequivocal rhythms of the snare drum, but the unison event is part of a triplet—the rhythmic language associated with the Latin instruments of the secco group. With this single note, the instruments of modified attack assert themselves as the mutable tissue of connection within the piece and successfully bridge the triple/duple gap in the secco music.

Modes of Interaction

I believe that *Ionisation* is a great piece of music. I further believe it can be heard and appreciated as a purely musical statement. It is among the first and remains perhaps the finest work of percussion music. However, I also believe that for anyone interested in the sociology of early experimental percussion music, and especially for those interested in modes of immigration by which "foreign" instruments become a part of a mainstream musical vocabulary, it contains important extramusical lessons. In the anthropology of instrumental evolution, how did the cymbal, for example, transform itself from a traditional instrument of the near Middle East to a sound with western utility but strong traditional associations (see Beethoven's use of cymbals in his Ninth Symphony) to a completely westernized instrument that every conservatory student must master? Had western composers simply discovered a Turkish sound that blended well with their European sensibilities? I don't think so. The appeal of the cymbal was precisely because it was foreign. The dissonance that resulted from its early presence in western music—its evocation of exotic culture and the sheer shock of its clangorous sound—provided the pressure for redefinition. Resolution of this dissonance meant that the new instrument was played in nontraditional ways in order to make it compatible with the sound world of the orchestra. Conversely the new sound also molded the context of the orchestra—aesthetic sensibilities changed and new music was made in which the cymbal could find its place in mainstream vocabulary. The cymbal found a home in the orchestra not because its path of immigration was frictionless, but because friction along the path provided the fuel necessary for reconsideration and recontextualization.

Ionisation presents a model for precisely this kind of dissonance between culturally disparate musical elements and the process by which meaningful reconsideration can be effected. Each of the three primary themes demonstrates the energizing force of dissonance to be found in the fluid negotiations across demarcations of acoustics, musical color, and culture. Dissonance in *Ionisation* is a powerful force of distinction, but beyond that it also provides the handhold by which differences might be reconciled. Since the secco theme features rhythmic dissonance between groupings of three and four, the most obvious path of reconciliation is through rhythm. Likewise it is through equilibration of phrase shapes in the resonant instruments, and of texture among the instruments of modified attack that forward momentum in the piece is fueled. Varèse calls his piece *Ionisation* with good reason. Uniting disparate forces into a convincing whole—the resolution of inherent dissonance—provides both the compositional imperative and the lasting poetry of the music.

The processes of rapprochement among dissonant elements in *Ionisation*—what I think of as *modes of interaction*—described in detail below, consist of four successively powerful transformational strategies: *juxtaposition*, *intersection*, *replacement*, and *radical filtration*. These strategies, presented in this order, serve to reshape the groups of affinity over the course of the piece.

Juxtaposition is the weakest of the four modes of interaction—and the easiest one to engineer. With juxtaposition, groups simply occupy the same space at the same time, but do not interact directly with each other. Overlaying one type of material over another enables interaction via osmosis. Note how dense and full of activity the music is in figure 2.5. The density creates a saturation of the musical space and the greater likelihood that the three groups of affinity will frequently be juxtaposed and will therefore commingle. Note also that at this early point in the piece the sounds of the three groups of affinity are allowed to mix while the identities of their original themes remain unaffected.

Intersection offers a more potent strategy for interaction among types of material. Here groups come into direct contact with one another by means of shared notes. We have seen an important example of intersection in the secco theme as snare drum accents are doubled by the *fouet* (slapstick) in bar 2 of rehearsal figure 1 in the score (see figure 2.2). These points of intersection importantly connect members of two different groups of affinity—here secco sounds and instruments of modified attack—thereby uniting quite different sounds into a single sonic alloy.

In many ways, intersection grows naturally out of juxtaposition. Juxtaposition floods the space with events. The more things that happen at any moment, the greater the likelihood that events will intersect as simultaneity. Accidental intersection is frequent in the example in figure 2.5, but later in the piece it becomes a powerful strategy in the purposeful moments of unification that connect instruments from different groups. In one of many such examples to be found in figure 2.5, the second half of beat three in the first bar is played simultaneously by tam-tam, bongo, and bass drum, effectively creating a momentary sonic alloy between members of the secco and resonant groups of affinity. Other simultaneities in this passage combine the guiro (a striated gourd performed by scraping the grooves with a thin stick) and bongos as well as the snare drum and maracas. These instances link the secco group to the instruments of modified attack. The strategies of juxtaposition and intersection thereby create an important and effective transition between the expository nature of the thematic materials in the introduction and full-blown interactive modality that informs the second half of the piece.

Replacement is an especially effective mode of interaction because it deals directly with issues of behavior and not just sound. With replacement, groups commingle by speaking each other's languages. The

Figure 2.5. Edgard Varèse, *Ionisation*, juxtaposition at bar 3 of rehearsal number 4. New York: Colfranc, © 1967. Used by permission.

maracas and tambourine of the modified attack group play articulated single notes in the quintuple rhythm of bar six (see figure 2.1). In this instance the instruments of modified attack adopt articulate behavior usually associated with the secco group.

The replacement strategy takes an important first step towards conciliation among the groups by first weakening the forces of attraction within the original groups of affinity. The goal of *Ionisation* is to resolve initially polarized relationships into fluid, multifaceted sonic plasma by the end of the work. In order to allow members of groups to combine with one another as free-floating sonic radicals, the initial forces of attraction within original groups must first be loosened. As new primary relationships develop, the potency of earlier alliances is inevitably diminished. Thus as both cause and effect of this process, the forces of connection within the original themes release to allow for the atomization and eventual redistribution of elements as parts of newly blended groups. Often the process of the dissolution of a group, its subsequent atomization into sonic components, and their eventual reassimilation as new structures takes place gradually and fluidly. The evolving treatment of the secco theme serves as a good example.

Recall the original secco theme from figure 2.2. Now notice the same theme in figure 2.6. Here a two-bar section of the original secco theme is heard again, but this time with darker sounding soft felt mallets on the snare drum. In this instance, as softer mallets, which are usually reserved for resonant instruments, replace the more customary snare drum sticks, the rhythmic identity of the secco theme remains but its color has changed.

Two bars later, the theme has been trimmed to a single bar and played on bongos. Replacement goes both ways: the theme changes color yet again, and at the same time the bongos abandon their association with the three-beat Latin-inspired phrase and play the "European" duple theme. The initial dichotomized relationship between bongos and snare drum has been narrowed considerably. By the time we next hear the secco theme it has been fractured into components so small that we are dealing effectively only with emblems of the theme. In figure 2.7, we see the syncopated sixteenth–eighth–sixteenth secco pattern expressed in the resonant language of the bass drums. The identity of the secco material has been sufficiently degraded by fragmentation that the coloristic language of the resonant instruments can permeate it. Resonant colors replace secco colors; secco rhythms replace resonant rhythms.

This one-two punch of fracturing and reorchestrating—the process of atomizing original material to make it permeable to the timbral language of other groups—allows Varèse to replace the music of one group with the instruments of another group by means of graduated paths of timbral equivalency. A path of timbral equivalency, expressed in the secco music through the examples above, shows Varèse's preoccupation

Figure 2.6. Edgard Varèse, *Ionisation*, theme at rehearsal number 4. New York: Colfranc, © 1967. Used by permission.

Figure 2.7. Edgard Varèse, *Ionisation*, emblems of the theme after rehearsal number 6. New York: Colfranc, © 1967. Used by permission.

with the linkage between sound and musical behavior. Secco material *sounds* increasingly resonant via the importation of resonant colors, and resonant instruments begin to *act* like secco instruments by speaking their rhythmic language. The seemingly unbridgeable polarity between two groups has lessened to the point of metamorphosis.

Timbral equivalency also assures an integrated narrative connection along a carefully scripted path: no matter how radical the transformation along the path might ultimately be, incremental steps of timbral equivalency mean that all modifications will be recognizably related to the original version. Small steps along the path of timbral equivalency prepare the way for just such a radical transformation in the coda (figure 2.8). Here the massive and resonant clusters of the piano, gongs, tam-tams, and bass drum convey secco rhythmic material. The secco theme consists of only of fragmentary, totemic remnants of the original rhythmic proportions—played this time at 1/4 speed as quarter note, half note, and quarter note. The secco theme as *behavior* still exists, but resonant instruments at the opposite end of the coloristic spectrum

Figure 2.8. Edgard Varèse, *Ionisation*, totemic representation of secco material by resonant instruments in the coda. New York: Colfranc, © 1967. Used by permission.

Figure 2.9. Edgard Varèse, *Ionisation*, radical filtration of ensemble as secco voice at rehearsal number 7. New York: Colfranc, © 1967. Used by permission.

have replaced the dry articulate language of the snare drum. Timbral equivalency, parsed as a series of incremental steps of coloristic replacement, makes even a transformation this stunning seem almost inevitable.

The gradual nature of a path of timbral equivalency seems gentle and organic compared with Varèse's most dramatic mode of interaction. At three critical junctures in the second half of the piece, *radical filtration* creates a powerful momentary unity of all available materials. With radical filtration, Varèse forces all instruments to speak a single language, straining all sounds through the same sieve, as it were. In figure 2.9, for example, *all* instruments speak as a secco voice. Resonant instruments are choked (or replaced in the case of the cymbal and gong players who play *cencerros*, the dry Latin cowbells); instruments of modified attack play single unadorned strokes. The prominence of triplets in the ensemble counterpoised against duple solo parts in the *tambour militaire* (military snare drum) and *tarole* (higher snare drum) reprises the "three against four" vocabulary of the snare drum and bongos in the original secco theme. (Radical filtration is the musical equivalent of a barn raising: whatever roles the resonant and modified attack instruments have been playing to this point are suddenly abandoned; they drop everything and come to the aid of the secco instruments.)

Radical filtration of material using resonant vocabulary takes place in figure 2.10. Using only the metallic sounds of *enclumes* (anvils), triangle, gongs and cymbals, the entire ensemble *acts* like the original resonant theme. As in the original theme, sirens and other instruments of modified attack—including the *frottez* of one cymbal plate rubbing against the other—comment on and profile the natural decay trajectories of the gongs and suspended cymbals.

A final brief but dramatic filtration through the voice of instruments of modified attack can be heard in the long tail of the siren in the fermata before rehearsal figure 12 in the score. Not every instrument can readily modify its attack. So instead of saturating the space with an entire ensemble speaking as modified attack, Varèse profiles this voice by an abrupt cutoff of all other sounds that launches the siren on its only solo voyage of the piece.

What resolution can there be to a piece that opposes three vividly contrasted groups of sonic behaviors? One supposes in some banal sense that there must be a winner among the three. A romantic European notion of form would lead to the ascendancy of one group. (Brahms might have acknowledged the rhythmic dominance of secco music through a grand unison reading of the snare drum theme with resonant instruments in tow as accompanimental voices.) But that would have forced Varèse to concede that there had been a favored candidate all along—a mainstream vocabulary into which foreign elements must

Figure 2.10. Edgard Varèse, *Ionisation*, radical filtration of ensemble as resonant voice, bars 51–55 (from two successive pages in the score). New York: Colfranc, © 1967. Used by permission.

necessarily be subsumed. But *Ionisation* models a culture of immigration: contact with "otherness" leaves nothing and no one unchanged.

Ultimately the goal of *Ionisation*, it seems to me, is to reconcile a high degree of musical and extramusical differentiation by converting the polarities inherent among Varèse's chosen array of instruments into a flexible, interactive environment in which initial differences are overshadowed by the promise of common cause. In this light, the coda seen in figure 2.8 plays the decisive role of apotheosis. It serves as the ultimate statement of the work, not as the canonization of one identity over another, but the embodiment of ideal process.

Surprisingly, Varèse sums up in *Ionisation* by introducing a new family of instruments not previously heard in the piece. Even more surprisingly, the new sounds—note the piano, chimes, and glockenspiel in figure 2.8—have direct ties to a European past, which the first part of the piece has seemed to disavow. Some have seen this as the ascendancy of the forces of melody over the brutishness of pure rhythm, and as such, proof that *Ionisation* achieved a new high-water mark of refinement and nobility among percussion pieces. When Chou Wen Chung visited UCSD in 2002 at the invitation of the composers in the Music Department, I asked him what he thought Varèse's purpose was in the last-minute introduction of pitched percussion in the coda of *Ionisation*. He answered quickly and surely that there were *no* pitched instruments in *Ionisation*. These new sounds, Chou held, were just a new batch of noises. My view is the reverse: that there are no nonpitched instruments in *Ionisation*. Each sound, no matter how noisy its surface, also acts as pitch and necessarily enjoins a rhetorical connection to all other pitches. In his final bid at rapprochement among the groups, Varèse calculates that if the pitches of every instrument must inevitably relate to the pitches of the piano, glockenspiel, and chimes, then they also necessarily relate to each other. (In a moment of uncommon relevance from my high school education I remember that if A equals B and B equals C, then A must equal C.)

Why did Varèse introduce instruments of pure pitch so late in the piece? I don't really know. But I do know that the focused ringing sonorities and environment of pitch at the end of *Ionisation* create the plasma of belonging in which all instruments both belong (and fail to belong) in the same measure. The final statement of perhaps the most significant work written for percussion is pure Lewis Carroll—"curioser and curioser." The secco theme—or what is left of it—is given to the resonant instruments. The piano and gongs play at a quarter of the original speed, while the *Grand Tam-tam (très profond)* imitates at 1/24 the original tempo. The snare drums have fully converted (by means of modified attack) to the crescendo/decrescendo shapes of the resonant theme. The only bit of original material still played by its original instrument is a one-measure quotation of the snare drum theme beginning in the fourth bar of figure 2.8. However, here Varèse asks for *voilé*, a muted covering of the drum, giving this moment a veiled, symbolic sense. When everything is other than what it initially appeared to be, when every role has been shared and every voice imitated, then what meaning does the word "foreign" have finally? I should like to sidestep an Aesop-style morality tale here. *Ionisation* does not propose a method by which we can all get along. But it does show that powerful interactions among disparate groups do not inevitably lead to a fight for space. Sometimes a space can be created in which fighting is not necessary.

From Ellis Island to the Golden Gate

Varèse opened the floodgates. *Ionisation* was not the first work for percussion instruments alone—among important pieces, both George Antheil's *Ballet mécanique* and Amadeo Roldán's *Ritmicas* predate it. But it was, as Borges said of Kafka, so important that it influenced even things that came before it. No one could hear *Ionisation* and not recognize its strength as a work of art, nor the lasting and legitimizing effect it had for composers of percussion music. It is a piece that one simply does not get used to. To this day I am as dazed by its cacophony and as stunned by the precision of its formal argument as I was when I first listened to it nearly thirty years ago. (That memorable moment took place on a brief trip home to Iowa City in the midst of a long tour with a regional blues band. The feeling of emotional vertigo—that everything I held true about music had suddenly been challenged—was in many ways responsible for my choice of a life in contemporary music.)

Ionisation cast a huge shadow over the percussion pieces that came in its immediate wake. A subtle rejoinder to Varèse's mammoth statement came in Henry Cowell's work from 1934, *Ostinato Pianissimo*. In many ways, *Ostinato Pianissimo* was a pivotal work for Cowell. It is a surprisingly delicate composition for a composer best known for inventing tone clusters that often featured fists and forearms crashing down on the piano keyboard. Cowell's gentle rebuttal to Varèse's heroic *Ionisation* prefigures Morton Feldman's ethereal *The King of Denmark* (1964) as an answer to Karlheinz Stockhausen's *Zyklus* (1959). To be sure, *Ostinato Pianissimo* is both gentle and clear. Supple melodic lines played by dampened pianos, bongos, tom-toms, rice bowls, and a solo xylophone cycle round each other in out-of-phase phrases of different lengths until they are reconciled in a brief flurry of *fortissimo* outbursts at the end of the piece. (See fig. 2.11.)

The rice bowls in particular give the work the flavoring of gamelan, but the truly Asian element of the piece is the multilayered cycling of phrases that comprise the form. Cowell was dealing in his own way with

Figure 2.11. Henry Cowell, *Ostinato Pianissimo*, bars 69–72. Philadelphia: Merion Music, © 1979. Used by permission of Carl Fischer, Inc., New York.

the same issues that confronted Varèse: percussion instruments were indebted to the musical languages of other cultures. But how much should a composer import from those cultures, and how might these elements be made to cohere? By borrowing the temporal structures of Asian music, gamelan in particular, Cowell anchored his rapport with non-Western percussion traditions not by borrowing surface sonorities, but to the deeper notions of form and process.

Cowell felt more at home in a world of cultural crossover than Varèse did. His childhood in San Francisco exposed him to a wide variety of musical and cultural influences from Asia. And the imprimatur of California as the exotic home of free-form experimentation lent credibility to his adventures in cultural matchmaking. Indeed California was rapidly becoming home to a long line of American iconoclasts. It has become a distinguished lineage: from Cowell to Lou Harrison, John Cage, Harry Partch, Kenneth Gaburo, Robert Erickson, Terry Riley, and the young Steve Reich. It seemed that the weight of inherited tradition was lighter in California. After all, a place where everything was new could hardly exact a penalty for new ideas. California was a place where anyone could try anything without worrying what Beethoven might have thought about it. The basic issues of early percussion music had not changed since *Ionisation*—how to reconcile multicultural musical vocabulary within the fundamentally western context of a musical composition—but when it came to experimentation, the question in California was not "why," but "why not."

First Construction (in Metal) (1939)

John Cage

John Cage's *First Construction (in Metal)* is not strictly speaking a California composition. It was created in Seattle while Cage was composer-in-residence at the Cornish School. However, *First Construction (in Metal)* is a piece with distinct Californian sensibilities. It took flight in a whirlwind of cross-cultural currents. And it smashed Cage's rapport with Arnold Schoenberg and Old World traditions to smithereens. Cage's break with Schoenberg, with whom he had studied briefly in Los Angeles, was stunningly reinforced by Schoenberg himself, who responded to Cage's invitation to a concert of percussion music by saying that he would not be free to attend such a concert "now or at any time."[3]

First Construction (in Metal) epitomizes an intertwining of two lifelong concerns in Cage's music. He was first and perhaps foremost a structuralist. For all of the apparent freedom in compositions from his indeterminate period, he remained committed to the need for discipline and process in composition. "Anything goes as long as nothing matters," he said once in a public lecture. He was also undeniably attracted to chance—to the inevitability that what would actually happen in a performance of music could not be completely foreseen by him or anyone else. A series of works for percussion ensemble, starting with his *First Construction (in Metal)* in 1939 and continuing with two more "constructions" and the radiant *Amores*,

---

3. Quoted in Alan Rich, *American Pioneers: Ives to Cage and Beyond* (London: Phaidon, 1995).

premiered in early 1943, were suspended between the forces of chance and structure. These are works that balance between the natural unpredictability of percussion sounds and the necessity to contain and define them in a musical composition.

The customary western solution for containing and defining the nature of sounds in a composition has been standardized notation. While notation is very good at telling a performer what note to play and when to play it, it has been at best a cumbersome mechanism for specifying the sound quality of percussion instruments. And since sound was of central concern to Cage and his contemporaries, and indeed anyone who composed using percussion instruments, notation became an especially vexing problem. There are, of course, plentiful variations of sound among different violinists all playing the same pitch at the same degree of intensity for the same length of time. We have learned to tolerate these differences and, on the highest level, celebrate them as interpretation. But with percussion even the simplest indication—cymbal with medium mallet, say—opens the door for a huge variety of sounds among different players. Some composers have sought to control the timbral unpredictability of percussion music by increasing the level of notational specificity in their scores. One thinks of Elliott Carter's pinpoint descriptions of striking areas and mallet construction in the 1966 version of his *Eight Pieces for Four Timpani*. However, the kind of detail in the Carter score, if executed scrupulously on different sets of instruments with different heads in different acoustical environments, assures precisely that no two results will be the same. In light of the ambiguities of percussive material, it seems that the more painstaking the notation, the less likely it can be reproduced with accuracy over time.

Cage was not too concerned, however, with making sure that each performance of his music sounded exactly the same. In fact his infatuation with percussion in the late 1930s and early 1940s flourished *because of* and not in spite of the ambiguities of percussive sonority. For a composer headed towards indeterminacy, the unpredictability of percussion was a natural first step. In *First Construction (in Metal)* he unleashes a metallic bedlam: thunder sheets, anvils, metal rods applied to piano strings, sleigh bells, Japanese temple bells, water gong, oxen bells, Turkish cymbals, gongs, and tam-tam. I have heard dozens of performances of this work and never have I heard the same set of sounds twice. In addition to the obvious matter of instrument and mallet choice, ringing metal instruments combine with one another to reinforce or cancel unique clusters of harmonics and fundamental tones. No conventional score can rein in all possible sonic options for this group of instruments. Cage punned once that the goal in life was to figure out what cage you were in and get out. If indeed Pandora were his guiding muse, he could not have picked a better *entrée* to the unknown than his construction in metal.

To contain sonic forces of such volatility, Cage opted for a formal architecture of almost puritanical strictness. The notional equation for Cage throughout his series of percussion pieces seemed to be that unpredictability of sonic content must be answered by predictability of form. With each piece the relative rigidity of form mirrored the volatility of his sound world. His *Third Construction*, for example, has a more forgiving form in direct response to the greater predictability of its sound world. The ultimate statement of this equation came in Cage's "silent" masterpiece from 1948, *4'33"*, where the sounds involved, if any, are the product of chance occurrences in the outside world. To secure this level of indeterminacy, Cage built a multisectional form precisely four minutes and thirty-three seconds long. He then filled that form with whatever might be sounding during that period of time. In *4'33"* a scrupulously constructed form is used to contain the greatest imaginable degree of sonic uncertainty.

Cage describes the global structure of *First Construction (in Metal)* in a foreword to the score as follows: "sixteen sections of sixteen bars and a coda of nine bars. Each 16-bar section is subdivided into phrases of $4+3+2+3+4$ bars. On the large scale there is an exposition of four 16-bar phrases $(1-1-1-1)$ followed by a 12-phrase development $(3-2-3-4)$ and a 9-bar extension $(2-3-4)$."

Cage allows no exceptions to his plan. There is no elongation of a 16-bar phrase to accommodate especially resonant or volcanic material, no variation from the constancy of the $4+3+2+3+4$ subdivisions. The development is separated from the exposition by an increase in tempo. Furthermore the development section itself is subdivided into groups separated from each other by increasingly faster tempi. The listener will note that the remarkable section marked "exceedingly slow" comes at the end of the first three sections of the development section. The excerpt in figure 2.12 is drawn from the opening of the piece and demonstrates the clarity with which Cage articulates the internal subdivisions within the basic 16-bar phrase. The first four bars foreground thunder sheets and string piano;[4] the following 3-bar section is a duo between piano and oxen bells; the 2-bar section that follows changes color completely with a trio for orchestral bells, brake drums, and Turkish cymbals.

Cage's formal strategy here is compartmentalization. Each subphrase of the opening sixteen bars of the piece is an internally coherent sonic unit: each is clearly marked by a unique set of colors, and none is so resonant that long decay times might confuse the form by bleeding across subdivisional boundaries. This critical sense of sonic unity can be cultivated in the 2-bar subphrase of orchestral bells, brake drums, and

---

4. Cage asks that an assistant to the pianist apply a metal rod to the piano strings while the pianist plays in order to produce ascending and descending siren-like sounds.

Figure 2.12. John Cage, *First Construction (in Metal)*, bars 1–11. Copyright © 1962 by Henmar Press, Inc., New York. All rights reserved. Used by permission.

cymbals, by careful choice of mallets. If the bells are played very softly with hard sticks to reinforce the upper harmonics of the brake drums and the cymbals are also played very softly with yarn mallets, perhaps midway between the edge and the dome to cultivate a high filtered noise, they can then complete the sonic unification by binding the bells to the brake drums. This reinforces my experience in general that a slightly underbalanced noise typically binds two strongly pitched events of the same register. Note Bartók's use of a soft tam-tam stroke to connect low piano chords in the opening of his *Sonata for Two Pianos and Percussion* as a prime example.

The formal clarity of the opening cannot be sustained, however. The piece begins to fill up with sound as the tempo becomes incrementally faster and the sound world increasingly more diverse and resonant. In figure 2.13 we see a sonorous and volatile passage drawn from near the end of the development. The enormous resonance of the piano, temple gongs, and thunder sheet tremolos along with a general increase in rhythmic complexity among the other instruments creates a chaotic and unstable sonic environment. Resonance often extends the presence of groups across formal subdivisions. Materials mix and collide and soon Cage's dignified formal plan is bulging at the seams.

In a passage drawn from still later in the piece (figure 2.14), the sheer quantity of noise created by the gongs and tam-tams threatens to rupture the form. Critical questions of interpretation arise here. Is it a reasonable goal in performance to control sound and use it as a means of representing form? Or is the point here that percussion sounds are so unpredictable and volatile and that any form must shape itself around the sounds? In short, do we let the form control the sounds or the sounds control the form? These questions point to the pivotal role Cage's works for percussion had in his evolution as a composer. In the late 1930s Cage himself was suspended between the formally determined structures of European modernism and his future path towards the aesthetic of Zen and indeterminacy. Any interpretation of *First Construction (In Metal)* must likewise embrace the ambiguous linkage between sound and form. An explosive performance that indulges the inherent chaos of metal percussion instruments negates the precision of Cage's formal sense; it misses the beauty of his mind. On the other hand, an overly cautious reading that seeks to control the incendiary musical environment of the *Construction* fails to acknowledge the risks Cage took along his path; it misses the beauty of his soul. (For me the most poignant moment in the recording of Cage's Harvard Lectures was the melancholy quality in his voice when he said that by composing *4'33"* he lost friends.)

An interpreter's choice of sounds takes on a very practical quality in what I see as the "red on red" problem in *First Construction (in Metal)*. That is to say that textural clarity diminishes in an ensemble of a single

Figure 2.13. John Cage, *First Construction (in Metal)*, bars 120–129. Copyright © 1962 by Henmar Press, Inc., New York. All rights reserved. Used by permission.

Figure 2.14. John Cage, *First Construction (in Metal)*, excerpt from near the end, bars 246–255. Copyright © 1962 by Henmar Press, Inc., New York. All rights reserved. Used by permission.

color. When metal sounds are heard against the background of other metal sounds, it is difficult to hear one line as independent from others. A performer's tendency is to use harder mallets on primary lines to distinguish them from the similarity of background voices. However, when the (now more brightly colored) primary line suddenly becomes secondary, other performers feel the need to compensate with harder sticks themselves to assert the primacy of their lines. The result is an escalation of attack, a problematic strategy since harder mallets produce noisier attacks and attack noises are by nature similar. Therefore the attempt to distinguish individual voices by playing them with harder sticks creates more uniformity rather than greater distinction. A form of compartmentalization like Cage's cannot function in an environment of coloristic uniformity and reveals again the critical mutual dependency of form and sound in the percussion music of John Cage.

The Big Chill

John Cage's *First Construction (in Metal)* is simultaneously a beginning and an ending. It was arguably the genesis of the fruitful polarity between indeterminacy and structure that would inform the next half century of Cage's musical life. However, the very germinal qualities of works like *First Construction*, *Ostinato Pianissimo*, and *Ionisation* locate them as fundamentally exploratory in nature. As adolescence assures old age (under the best of circumstances), a period of exploration inevitably prefigures a more settled phase of consolidation and development. With early percussion music there was a sizable gap between the phase of exploration and the beginning of the mature language of development. The series of major percussion ensemble works that began in the early 1930s with *Ionisation* and Roldán's *Ritmicas* concluded in 1943 with Cage's *Amores* and Carlos Chavez's *Toccata para instrumentos de percusión*. Then there was nothing. The end came as suddenly and unexpectedly as did the beginning. Following Cage, Varèse, and Cowell came almost twenty-eight years of near silence from percussion. The next great American work for an ensemble of percussion instruments arrived, in my opinion, in 1971 with Steve Reich's *Drumming*.[5]

Why the big chill? There are undoubtedly numerous and interrelated reasons. Perhaps the novelty of new percussion sounds had worn thin. Or maybe those composers continued their experiments with

---

5. Lou Harrison's major percussion work, Concerto for Violin and Percussion Orchestra, was written in 1959. I do not discuss it because of the central role of the violin. Reich's *Drumming* includes voices and piccolo, of course. I include it as a percussion ensemble work since the nonpercussion parts function in a largely supportive role.

novel sounds by turning to new sources. We know that Varèse composed very few pieces of any kind through the late 1930s and 1940s. His music needed the kind of noisy punch in the guts that only the fledgling discipline of electronic music could provide. Except for *Density 21.5*, his only published composition from the 1940s, he would wait until 1954 and his electroacoustic masterpiece *Déserts* before again exploring noise as primary compositional tool. Perhaps the very source of his interest in percussion—the newness of the noises—proved to be too expendable as compositional collateral. Listeners had accepted percussion sounds into the mainstream of contemporary music. And for Varèse and others that had been the kiss of death.

Perhaps the outbreak of World War II dampened the spirit of unbridled experimentalism that had dominated the 1920s and 1930s. Perhaps the military history of many European percussion instruments made them distasteful to composers. Certainly Varèse's sirens were colored with a new emotional aura in light of air raids. (I performed *Ionisation* during my studies in Germany in the early 1980s. Even at the distance of thirty-five years from world war, the sounds of sirens were an unsettling reminder to many audience members old enough to remember the war.) Or perhaps wartime xenophobia had transformed the culturally vivid sounds of percussion from exotic to merely foreign.

Perhaps the reason was more basic: we get tired of new toys. Percussion had been the playground of the adventurous and curious. Once curiosity had been satisfied, experimentally minded composers moved on. Percussion was no longer new, but it was also not mature enough to support an enduring discourse capable of slow and meaningful development. Anvils by themselves were no longer shocking. Yet, what did one do with a nonshocking anvil? There was no language to make sense of them, no ability to generalize them as a part of a broadly shared matrix of meaning. Likewise, once audiences had heard a handful of pieces with a world-tour approach to multiculturalism, the simple presence of multiple cultures failed to stimulate in the same way.

There was, however, one overriding difference between percussion at the time of Varèse's *Ionisation* and the percussion of Steve Reich's *Drumming*: the presence and capacity of the percussionists themselves. Nonpercussionists—dancers, other instrumentalists, and friends of the composers—played the music of Cage, Cowell, and Varèse. Early percussion music by Cage and Lou Harrison notably has no snare drum rolls or timpani parts since these specialized techniques were thought to be beyond the players of the time. On the other hand, contemporary percussion music in the 1970s was performed by highly skilled percussionists with a wide knowledge of percussion technique and contemporary music. When Steve Reich formed one of the first ensembles of percussionists to develop his work *Drumming*, he also created a mechanism of perpetuating percussion music. Some of Reich's early collaborators were also founding members of the legendary Canadian percussion group Nexus. These percussionists suddenly found themselves in a group without much percussion music to play. The need for repertoire resulted in cycles of commissioning, interpretive development, recording, and teaching that have produced both great music and a self-perpetuating dynamic in what might be called the second school of percussion ensemble music.

Why the big chill between 1943 and 1970? Why didn't Stravinsky compose a piece for an ensemble of percussionists? Why did Varèse never write a percussion solo or Bartók a chamber concerto? Perhaps the answer is simple. Maybe nobody asked them. It was the Reich/Nexus percussionists who started heating things up again. And beyond them, there were groups in Europe like Les Percussions de Strasbourg and Kroumata in Stockholm, and along with them, soloists like the Americans Jan Williams and Ray DesRoches. Christoph Caskell in Cologne and Sylvio Gualda in Paris were doing the same thing. They asked, begged, insisted on new music for percussion. And it is with very great thanks to them that we have music like *Drumming*, Iannis Xenakis's *Persephassa* and *Psappha*, Charles Wuorinen's *Janissary Music* and Morton Feldman's *Crippled Symmetry*.

Much about the politics of culture has also changed. A piece like Cage's *Third Construction*, with its instrumentation drawn from a dozen world cultures, might seem less like experimentation and more like appropriation in today's climate. A deepening critical discourse has illuminated the mechanisms of cultural sharing and evolution. We have rightfully become suspicious of the universalizing pressures of monoculturalism. Indeed as the opportunities of living in a culturally fluid world have risen, so have the stakes. With many thanks to Varèse, Cage, and Cowell, today's percussionists enjoy an unprecedented range of cultural exchange. If this can be understood in a reflective environment that balances the opportunities of cultural exchange with the need for stewardship of diversity, then we will have successfully translated the explorations of early percussion music into the cultural realities of the new century.

The Gap-Toothed Smile

After the explosions in percussion music that marked the 1930s and early 1940s the silence that followed was, as they say, deafening. Young percussionists today often innocently presume that a rich and lasting repertoire for percussion is and always has been inevitable. But I don't think there was any real assurance of survival during its long period of dormancy in the middle of the century. Interesting and virtuosic percussion music might well have been a passing phenomenon: a doomed species like the futurists' noise contraptions, momentarily interesting but quickly lost to the crosscurrents of history, rather than an enduring organism like the string quartet. With the chaos of radical artistic change in the wind and the storms of war on the horizon, the waters of the mid-twentieth century were rising fast. There was no guarantee that every worthy creature had boarded the ark.

But of course all was not lost. There was noise at the end of the tunnel. A new generation of composers and percussionists began to translate the experiments of Cage, Varèse, and Cowell into a language that would be relevant to the late twentieth and early twenty-first centuries. Thus adventurous new work came via commissioning, improvising, and creating new technologies. In this regard I was pleased to note recently that when a student asked me how I find new music to play, I could think of only two solo pieces that I have learned in the last fifteen years that I did not commission or premiere. The two exceptions were fortunate invitations to learn *Silver Streetcar for the Orchestra* and *Sen VI* as part of residencies that Alvin Lucier and Toshio Hosokawa gave at the University of California, San Diego. Other than these two works, everything else for me has been brand new. It is of course a luxurious situation to have such a large amount of control over one's own fate. But it is also a welcome reminder of the enormous responsibility that each percussionist alive and working today bears towards the construction of a meaningful repertoire. Simply put, without these efforts we would have nothing to play.

Commissioning new music is often a frightening and sometimes a discouraging experience. I will never forget commissioning Charles Wuorinen's *Percussion Duo* with the pianist James Avery. It was the first time I had ever commissioned a new piece of music, and somehow it came as a surprise to me that, if I could not find the funding necessary to satisfy the contract we had with Charles, I myself would have to pay. When that unhappy realization came I was stricken with the kind of financial paralysis that comes from growing up in a frugal farming family. How could we afford it? However, my wife Wendy, to her everlasting credit, took me by the hand, led me to the bank, withdrew approximately one-third of our entire savings and handed it personally to the commission coordinator at the University of Iowa where we were both students at the time. I remember thinking that this had better be a damn good piece or I can't come home.

Of course there are other ways to create new work besides commissioning. Improvisers have added immeasurably to the compendium of new percussion music and to the means by which it can be made. Two new classifications, performer/composers and e-percussionists working with a variety of electronic media, have likewise created both new music and new modes of creation. I have never been interested in becoming a composer myself, and although I sometimes have been an enthusiastic improviser, most dispassionate accounts would indicate that I am not very good at it. So my choice has been to commission: that pact of duality whereby the ideas and conceptions of a composer abut directly with the interpretations and capacities of a performer. I think in fact that the inevitable frictions along this path have made it especially appealing. I happily attempt to learn, embody (and sometimes even contravene) the language I discover in a composition by another person.

My strategy in commissioning has been largely hands-off. I rarely indicate to a composer what kind of piece the new work should be. Questions of how long or how difficult, whether it should include or reject technology, the presence or absence of new instrumental resources and techniques are left completely up to him or her. In essence I commission the composer of a piece of music, not the piece itself. It is precisely the necessity to clarify and detail the qualities of a new work with that composer over the course of composing and rehearsing the piece that draws me to the act of commissioning. The amount and quality of contact has varied widely, as one might suppose it would, with individual composers. My work with Roger Reynolds took place on at least a weekly if not daily basis for more than a year and a half, during which time *Watershed* was discussed, composed, learned, and refined. We met subsequently for nearly two years to define and codify the performance practice of the piece into a workable score that other percussionists could also play. With Brian Ferneyhough in the case of *Bone Alphabet*, I received the score in the early summer of 1991. Besides seeing him regularly in faculty meetings at the University of California, San Diego, where we were both teaching, our next contact was in February of 1992 at the dress rehearsal for the premiere of the piece. Both ends of the spectrum of contact and collaboration have advantages and disadvantages.

Commissioning the series of pieces for cello and percussion with my duo partner Maya Beiser has had its own particular qualities. From composers with whom we worked as members of the Bang on a Can All-Stars, including Julia Wolfe, Lois Vierk and Nick Didkovsky, to composers like Martin Bresnick, Robert Rowe and Chinary Ung, our commissions have had to make sense of the unusual sonic resources that a duo for cello and percussion offers. Any use of the idiomatic clichés for either instrument—an attempt to treat the cello as pretty and fragile or the percussion as bombastic and overpowering—would be destined for failure. The key to success in these commissions was finding the slim area of overlapping possibilities between the two instruments. For that reason we really needed to know the composers we commissioned, or more to the point, they really needed to know us. We often had to demonstrate what might or might not work. Sometimes we succeeded. I remember explaining our commissioning proposal to Chinary Ung with the notion that an untested instrumental combination like cello and percussion might open up new doors to secret sounds. His long silence and sly smile after my sales pitch was the real-life version of a cartoon light bulb glowing with a new idea. File that one under winning some.

Even after the flurry of creative activity in percussion in the past forty years, the percussion repertoire remains small and selective. Percussion music today is a gap-toothed smile: it features a few strong iconic prototypes with lots of spaces in between. There is *Psappha*, and its many imitations; *Zyklus* and *The Anvil Chorus*, also with a string of impersonators in tow. One of the principal goals in commissioning new percussion music, it seems to me, is to make the repertoire less clannish. We needn't suppress the imitations of major works—some of them are worthy pieces of music—but we should be looking for ways to fill the gaps.

Below I detail three very different encounters with composers that were designed to find and fill the gaps as I saw them. I know each composer well. Each of the three—George Lewis, Michael Gordon, and John Luther Adams—was and, as a true barometer of the success of the collaboration, continues to be a friend. Each stamped his music with an undeniable and highly distinctive musical voice, and the new pieces afforded me a close-up view of the compositional process of each composer. The result in each case was an energized process of learning the score, a closer friendship and ultimately a fine piece of music.

A Question of Belonging

North Star Boogaloo (1996)

George Lewis

To say that I pestered George Lewis for the piece that eventually became *North Star Boogaloo* is not much of an exaggeration. Lewis, the brilliant composer, trombonist, improviser, music scholar, and technologist, was in demand. By 1996 our interactions together as faculty members at the University of California, San Diego, along with numerous performances together in various contexts, had led us to the point where the next logical step in our collaboration with each other was for George to write me a new percussion piece. There were the usual initial considerations—it was important to decide upon an instrumentation that was both rich enough to enable variety and limited enough to provide focus. There was also the issue of music technology. From the outset George wanted to combine a small percussion set-up—thus establishing a limited range of percussion sounds to be played live—with a technological system activated in real time that would radically multiply the number of available sounds including many nonpercussion sources. The idea was that sound files would be available for playback via pedal-activated triggers, or in our more elaborate discussions, through more interactive means like a computer with score-following capabilities. For a variety of reasons George opted for a straightforward arrangement of live performer and prerecorded tape. This decision obviously alleviated many practical difficulties of performances on tour. Beyond that it also answered the pressing question present in any piece of music for live performer and electronics: who is following whom?

Early works for instruments and electronics were almost invariably compositions for tape. (Exceptions include a small number of works for amplified and/or filtered instrumental sounds such as Stockhausen's *Mikrophonie*.) Tape was necessary because computer technology was simply not sophisticated enough to allow a flexible engagement between instrumentalist and electronics in real time. Electronic sounds that are fixed on prerecorded tape provided (and still provide) some undeniable advantages for the composer. He or she can work with tape as a sculptor might work with clay, actually shaping and constructing a sonic object that will be heard directly by a listener without the need for an interpreter. More than one composer has noted that by eliminating interpreters one also eliminates poorly prepared or shoddily executed interpretations. Using tape inevitably poses a trade-off though: composers gain control but lose flexibility. The best works in the tradition of percussion and tape—and I would include Stockhausen's masterful *Kontakte* as the first and still foremost of these—are coloristically rich, temporally precise, and formally provocative. But they are often rigid and unforgiving in performance—horrible duo partners in essence. The tape "plays" its part exactly the same way in each performance, no matter what the acoustical qualities of a given hall or the emotional perspectives of a given performance may be. The performer must always follow the tape (although in good performances, players find a way to suggest that the tape is following the live playing).

Creating a more flexible interface between electronics and performers through real-time music technology allows the electronic part to "listen to" and engage with the live performer as a real duo partner. However, there are still limitations. Real-time electronics operate on the paradigm of transformation: a sound must first be played in order for it to be modified. In essence the electronics then necessarily follow the performer (although in good performances the performer can find ways to signal shifting fore- and background relationships so that it sounds as if the electronics are leading the live performer[s]). In many recent works a combination of preconstructed sound files and real-time modifications of performed sounds can combine leading and following roles.

The use of tape in *North Star Boogaloo* ensures that the performer will follow the electronics. But here the question of who follows whom becomes not just a practical detail of performance with electronics, but a critical component of the expressive axis of the piece as well. *North Star Boogaloo* is based on Quincy Troupe's poem by the same name, and unlikely as this may first seem to be, it examines the relationship between the North Star and basketball. The North Star has played a central role in celestial navigation in this hemisphere literally for ages. And more to the point of George's piece, the North Star was the singular guiding light that led slaves to freedom as they escaped the plantations of the South and headed north. Basketball as a modern-day North Star beckons to many, especially to young African Americans, who have seen it as a beacon to the kind of freedom that comes from fame and affluence.

So in *North Star Boogaloo* the player follows the tape. This must be the case. The electronic sounds would no more react to the actions of a performer than the sky would reconfigure itself according to the needs of a navigator. Furthermore the percussionist, as follower, has only a few sonic options at his or her disposition. These include five basic skin instruments ranging in size from tambourine to timpano, as well as a small bell and a rain stick. To the contrary, the tape part, as sonic template and spiritual map of the piece, is packed full of possibilities. There are hip-hop beats, quotations from basketball players and commentators, sound effects and, at center court, Quincy Troupe reading his poem. Against the rich variety of the prerecorded sounds, expanded into multilayered complexity through looping, multitrack recording, and lightning-fast edits, the live percussion can sound simple and quotidian. The player can seem like a small point lost somewhere on a giant map. But herein lies the beauty of *North Star Boogaloo*: ordinary people can locate themselves in the giant map of the universe. We can navigate vast spaces and effect dramatic transformations in life if the simple tools available to all of us can be wielded with skill and steadfastness. It's all a question of sharpening the tools and learning to use them.

In *North Star Boogaloo* a principal tool of performance lies in the intimate correlation of the rhythms of language and the rhythms of drumming. The need for drumming to follow language and to engage the consequential linkage of, in Troupe's words, a "poet's word dribble" and "a drummer's paradiddle," is a major guiding force in the piece. In order to push the ordinary percussion sounds towards the sonic complexity of the voice, I expanded the vocabulary of the drums to include colorful, almost noisy, versions of the consonants, fricatives, and labials found in speech. A normal note on a drum that in Elliott Carter would mean "a note" might be represented in the music of George Lewis by the click of a stick, a buzzing overpressured stroke, or a bent pitch produced by elbow or stick pressure on de-tuned tom-toms. Of course this was hardly my idea. Great jazz drummers have been doing this for generations. Players like Tony Williams and Roy Haynes seemed always to have understood that great jazz drumming was more about an incantatory than a purely rhythmic experience. An "incantatory experience," that is to say an encounter with performed rather than written or casually spoken language, relies on the use of inflection to create meaning. That is to say that sense and expression devolve not just from the meanings of the words *per se* but from the contour of vocal phrases, the sonic qualities of the voice, and even the sense of the proximity of the speaker. The jazz crooner who seems to whisper in our ears and the shouting rapper both maximize the incantatory qualities of language and communicate effectively with the voice far beyond the mere meaning of words. In *North Star Boogaloo* word and drum stroke, as expressive equivalencies, must be interchangeable. In purely technical terms the percussionist must mirror the inflections of the spoken language on the tape by creating a supple and fluid fore- and background sense in performance. On the smallest scale the percussionist must be able to represent the attack and proximity of consonants as well as the indistinct and swallowed sounds of diphthongs. But fluidity of inflection applies to rhetoric on a larger scale as well. In *North Star Boogaloo* there is vigorous assertion and whispered aside. Any percussionist who wants to play it has got to be able to mumble as well as shout.

Information management poses another challenge for a performer of *North Star Boogaloo*. There is so much happening at any given moment—percussion playing, Quincy Troupe reading his poem, hip-hop beats in both 4/4 and 3/4 meter, Michael Jordan saying "I feel like an artist when I create" (with Charles Barkley in rebuttal, "I don't want to be like Mike"). Inevitably a certain amount of chaos is built into the piece, but desensitization is a bigger problem than messiness. The piece is nearly fifteen minutes long, and there is a real danger that the initial burst of energy—the saturation of colors, rhythms, and effects—cannot be sustained and might eventually lead to exhaustion and numbness. This means that the percussionist must use "effects" sparingly. A decelerating double-stroke roll on tambourine that accompanies broadcaster's voice announcing, "there's the finger roll and the foul" happens twice. To prevent this gesture from losing its effectiveness it must not be repeated verbatim. My solution was to play down the second instance of the tambourine roll in order to recreate it as a brief recollection of the first.

Likewise, the moment of greatest density of materials—a beautiful passage with a drum-machine track and live drumming that amplifies a description of a Roy Haynes drum solo—must be played for all it is worth. But this inevitably means that no other section should be rendered so vividly. Interpretative strategies in *North Star Boogaloo* require spending a performer's capital of passion and engagement slowly and carefully.

The flood of musical and cultural information in *North Star Boogaloo* is both appealing and challenging. It pushes the percussionist towards a multifaceted interpretation in order to bridge the large number of disparate elements in the piece. As a performer of *North Star Boogaloo* you are the link between words, rhythms, sound effects, and the poignant metaphor of the piece as a search for liberty and communality. Can any single performer be all of these things? I found that I could not. On one hand I was very comfortable with the *tasks* of the piece. I liked the challenge of imitating speech sounds on the drums, and I was also well prepared to tackle the work's more difficult polyrhythmic passages. Pieces like *To the Earth*, *Toucher*, and *Le Corps à Corps* had prepared me for mixing language and percussion sounds. And frankly, ever since I learned *Bone Alphabet*, even difficult polyrhythms have not posed serious problems. On the other hand I felt uncomfortable playing along with the hip-hop rhythms on the tape, which, at least in the cultural context of 1996, had been almost the exclusive province of African American musicians. (A bigger problem yet was how to look and act during pauses in the playing while the taped hip-hop music went on alone. How should I act when there are no tasks?) Likewise my passing acquaintance with the drum set left me insecure with the imitations of jazz drum solos in the piece. What was *I* doing up there playing this music? In one sense I took comfort and confidence from the fact that George Lewis had written the piece for me, and if he had thought it was inappropriate for me to play this music he certainly would not have given it to me to play. I must confess, however, that in my first few performances I concentrated on the aspects of *North Star Boogaloo* I felt most comfortable with. In their essence my first performances were strong on defensibility. I didn't try to do anything that I wasn't expert at. But what constitutes expertise in a piece about searching? You can be expert only if you have already found whatever you are looking for (or know how to find it). So the aspects of *North Star Boogaloo* that were about searching, aspects of the piece in which I could never be expert, slowly began to beckon. In an early performance of the piece at Lincoln Center as a part of the Bang on a Can Marathon, I had a sudden flash of the image I was presenting: a white middle-aged, classically trained percussionist intently focused on accurately rendering hip-hop rhythms to a mostly white, mostly middle-aged audience. I was Ward Cleaver in a pick-up game of basketball on a Harlem playground. That sudden feeling of not belonging, of never being able to belong, made me feel momentarily ridiculous and, later, profoundly sad. You see, after my performance was over I went back to being an expert percussionist playing music I was expert at. I knew where I was, where I was going, and exactly how I was going to get there. I had only momentarily dipped my toe into the waters of not belonging, of never belonging. I didn't actually have to live there. But in my moment of cultural vertigo, which came from feeling like an outsider, I felt the fear of being lost and glimpsed the pull of the North Star. For this reason George taught me an important lesson on a personal level. On a musical level *North Star Boogaloo* made me realize more strongly than ever that exploration and comfort would never be conveniently mated. I also began to wonder about the nature of expertise. Could the desire to be expert ever be compatible with the search for new forms of musical and personal expression?

A Question of Expertise

XY (1997)

Michael Gordon

If ever there was a piece that needed an expert, it is *XY*. Depending on which version of the story you believe, *XY* was named after the horizontal and vertical vectors on a two-dimensional graph or after the male chromosome, since Michael composed the piece during the time that he and his wife Julia Wolfe were expecting their son Lev. Either way, it's difficult music, both to learn and to execute.

I premiered *XY* in October 1998, but I did not commission it. Evelyn Glennie, the distinguished Scottish solo percussionist, had commissioned it. However, in response to my request to play the piece as a part of a large retrospective of solo percussion music that I presented in New York that year, she generously released the premiere to me. The piece required about four months of steady work to learn and memorize, a very long time (and great deal of expertise) indeed for a piece that features such a high degree of repetition.

What makes *XY* so hard? In the first place the polyrhythmic component of the piece is sometimes very complex. The work begins with both hands playing in sixteenth-note subdivisions, in other words in a ratio 1:1 between the hands. The polyrhythmic structures subsequently move to the increasingly complex ratios of 3:2 (where one hand is in triplets and the other in eighth notes), 5:4, and 6:5, with a little bit of 5:3 and 12:5 at the very end of the piece. Furthermore with each increasingly involved polyrhythm, the patterns

Figure 2.15. Michael Gordon, *XY*, crossing patterns, bars 241–246. Copyright © 1998 by Red Poppy (ASCAP). All rights administered by G. Schirmer, Inc. (ASCAP). International copyright secured. All rights reserved. Reprinted by permission.

across the five drums also become more involved. The simple sixteenth-note music of the beginning has minimal melodic profile. However, in the 6:5 example shown in figure 2.15, notice that the quintuple component is parsed as a pattern in four across two drums while the six is phrased in groups of two across two drums. This additional subdivision, along with the fact that the first notes of the groups rarely line up effectively imposes a polyrhythm on top of a polyrhythm. (This seems a fitting moment to apologize to my high school math teacher, to whom I maintained passionately that algebra would have no relevance in my adult life.)

Another source of difficulty is the "XY" effect. Thinking for a moment of X and Y as the horizontal and vertical dimensions on a graph, whereby the horizontal aspect equals time and the vertical aspect amplitude, one can easily diagram the piece as a series of cross-fading crescendo and decrescendo patterns. The piece starts with the right hand playing *forte* sixteenth notes and the left hand at *piano*, also in sixteenth notes. Then the hands exchange dynamics. Over the course of three measures the right hand gets softer while the left gets louder. As the piece progresses, the phase length—the time it takes to completely exchange dynamic markings between the hands—changes from three measures to two measures and later to a single bar. As the phase lengths become shorter, more difficult polyrhythms are utilized. In short, complexity in *XY* is generated progressively as ever-greater rhythmic information is crammed into increasingly smaller periods of time.

Now for the truly hard part: these rhythms must be played as fast as possible. (The indicated tempo of M.M. 202 is too fast to be playable. In my opinion a speed approaching M.M. 144 is a more practical tempo choice, given the need to sustain fifteen minutes of vigorous drumming.) Here's where things get dicey: it is one thing to play a rhythm of 6:5 accurately; it is another thing to hold it cleanly at breakneck speed. In my experience the polyrhythms in *XY* go by so fast that the music cannot be "counted." If my brain cannot track polyrhythms at this speed, then they must be played from a physical rather than rational reflex and fine-tuned as well as possible by the ear. Further confounding the issue is the "*XY* effect," the constantly changing dynamic relationship between the hands. Take the 6:5 rhythm again. If the hand playing the six is the louder one, it easily obscures the hand playing the five at the moment of greatest dynamic difference between the two. The performer then must execute a quintuple rhythm that is both too fast to count and too soft to hear. In the absence of rational and auditory control over the polyrhythms, a player depends *entirely* on a learned physical response to execute the material. You know for sure that you are playing the correct rhythm only when the hand that was soft becomes loud enough to hear. Of course at that point the loud hand becomes too soft to hear and the problem reverses itself. Fortunately, at the midpoint of each cross-fade the hands are balanced and momentarily, at least, you get real polyrhythmic equilibrium. But this does not keep the hands from going astray at the extremes of the dynamic spectrum where the ear cannot correct problems. At the instant of most extreme dynamic difference between the hands, you often cannot tell if the rhythm is accurate or often even if you are playing the correct drums. Quality control in *XY* can be maddening.

So how do you know if you are right if you can't hear what you are doing much of the time? An honest response might be, "Who cares?" If a performer standing directly over the instruments cannot tell whether the performance is accurate or not, then accuracy loses its meaning. What difference does it make if it's right but you can't hear it? Don't give up here though. This is precisely the point at which *XY* gets interesting. I found that polyrhythms played very rapidly, as in *XY*, begin to take on a harmonic rather than a purely rhythmic quality. When both hands play sixteenth notes—a rhythmic ratio of 1:1—the resulting polyrhythm resembles pitch unison. Its rhythmic unity is absent of friction in the same way that the pitch unison is. On the other extreme, the components of 6:5 rub against each other like out-of-tune notes. They act as rhythmic dissonance in other words. Triplets and eighth notes together—a ratio of 3:2—create a relationship that sounds open and vaguely consonant, much like the interval of the perfect fifth does with its three to two ratio of vibrations. Viewed this way *XY* is fundamentally a work built on interactions among harmonies. Polyrhythms that tend towards dissonance appear to "cadence" when they are followed by more consonant polyrhythms such as the example in figure 2.16 where a rhythm in 6:5 resolves to one in 3:2.

So again, how do you know if a rhythm is being played accurately when the individual notes go by too quickly or quietly to be heard? You tune it! You can sing a perfect fifth against a given tone even if the

Figure 2.16. Michael Gordon, *XY*, 6:5 resolving to 3:2, bars 307–312. Copyright © 1998 by Red Poppy (ASCAP). All rights administered by G. Schirmer, Inc. (ASCAP). International copyright secured. All rights reserved. Reprinted by permission.

vibrations go by too quickly to be heard because the interval of a fifth has a *sound* that tells you when it is correct. The same holds true for rhythms of 6:5, 5:4, or 3:2. You just have to be able to recognize the sound. Once I identified "the harmonic qualities of polyrhythms" as my principal point of departure in an interpretation of *XY*, everything else about the interpretation seemed to fall into place. For example, some kinds of pitch relationships among the set of five drums made rhythmic harmony easier to hear than others did. I therefore spend a greater than usual amount of time with my wrench in tuning the bongos and congas when I play *XY* than I do in many other pieces. Mallet choice also makes a difference. Hard wooden mallets seemed to render the rhythmic harmony with greater clarity, perhaps by making the chattering of dissonant polyrhythms more grating, than the euphonious quasi-tremolo sounds produced by softer sticks did. Solutions to an entire set of seemingly unrelated performance problems seemed to flow easily after this core issue had been articulated. The correlation of rhythm and harmony acted as the DNA of an interpretation of *XY* and gave rise to an integrated and organic performance.

As tantalizing as it might be to declare victory at this point, I must acknowledge that mine may be a personal and irreproducible solution. Could it be that such a seemingly rich source of ideas might be only a fetish—a personally provocative rather than universally applicable solution? Conversations with the few other percussionists who have played *XY* tend to support the view that each of us has found a personal and quite different point of entry to technical and interpretative questions. I began the discussion of *XY* by saying that this was a piece that required an expert percussionist. But what kind of expertise is not, by definition, transferable to other performers or at least applicable to similar problems confronted by the same performer? What kind of performance practice results when two performers use two different sets of skills to solve the same problem, when expertise is a floating raft rather than a firmly anchored platform? Of course the situation for percussionists is not always that extreme, but no other instrument and no other repertoire requires as personalized, mutable, and self-constructed set of skills as does playing percussion. Perhaps expertise in percussion playing implies the ability to create and individuate a new set of skills for every problem. Is adaptability—expressed in more Darwinian terms as the evolutionary fluidity necessary to contrive new solutions for new problems—the *real* expertise of the percussionist? A new score arrives and you are left wondering, in Dorothy Parker's famous words, "Ah, what fresh hell is this?"

A Question of Place

The Mathematics of Resonant Bodies (2003)

John Luther Adams

The realization that expertise in percussion playing might mean nothing more than the ability to cope with an endless supply of fresh dilemmas led me back to an essay written by Stephen Jay Gould. The relevant passage comes from his book *Ever Since Darwin*,[6] and in it he claims that individual members of a species living at the edges of populations evolve more rapidly and radically than do individuals positioned closer to the centers of population. The notion is that the forces of nature are more brutal at the edges of a communal population; therefore they exact a greater need on the part of individuals on the fringe to adapt. At the edge everything is rawer and less certain: space seems larger but poorly mapped, possibilities appear greater but are only vaguely defined. I could not stop myself from making the leap. In the community of musicians, were we percussionists necessarily more adaptable because we were living at the edge of the herd? This question and others led me north to Alaska and to a fascinating conversation with the composer John Luther Adams.

That conversation took place just before a solo concert I performed in November of 2000 at the University of Alaska in Fairbanks. I had arranged the recital through the percussionist Scott Deal in order to meet with John—who makes his home in the forest near Fairbanks—and talk to him about the possibility of commissioning a new percussion solo. As the Alaska trip came closer I began to regret having to go. To be honest it was a musically and personally trying period of time for me, and I was having some

6. Stephen Jay Gould, *Ever Since Darwin: Reflections in Natural History* (New York: Norton, 1977).

difficulty finding any enthusiasm for the long flight from San Diego into the beginnings of the subarctic winter.

John Luther Adams and I began that day by talking about John Cage and the fragility of his legacy, especially in the newest American music. The conversation turned (again) to issues surrounding the notion of *place*. We discussed how and to what extent the cultural, historical, and even geophysical considerations of *where* influence the pressing questions of *what* and *why*. It occurred (again) that the real courage of Cage was that he was willing to make a small mark in a big place. He began to map the enormous musical space he roamed over the course of his life by saying simply, let's start here. And of course, to the lasting benefit of percussionists everywhere, by *here* he meant his music for percussion ensemble from the late 1930s and early 1940s. But the poetry of Cage comes from the enormous reverberation that his simple mark of starting *here* implied. Cage's first footfalls in the new landscape of percussion music echoed with the sure knowledge that his was a vast space.

During this conversation dusk began to fall and the vista outside the picture windows of John Luther Adams's studio melted into a minichromatic study in white and gray. The foreground hills, increasingly in shadow, posed as a modest and austere dress rehearsal for the Alaska Range, which rose starkly and dramatically in the distance. At some point Adams asked me to look at the percussion instruments he had on the shelves against the wall of his studio—there some temple bowls, wood blocks, and a pod rattle. On the reverse side of each, handwritten on a piece of masking tape, was the name John Cage. These were Cage's personal instruments, the very ones he had used at the time of the composition and premiere of his early percussion pieces. They had been left in storage by Cage after his final move to New York City and given to John Luther Adams for guardianship in 1993 with the blessing of Jasper Johns after Adams won an award from the Foundation for Contemporary Performance Arts (established by Cage and Jasper Johns). As if on cue the sky faded to black and I stood there holding a Chinese tom-tom. I played a little of the opening of *Amores* on *his* instrument and felt very much indeed like a small mark in a large space.

That moment reflected the dilemma of the project that John and I had been discussing—the dilemma in fact of every commissioning project I have ever undertaken. In unbounded space, when you can strike off in any direction, how do you decide what to do? Perhaps not surprisingly, in light of Adams's long-standing advocacy of issues promoting environmental protection especially in the Arctic National Wildlife Refuge, our conversation turned to the issues of environment, topography, and scale as potential source ideas for a new percussion solo. We were poised to do something big.

To set the stage, a few months earlier I had premiered James Dillon's mammoth *La Coupure*, commissioned by IRCAM, the center for the advancement of electroacoustic music housed around the corner from the Centre Pompidou in Paris.[7] (See the discussion of *La Coupure* in chapter 4). *La Coupure* is a sophisticated and complex solo piece of about sixty-five minutes duration. One of the main problems I had in interpretation was managing the size and scale of the form. In short I often felt lost. This was a new and unsettling experience for me. Many conventional percussion solos are about ten to twelve minutes long. Their inherent similarities—of length, of instrumentation, and frequently of formal design—mean that you almost never feel lost. (If it's the eight-minute mark, it must mean a cymbal crash; at eleven minutes, diminuendo, wind chimes, and slow fade to black.) I realized after learning *La Coupure* that I *wanted* to feel lost in a piece of music. I craved it. Or perhaps more accurately, I loved playing music that impeded the conditioned interpretative responses that come from always and automatically understanding where you are and where you are going. In this vein I challenged John to create a new piece with an unmapped topography, a new kind of piece of sufficient length, rigor, and difficulty to thwart any standardized approach in interpretation. He did not disappoint me.

The Mathematics of Resonant Bodies is about seventy-five minutes in length, composed in eight movements. Each movement is scored for a single instrumental color and accompanied by its "aura," a prerecorded, computer-generated manipulation of that color. *The Mathematics of Resonant Bodies* consists of:

burst for four snare drums
rumble for bass drum
shimmer for eight triangles
roar for tam-tam
thunder for eight tom-toms and two kick drums
wail for low air raid siren
crash for eight cymbals
stutter for four snare drums

7. Institut de Recherche et de Coordination Acoustique/Musique.

From the standpoint of process, each movement in *Mathematics* is essentially identical. Three movements—*rumble*, *roar*, and *wail*—consist of music where formal concerns revolve around amplitude. Another three movements—*shimmer*, *thunder*, and *crash*—explore rhythm. In the two movements for four snare drums, *stutter* and *burst*, Adams explores a density-based process by gradually hollowing out and then refilling a basic nine-bar phrase. Each of the three process types involves a simple operation of expansion and contraction: the amplitude movements utilize crescendo/decrescendo figures; the rhythmic movements involve accelerations and decelerations; the snare drum movements achieve variation in density by manufacturing and relocating silence. Change in each movement starts small then grows larger and finally retreats. By way of illustration, note the complete score for *wail* in figure 2.17. As one of the "amplitude" movements, *wail* consists of a progression from short and small crescendo and decrescendo figures to gradually longer and more extreme crescendos and decrescendos. The first hairpin figure from soft to loud and back takes about ten seconds and spans a dynamic range from *pianississimo* to *piano* and back. The climax comes at the midpoint of the movement with the only real *fortississimo*. This central hairpin shape takes more than three times as long to complete as the first figure. After the midpoint of the movement is achieved, the process reverses itself in a strict retrograde. This pattern of increasingly potent and lengthy crescendo and decrescendo figures and their retrograde is the same for *rumble* (bass drum) and *roar* (tam-tam) as well.

For *shimmer*, *crash*, and *thunder* the amplification of phrases from small to large (followed by the retrograde of the process each time) applies to accelerating and decelerating rhythms. For example, *thunder* starts with sixteenth notes, decelerates to eighth notes, and accelerates back to sixteenth notes over the course of its first phase. Its second phase spans rhythmic increments from sixteenth notes down to quarter notes and back, the third phase from sixteenth notes to half notes and back. Any given phrase of *thunder* actually consists of two to six simultaneously unfolding deceleration or acceleration shapes. This polyphonic aspect creates complex crossing patterns and minidramas of collusion and fragmentation within the phrases.

The two movements for snare drums are equally complex and equally rigorous. Notice how the excerpt from *burst* shown in figure 2.18 is launched by a very rapid and loud single-stroke roll in subdivisions of nine notes to the quarter on a single snare drum. The unwavering, monolithic noise is first disrupted as the roll circulates around the group of drums to form noise melodies. Later small silences are inserted into the music to create rhythmic complexity. In essence Adams creates rhythm by replacing

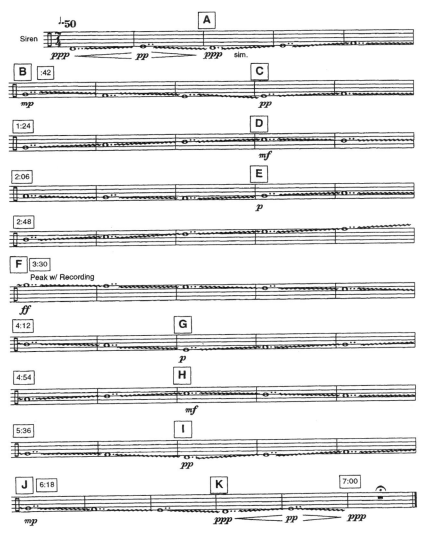

Figure 2.17. John Luther Adams, *The Mathematics of Resonant Bodies*, "Wail." Copyright © Taiga Press, 2003. Used by permission.

Figure 2.18. John Luther Adams, *The Mathematics of Resonant Bodies*, from "Burst," bars 136–162. Copyright © Taiga Press, 2003. Used by permission.

notes with silences. In the rapid groups of nine, the 2nd and 8th notes are removed first. Then notes 4, 5, and 6 are suppressed. These proportions are transposed to the next larger scale, quarter notes, where the 2nd and 8th, then the 4th, 5th, and 6th quarter notes are removed. Finally on the largest scale—the measure—in each of the nine-bar phrases, the 2nd and 8th followed by the 4th, 5th, and 6th bars are suppressed. The music progressively empties itself of sound in proportions of rhythm and rest that start at the smallest rhythmic increment and work towards the increment of the entire phrase. *burst* starts with all 243 possible rhythmic subdivisions in a nine-bar phrase played at *fortissimo*. (The figure of 243 possible notes comes from the 27 quarter notes in each basic nine-bar phrase, each of which is divided into nine parts.) By the end of the "hollowing out" process only 32 of the possible 243 subdivisions is played—this time at *pianissimo*. Silence punctuates noise until a critical threshold is crossed, and then it is rhythm that seems to punctuate silence. At the moment of greatest silence, the process then reverses itself and the phrases begin to fill up again.

At first the rigor and authority, not to mention the ubiquity and similarity, of these structures of expansion and contraction perplexed me. After all, John and I had talked about making a piece without conventional signposts—an "environmental" rereading of Cage's indeterminacy where we were not to know whether the event lying announced just around the corner would be terrible or placid or brutal or banal. We had seen enough false drama in contemporary percussion music where the monumental peak you just scaled turned out to be Disneyland's Matterhorn placed conveniently along your path. I wondered if the predictability of shape and structure in *Mathematics* might be just another kind of map, another way of knowing for sure what lay ahead? However, John convinced me, in ways and at moments that he was unaware of, that it was *my* reading of an environmental music as a series of unannounced dramatic events that was mistaken. White water or an avalanche lurking just ahead, complete with a movie score swelling tumultuously on cue as each drama unfolds, was the real Disneyland. A more accurate reading of "real nature" was rooted in the pervasiveness of design, repeated in numbing quantities on all levels of scale from the microscopic to galactic. By asserting that small shapes can be amplified to make larger versions of themselves or reduced to create miniatures, Adams invokes natural design in an equation that Cage understood in the context of his early percussion music (and that James Tenney and a few others also understand). Simplicity and universality of design can be multiplied by the energy and uncertainties of performance to yield complexity in perception.

At first glance *Mathematics* seems to satisfy this equation on the grounds of simplicity and universality. Recall that each movement features a process that is practically identical to every other movement in terms of shape and proportion. Small shapes grow larger and more vigorous and then reverse themselves. Or in the case of *burst* and *stutter*, structures empty and refill themselves. At first one is tempted to think of the piece as a study of process itself, a beautifully articulated and fully realized look at crescendos or accelerandos for example. But this is the beauty of the Cage theorem. Simplicity of rhetoric implies complex and highly interconnected modes of perception. As a result you cannot view a single parameter in isolation. As soon as you think that *roar*, for example, is only about crescendos and decrescendos, you begin to notice that it is also a piece about melody. A crescendo on a tam-tam activates a highly complex and gradual excitation of harmonics from low to high, and automatically produces a kind of slowly rising tide of pitched noise. Furthermore, a decrescendo on the same instrument does not simply reverse the process as waters might recede after the crest of a flood. Harmonics, especially in the medium high range, tend to persist once they are activated. (Any percussionist who has cultivated a beautiful tone by bowing a tam-tam and then tried to change notes can attest to the stubbornness of sounding frequencies in ringing metal instruments.) On its descent the tam-tam sound loses the luster of its mid-high partials more slowly and irregularly than it gained them. Tones persist and the decrescendo seems to accrete around nodal pitches. That which rose as noise recedes as melody.

Or take *thunder* (figure 2.19), which at first appears to be a study of pure rhythm parsed as concurrently unfolding deceleration and acceleration structures played on tom-toms and bass drums. But this movement is also about texture and the mutability of perception. Here we see that the quality of polyrhythmic interaction changes radically according to the proximity of speeds between the parts. To understand this take a polyrhythm of 5:4, for example, where the constituent elements are close to each other in speed. This rhythm tends to highlight the sense of rhythmic friction between two competing forces. A rhythm like 17:2 (or why not take a really extreme example like 751:2) where the components are of very different speeds seems more like fast music with occasional interruptions. The former rhythm highlights the vertical interactions of competing rhythmic components, the latter acts horizontally as a line with internal markers. In *thunder* the complete statement of deceleration starts at M.M. 176 with sixteenth notes in the hands and quarter notes in the feet, and concludes in a rhythmic unison at half-note speed. In other words the polyrhythm converges—during the time the upper line in *thunder* has decelerated to an eighth of its original speed the bottom line decreases to only half of its original speed. Perceptually the relatively large difference between the sixteenth notes and quarters (a 4:1 ratio of speeds)

Figure 2.19. John Luther Adams, *The Mathematics of Resonant Bodies*, from "Thunder," bars 84–104. © Taiga Press, 2003. Used by permission.

means that music at the fast end of the spectrum acts horizontally. It sounds like a fast and forceful upper voice that is punctuated by the slower pulse of a bass drum. At the bottom end of the spectrum of speed, the convergence of the two rhythms as they approach unity positions them within a single perceptual plane. In other words, they are heard as a polyrhythm. The fascinating part of the process is the change from horizontal to vertical modes of perception, from line to "polyline." At the volatile midpoint of the process, friction between the lines increases as their speeds approach each other and the strong sense of horizontal unity within the phrase fractures. The upper line loses momentum and becomes grainy as it slows. Entering the rhythmic sphere of influence of the slower line, the two become bound together perceptually, and finally the polyrhythmic friction brings the two lines into unity and stasis. Natural metaphors for this process abound. With sufficient velocity and momentum a rock will skip along the surface of water in defiance of gravity until it slows and eventually sinks. (Note that the horizontal becomes vertical and two very different vectors are united in stasis.) Or equally unambiguously, "love at first sight" begins to cool and dissipates into low-grade combat where passion loses steam through alternating quarrels and halfhearted reconciliations. It finally grinds to a halt. (Note that the steady application of low-grade friction can trump even powerful forces.)

At last I see the "environmental" qualities in Adams's music. The fact is that this music is not about the environment alone, but about the position of an individual in the environment—about the place of a person among environmental forces outside his or her control. John's piece is about a singular presence in an ambiguous place. Let's return to the basics of *The Mathematics of Resonant Bodies*: it is a work for solo percussionist and electronics. And it is here in the electronic component, what the composer calls the *aura*, that we find some enlightenment. The *aura* is the virgin landscape, an untraveled place, which a human performer seeks to traverse. John has often spoken to me about the presence of the soloist in *The Mathematics of Resonant Bodies* as a musical version of, in his words, "the 'zip' in a Barnett Newman painting: a solitary vertical presence that both divides and unifies a vast horizontal field of color."

The environment in John Luther Adams's world asserts itself in terms of deep and immutable simplicity. Its dispassionate and sometimes terrible force is awe-inspiring, but it is the fragility of the human position within this environment that gives us poetry. We often don't know where we are or what we should be doing. Who does, after all? In spite of our uncertainties, however, we must traverse the unknown space.

We must strike out in a plain and evident direction, because in this music, just as in the natural topography that inspired it, the absence of a position is not acceptable. For the future performers of *The Mathematics of Resonant Bodies* or *XY* or *North Star Boogaloo*, just as it was for Varèse when he arrived in New York, it is not just *what* we are doing, but *where* we are doing it that counts.

Learning *Bone Alphabet*

On my first day as a faculty member at the University of California, San Diego, in 1991, I asked my new colleague Brian Ferneyhough to compose a percussion solo for me. The invitation was not as abrupt as it may sound. I had known Brian for years. We met in 1982 when I was a student at the Staatliche Hochschule für Musik in Freiburg, Germany. where he was teaching composition. Later we were both members of the faculty of the Internationale Ferienkurse für Neue Musik in Darmstadt. I was (and continue to be) very interested in Ferneyhough's music. The immediacy of percussive attacks and the possibility for creating a diverse and highly contrasted sound world seemed to make percussion a perfect medium to represent Ferneyhough's precise polyrhythmic language. Yet, he had not written a substantial work for percussion. Exploring this natural partnership was my first motivation for inviting him to compose a percussion solo for me.

The other reasons for approaching Ferneyhough for a new piece are more ambiguous. In 1991 solo percussion music was rapidly becoming a classical medium. Although the repertory was new and still quite small, a few strongly defined types of works were emerging. The extant pieces were almost exclusively titanic in scale and posed technical demands of heroic proportions. Furthermore, they usually featured large instrumental set-ups and a straightforward narrative sensibility in construction. In short, solo percussionists, who had started three decades earlier by exploring new intellectual and aesthetic ground, were slowly but surely reprising inflated nineteenth-century solo models. The percussion repertoire was becoming Liszt scored for drums, marimbas, and gongs. I believed that Brian would write a physically and intellectually demanding piece, but one with an original, perhaps purer take. Apparently Ferneyhough also saw the problem. His initial reply to my request was that he had no interest in writing a percussion solo. He put it this way (more or less): that the momentarily vivid and diversified sonic material of percussion could not be sustained as a successful solo composition in the absence of means to create large-scale architectural robustness. Since I agreed with him, I took his resistance as a good sign.

I clearly recall this persuasive argument emerging over the course of our first conversation about the piece that would become *Bone Alphabet*. We stood outdoors in the thin January sunshine of La Jolla. As Brian walked away he turned suddenly and asked, just in case, what kind of piece did I have in mind? I replied only half-jokingly that I wanted a set-up of instruments small enough to pack in a suitcase and carry onto an airplane. He called a few days later and suggested a solo piece with an extremely limited set-up consisting of only seven small instruments; instrument choice would be left to the player. By April I had several sketches of the basic rhythmic material for *Bone Alphabet*, and I had a completed score of the piece in August of 1991.

The idea behind the severe limitation of sounds reverses the usual psychology of multiple percussion pieces. Pieces with very large instrumental arrangements tend to weaken a listener's ability to track important events. It's simple market economy—when many sonorities are available at once, the value of any one of them is reduced. By contrast, with a much smaller set of sounds each sound becomes more valuable. The global limitation of instrumental colors in *Bone Alphabet* quickly focuses the attention of a listener on the complex web of rhythmic and polyphonic interactions that form the center of the work's musical vocabulary. This spare sound world and a constantly shifting syntax of rhythmic "comportment" (using Ferneyhough's word for the localized behavior of elements within the piece) give the piece its structural and expressive axis as well as its title, *Bone Alphabet*.

The inevitable virtuosity of any Ferneyhough piece was also attractive. In *Bone Alphabet* I hoped to explore new horizons of physical and intellectual difficulty. I was not disappointed. A quick look at any bar of *Bone Alphabet* will reveal that this work is one of the most demanding pieces of the entire solo percussion repertoire. The piece features lightning-fast rhythms, polyphony including as many as four independent lines, and rhythmic and polyrhythmic structures I had never seen before. I began practicing in August 1991 for the premiere in February 1992—it took more than six months of continuous practice (a total of nearly a thousand hours by my calculation) to master and memorize a piece of about ten minutes in length.

Learning

In retrospect I realize that the challenge of learning *Bone Alphabet* had been my primary, albeit initially unconscious, reason for asking Brian to compose it. Ferneyhough's original comment to me about percussion music—the implication of which was that percussion solo music had been codified into just a few kinds of pieces—seemed to extend into the domain of learning as well. If percussion solos were becoming increasingly similar and predictable, then so too were the practice strategies involved in learning them. My hope with *Bone Alphabet* was to shatter the inherited strategies of learning a piece of percussion music. Indeed, Brian's new piece proved impervious to the usual approaches of learning a new work. It was nearly impossible to sight-read even a single measure at any tempo. (Early progress on *Bone Alphabet* was excruciatingly slow. I spent the first week of practice simply trying to understand, calculate, and memorize the polyrhythmic structure in the first three sixteenth notes.) It became apparent as I learned *Bone Alphabet* that I had never focused on the process of learning as an act distinct and separable from interpretation or execution. As I searched for new models of learning I noticed that even in academia, people speak a great deal about education and almost never about learning. Learning, especially at a high-powered research university like the University of California, seemed to have an almost unseemly air of practicality about it. Learning is measured by a palpable change of state: you have learned if you can do, think, realize, or notice something that you formerly could not.

In the predominating view of contemporary music, especially of institutional contemporary music, learning has really meant learning to think. The last one hundred years of composition in the arena of western art music has been arguably a celebration of the brain. A quick walk up the stairs at IRCAM, for example, takes you by a photo gallery of famous composers who have been associated with that prominent institution. Each photograph displays the intense, searching gaze of people who are thinking about their art. Thinking hard. Musical performance, however, clearly places the emphasis on learning to *do*. A musical version of the Cartesian paradox—the presumption that somehow body and mind, thinking and doing, are separable—is simply no longer valid. The best performers are people who can think *and* do. As the sole musician in a long line of farmers, I learned early that an idea is only as good as the work that sustains and continues it. There is nothing cool or theoretical about growing corn.

In percussion music—arguably the earthiest of the musical arts—thinking and doing can be tracked as the parallel attainment of understanding and facility. The mental and physical double spoor of grasping and *grasping* quickly becomes intertwined and indistinguishable. Start on one side of the equation and you soon end up on the other. Performing involves the development of intelligence in the body and tactility in the mind. For me, *understanding*—the immediate progenitor of interpretation and art—comes as the direct result of working with muscles. (I think about a new piece almost invariably *at* the instruments, as I play, and in direct response to the sounds I hear.) And clearly *facility*—the basic ability to execute ideas—is meaningless without ideas to execute.

"God is in the details," as the saying goes. You might say that the secret of deeply expressive moments in music lies in the details of an organic union of physical and mental nuance. The synergy of those modalities as a state that is both thoughtful and absent of thought, refined and instinctual weaves the fabric of a convincing performance. It is not surprising that the most profound examples of musical expression are neither strictly cerebral nor corporeal but built from some ineffable combination of both. After all, life's great moments—matters of birth, life, love, and death—are much more than thoughts or impressions. They are sensed by a complete human organism simultaneously as emotional, physical, and intellectual impact. Why should the experience of the most sublime and powerful moments of musical expression be any less completely rendered or received? And why should the process of learning complex and meaningful pieces of music not also mirror this essential union of intellectual, physical and spiritual properties?

Unfortunately the path to the Promised Land—the rich delta where the mental and manual meet—is not clearly signposted. Difficulties start with the realization that the brain and body learn at different rates. The brain might quickly understand a passage that takes the body weeks to master. As a compensatory mechanism, the situation is often reversed in performance. The body—or at least what one might call a physical sensibility—responds to subtleties in the musical environment with a speed and authority that the brain cannot match. To rectify the difference, traditional performance pedagogy attempts to speed up the physical process to match the mental one. Sight-reading skills are practiced so that the gap between seeing the score and executing it in performance is reduced to a bare minimum. The body is trained to act and react as quickly as the eye and the mind. In many ways "performance practice" is not much more than a compendium of shortcut strategies designed to accelerate the learning curve of the body. Learning is streamlined by opting for methods that have been known to work in the past and avoiding those that have not. Fingerings, bowings, and mallet choices are passed down over generations from teachers to students until they attain almost biblical importance. From the standpoint of productivity it makes sense. The wisdom of tried and true strategies produces efficiency and speed. Not coincidentally however, conventional learning strategies also produce a distressing uniformity in the final musical results.

The ability to learn music quickly—a principal criterion for success in the fast-paced world of professional musicians—reduces the importance and frankly the pleasure of learning as an independent activity. After all, learning is a singular experience. However often one may play a piece, one learns it only once. The trade-off is clear: after a piece of music has been learned, it becomes something concrete and public; it can be performed for other people, recorded, and discussed. But it no longer exists in a utopian state of pure possibility. A new piece, once learned, breathes the air of Kansas rather than of Oz. Its universe of possibilities has been drastically limited by the hard facts of performance in the real world. One of those hard facts is that performances of notated music are designed to be repeatable. The performer must develop a concrete interpretive stance and the muscular reflex needed to execute it. This solidity is necessary for performance, but I always regret losing the realm of imagination and possibility that characterizes learning. With performance, the fragile adolescence of a work of art has ended and, in music as in life, a misspent youth cannot be relived.

Learning as slowly as possible cultivates the full benefit of plasticity and possibility. Slow learning is an important precept in my personal practice. It disentangles the complex trajectory of learning a piece of music and separates it into three distinct stages. In order, they consist of a *conceptual* phase, a *soft* phase, and a *refinement* phase. In the *conceptual* stage, a performer fantasizes about what a piece might sound like and how it might eventually fit into his or her repertoire. He or she also addresses the critical question of why learn this piece and why now. (Many pieces in the solo percussion repertoire are difficult works that might take the better part of a year to learn. Questions of motivation should be addressed early.) In the second stage of learning, the *soft* phase, a serious and consequential practice schedule has started but interpretation is in maximum flux. It is a time when ideas are tested and physicality is trained. Here the brain and body learn from each other—boundaries between the two are maximally porous and their rapport is mutually informative. With the conclusion of the *soft* phase, a stage of *refinement* begins. In this phase most interpretive decisions have been made, but execution must be made reliable and converted to physical reflex. In this stage a critical moment arrives as the music, which has been stored as notation on paper (or in the less scripted repositories of oral tradition or improvisational constructs), is relocated to the musculature of the performer.

In particular, slow learning prolongs the critical *soft* phase. A simple lesson from evolutionary biology seems relevant here. The relative sophistication of human beings as mature creatures is prepared by an extended period of development. The change between infancy and adulthood is large; therefore a prolonged period of construction as childhood and adolescence is needed. By contrast, animals to which maturity comes rapidly—think of how quickly kittens become independent and fickle cats, for example—change relatively little from birth to adulthood. With a piece of music the importance and complexity of performances over the long term is directly related to the length and quality of its soft developmental phase. Complex music, like complex organisms, requires a lengthy period of development. Extending the soft phase of learning sustains the period of the most intense communion between player and music, and brings as a result greater richness and sophistication to the final product.

Avoiding Perfection

Nominally the goal of learning is the preparation of a *representative* performance of a piece of music. But what does it mean to represent a piece of music? The initial need to develop the physical capacity to play a piece of music—clearly necessary if public performance is the ultimate goal—curates a view of learning as *perfecting*, the focus of which locates the integrity of a performance experience as accuracy of presentation. A more fluid view of learning as *development*, over both the short term and the long term, foregrounds a flexible environment of exchange between the piece and the player. Unfortunately, western performance practice is suspicious of too much flexibility. It teaches us that the score, the shroud of classical music objectified, is sacred. Performers learn that to venerate this music means devotion to a faithful reproduction of the score. The paralyzing need to *perfect* mistakenly places emphasis on the first few performances of a piece and neglects the rich experience of evolution over the long term.

I approached *Bone Alphabet* and other similarly demanding works from the solo repertoire with the idea that I would play them over the course of my lifetime as a performer. Learning therefore was defined in the broadest terms as both perfecting the capacity to execute the score accurately and as curating an evolutionary imperative that would allow the piece and my relationship with it to develop slowly over years. I do not relinquish my goal of an accurate performance, but I do resist developing a fixed interpretation of a work. Multiple performances from memory tend to cement musical information into rigid physical reflex—the more you a play a piece in a certain way, the greater the likelihood that you will continue to play it that way. On the contrary, long-term evolution of interpretation requires plasticity of materials. One must be able to change tempi, foreground/background relationships, and even instrumentation as the occasion requires.

The notion of long-term plasticity is not new to performers of eighteenth- and nineteenth-century classical repertoire. One does not learn the Brahms Violin Concerto to play it only once. However an overly devout reading of the "new" in new music often means that pieces of contemporary music are learned for a single performance. If one expects never to return to a piece of music, there is little need for a learning strategy designed to support multiple performances. I approached the development of an interpretation in *Bone Alphabet* as a process that would last decades rather than months.

Interpretation—either on the long or short term—in a score as highly inflected as *Bone Alphabet* is itself a problematic matter. Two rhythms that sound *almost* alike in a performance of Brahms, for example, usually mean that a performer is bending one of them for expressive effect. The same two nearly identical rhythms in *Bone Alphabet* are in fact likely to be notated as two different rhythms. A performer who modifies

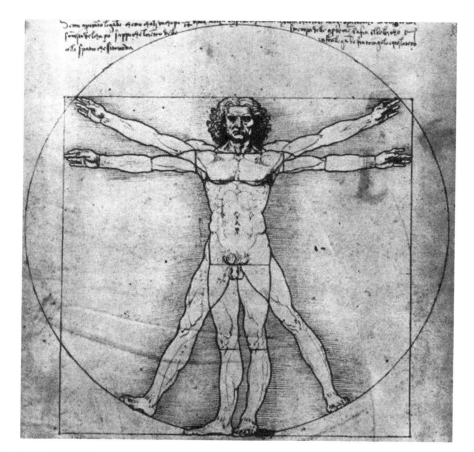

Figure 3.1. Leonardo da Vinci, Drawing of the proportions of the human figure, after Vitruvius.

rhythm in Brahms will be thought of as expressive; in Ferneyhough he or she probably will be though of as inaccurate. During a rehearsal of *Bone Alphabet*, Ferneyhough once defined interpretation as "meaningful deviation" from the printed score. In fact deviation sometimes looks like imperfection. Glenn Gould bends rhythms or highlights middle voices in his second recording of Bach's "Goldberg" Variations. Sylvio Gualda alters tempi in *Psappha*, a work he premiered and has championed for nearly thirty years. These deviations are products of a musical sensibility that has been filtered over the course of decades through the minds and bodies of performers. Their interpretations may be superficially inaccurate, but in my opinion they are marked by a "rightness" that transcends correctness.

Embracing plasticity does not mean celebrating inaccuracy. It simply acknowledges the inherent mutability of the bodily memory. Human performers are notoriously unreliable and unstable as computers. We can store a great deal of musical information, but over time it is sifted through a warren of physical habituation and the vagaries of memory. In short, music slowly warps itself in our image. The longer information is stored, the more firmly planked it becomes as bodily memory and reflex. The passage of time produces an ever-greater level of corporeal filtering and, as a result, an ever-smaller likelihood of unimpeded recall. In my experience with *Bone Alphabet*, long-term evolution has been the result of the simple dualities of the body as they exert a mollifying influence on the complex ratios of Ferneyhough's rhythmic language. A quick glance at Leonardo's famous sketch of the human body shows that we humans are creatures more or less constructed in ratios of twos and threes (see figure 3.1). A rhythm of 7:5 played by a body with the proportions of 3:2, will, over time, likely lean towards 8:6. The challenge of interpretation over the long term is to draw the line of "meaningful deviation" between a perfected representation of the score and the fluid evolutionary forces of bodily memory.

Bone Alphabet

Bone Alphabet (1992)

Brian Ferneyhough

The initial stages of learning *Bone Alphabet* were one-sidedly devoted to the goal of accuracy in representing the score. But before I could start practicing I first had to choose and arrange the seven instruments required by the score.

The score to *Bone Alphabet* leaves this choice largely open to the performer. This makes *Bone Alphabet* unusual among Brian Ferneyhough's compositions. In conversation with James Boros, Ferneyhough said: "Thinking about composing means, first of all, thinking about the specific nature of the instruments to be employed. I am very concerned that the things I ask an instrumentalist to do be instrument-specific . . . ensuring that one could not imagine any other instrument playing the material in the same way."[1]

---

1. Brian Ferneyhough and James Boros, "Shattering the Vessels of Received Wisdom," *Perspectives of New Music* 28, no. 2 (1990): 6–50.

Ferneyhough found, however, that percussion sonorities are not easily specified. Nor are they easily summoned in performance. Even under the most controlled circumstances, where a composer knows a particular array of instruments and carefully specifies mallets and striking areas, there can be no assurance of being able to reproduce certain sounds exactly from performance to performance. Add to that variations in technique among different performers—not to mention what any given performer might understand by the word "gong" or "hard mallet"—and one can begin to see the enormity of the task involved in specifying and notating percussive sonority. For a composer like John Cage, who was attracted to exactly this kind of sonic indeterminacy, percussion was a world full of the best kinds of surprises. For Brian Ferneyhough, with his meticulous sensibilities of color, percussion was a swamp of sounds with clearly defined attacks but poorly defined colors.

Ferneyhough's solution in *Bone Alphabet* was to leave the specific choice of sounds open to the performer. In his preface to the score, Ferneyhough indicates that instruments should consist of sounds organized consecutively from high to low where adjacent instruments must not belong to the same family. Here a non-"family" relationship among percussion instruments means simply that adjacent instruments are to be made of different materials. My seven instruments from high to low include:

#1 high wood block
#2 high bongo
#3 small Chinese opera gong (muffled quite heavily with an audible glissando upwards)
#4 medium tom-tom
#5 medium-low cowbell
#6 low wooden tom-tom (of the sort required for Stockhausen's *Kontakte*)
#7 low tom-tom (as low as possible with a faint glissando downwards)

Important considerations behind these choices dealt first of all with register. Pronounced differences of sonority tend to overshadow differences in pitch. (Ask anyone what the difference between a wood block and a tuba is. The answer will likely reflect the differences in their sound colors rather than the fact that one produces high and the other low tones.) However, the strongly vectorial nature of Ferneyhough's melodic lines demanded an appreciable scale of sounds with similar decay profiles arranged from high to low. Therefore sounds with similar attack and decay profiles were chosen so that a listener would understand lines as changes in register—and thus melody—rather than changes of color or texture. Controlling the resonance of instruments became a critical criterion of creating attack/decay similarity. Because of the very rapid rhythmic material, sustaining instruments proved inappropriate. My choice was dry instruments that featured a graduated scale of duration. In my set-up lower instruments ring slightly longer than the higher ones, with the goal of equalizing the affective force of each. The sharper attacks of the higher instruments are balanced by the more massive sound of slightly more resonant lower instruments. Furthermore, since there would be no time for changing mallets, all instruments would have to respond to a single set of four mallets consisting of a pair of hard and soft sticks in each hand. I usually hold soft sticks as my outside left and inside right mallets and hard sticks as the inside left and outside right mallets. Since, with my technique at least, inside mallets are more dexterous while outside mallets have greater force this distribution assures parity of both strength and maneuverability between hard and soft sticks. Both instruments and sticks were chosen so that strokes of equal force would produce equal dynamic response across the range of sounds. There would be no time in the torrent of cross-rhythms to balance the instruments; thus a fundamental parity of sonic force was necessarily an intrinsic feature of the set-up.

In *Bone Alphabet* texture shifts kaleidoscopically between monophonic linearity and polyphony with as many as four lines. The instruments had to be different enough from one another to be able to project clearly perceivable polyphony yet compatible enough to be melded together into a single line. Polyphony required that each instrument project an indelible and identifiable character. The gong must be identifiable as a gong in any polyphonic texture, played at any speed, and in any rhythmic context. It seems simple enough. However, in rapid alternation even instruments constructed of different material, such as the vibraphone and marimba, have similar enough harmonic spectra to be easily confused. On the other hand, in order to accommodate monophonic sections of the piece, instruments needed to knit sufficiently well together to form a single line. These dual necessities meant that sounds on either extreme of a scale of individuality were inappropriate. Sounds of maximum identity, an array consisting of snare drums and crotales to cull an extreme example, could never be fluid enough to mesh as a single line. Highly combinable sounds like cymbals and tam-tams could never project multiple polyphonic ideas. Eventually it became clear that freedom of choice in the instrumentation of *Bone Alphabet* was largely illusory. The number of possible instrumental configurations that satisfied the rhythmic and textural conditions of the score—and did not at the same time pose insoluble performance problems—was very limited indeed.

Brian once told me in conversation that an ideal instrumentation for the work was one that was "maximally Protestant." Straitlaced, yes, but not bland. Coloristic nuance—produced by subtle changes of mallet choice, striking area, and stroke speed according to the dictates of the musical context—was my initial solution to what I perceived as the looming challenge of the piece: how to engineer a work of ten minutes in length with only seven sound sources. Decisions about instruments and mallets were made in a flurry in the first few hours of practice. By the end of the first day I had constructed a set-up that has remained constant over more than a decade of performances. The rest of the learning process—calculating and learning rhythms and memorizing the piece—proved, on the other hand, to be much more involved.

I began learning the rhythms in *Bone Alphabet* by gluing an enlarged copy of each measure on an individual sheet of graph paper. I then calculated the exact position in time of each note and graphed the rhythm proportionally onto the paper. Seeing the rhythms this way helped clarify very small distinctions among similar rhythms. I then mapped rhythms onto instruments, deciding quite quickly which note or line would be played with which of the four available sticks. Finally I memorized that measure before going on to the next one. This multistep process involved some stages that took a lot of time and others that went very quickly. The advantage to this approach was that quick decisions in matters of mallet choice and sticking lent a sense of spontaneity to those elements, which in final performance should sound fluid and uncalculated. By contrast, spending a lot of time on the bedrock of rhythm meant that the structures most central to the composition were the least mutable in performance.

Since my strategies for memorization lean heavily on physicality, bodily gesture quickly became an indispensable tool in support of memory. I immediately translated rhythm (the temporal interval between notes) to physical space (the height of a stick or the angle of a forearm). As a result, from the first days of practice the piece became a corporeal (and by extension, a theatrical) form whereby gesture was not the incidental byproduct of performance but integral to a nascent interpretive point of view. *Bone* Alphabet became, in Ferneyhough's words, an instrument that framed "a theater of the body,"[2] a corporeal space, in effect, for the disposition of actions.

Rhythm

In *Bone Alphabet* meters are simple and tempi are slow. Compare this with his use of constantly shifting "irrational" meters in the percussion duo, *Fanfare for Klaus Huber*, where meters like 5/24 and 7/20 dictate that a performer's internal tempo sense change quickly among rapid subdivisions. To clarify, a 24th note is

2. From an unpublished interview with Brian Ferneyhough by Arun Bharali (November, 1992).

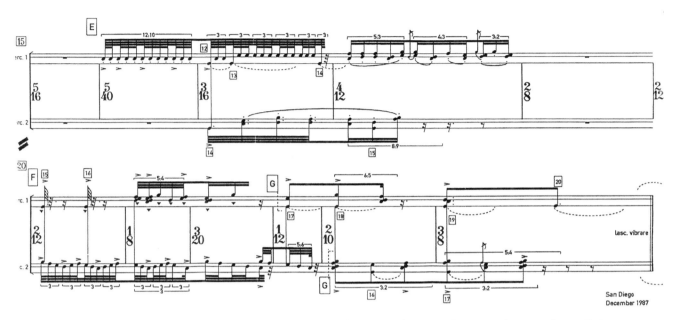

Figure 3.2. Brian Ferneyhough, *Fanfare for Klaus Huber*, bars 15–end. Copyright © 1987 by Hinrichsen Edition, Peters Edition Limited, London. All rights reserved. Used by permission.

1/24 of a whole note in the same way that a sixteenth note is 1/16 of a whole note. A 5/24 bar is then five sixteenth-note triplets long; a 7/20 bar is seven sixteenth-note quintuplets. The constant presence of such small subdivisions of time in the *Fanfare* means that a performer must "think fast." By contrast *Bone Alphabet* asks the percussionist to hear rhythm as a rapid elaboration *against* a slow and stable temporal backdrop. The hands may move fast but the tempo and therefore the speed of a performer's internal clock is slow (see figure 3.2). Ferneyhough achieves density by in *Bone Alphabet* by layering rhythms into dense polyrhythmic constructions.

Eventually, several strategies emerged as means for solving polyrhythmic problems. These strategies involved: (1) solving polyrhythms by means of calculating the least common multiple of their constituent components, (2) translating rhythms into differences of tempo, and (3) identifying a primary line in each

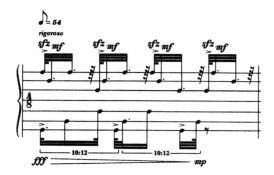

Figure 3.3. Brian Ferneyhough, *Bone Alphabet*, bar 1. Copyright © 1991 by Hinrichsen Edition, Peters Edition Limited, London. All rights reserved. Used by permission.

polyrhythm into which opposing rhythms could be folded. Very often a given bar of *Bone Alphabet* required a mixture of techniques.

In instances where two or more rhythmic lines share both beginning and end points, a method of calculating the least common multiple of the rhythmic components works well. Bar 1 (see figure 3.3) serves as a good example. In clear two-part polyphony the lines start together and then meet again on the second half of beat 2. The upper line in 32nd and 64th notes is quite straightforward; the lower line divides the twelve 64th notes—one and a half beats—into ten parts, thus the indication 10:12. A second phrase begins on the second half of beat two and continues the 10:12 ratio for the remainder of the measure.

A very simple grid can be constructed for this kind of polyrhythm by multiplying the denominators of the two components together. The upper voice is expressed in 64th notes, or 12 units for the beat and a half, and the lower voice is expressed in 10 units. Thus a grid based on the multiple of the two rhythms contains 120 increments and will account for each note of the polyrhythm. This grid can be simplified by taking the least common multiple of two rhythms—in this case 60 (see figure 3.4). Using the least common multiple the grid provides an index for every note of the polyrhythm. Note, to preserve the convenience of having major subdivisions of the rhythm correspond with multiples of ten, one must begin counting the first note as zero. This way the second 32nd note is counted as ten and not eleven, the second 32nd as 20 and not 21, and so on.

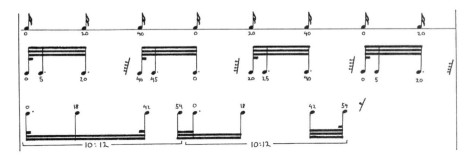

Figure 3.4. Brian Ferneyhough, *Bone Alphabet*, grid of 60. Drawing by Steven Schick.

The least common multiple grid works very well when polyrhythms begin and end together and where the resultant least common multiple is not so large as to render subdivision by a performer impractical. Simple two-part polyrhythms are usually solvable this way. With more difficult rhythms involving three- and four-part counterpoint, or where the components of the polyrhythm do not begin and end together, I produced grids of extremely large common multiples. True, this did locate each note exactly, but I would have to subdivide each pulse into several thousand parts. This would clearly be impractical as a learning or performance strategy.

The second bar of the piece, seen in figure 3.5, is just such an instance. There are just two lines, but the rhythms do not have common beginning and ending points. The 6:7 rhythm starts its second cycle between the last triplet of the second beat in the right hand and before the beginning of the third beat. Exactly where between those two beats is of course the question. This passage is compounded by the difficulty of deciphering the nested polyrhythm in the lower line. Note: a nested polyrhythm is a polyrhythm within a polyrhythm. It is a rhythmic shift *within* a rhythmic line and is often perceived as a momentary surge or ebb of speed within the line.

I clearly had some disentangling to do. The rhythmic marking of 6:7 indicates to play six notes in the time it would take to play seven 64th notes—six in the time of seven in other words. The nested polyrhythm of 4:3 further indicates that the last three of the 6:7 notes are to be divided into four parts. You would be correct to observe that it is impossible to think six in the time of seven while subdividing four in the time of three. The impossibility of solving this rhythm was crushing. I was greeted with failure after only a week of practice.

Figure 3.5. Brian Ferneyhough, *Bone Alphabet*, bar 2. Copyright © 1991 by Hinrichsen Edition, Peters Edition Limited, London. All rights reserved. Used by permission.

I started towards a solution by converting the nested polyrhythm into a tempo. Instead of trying to think two rhythms against a basic tempo simultaneously, I translated the 6:7 indication of rhythm into a change of speed. The rhythm 6:7 became a new basic tempo 6/7 as fast as the given tempo of eighth at M.M. 54, or M.M. 46.3. (Note that this works with all polyrhythms: the rhythm 3:2, a simple triplet, can also be thought of as a tempo 3/2 faster then the speed of the basic tempo.) The resulting unnested polyrhythm becomes a manageable four against three. This became a general strategy whereby I replaced the outer ratio of all nested polyrhythms with tempo changes.

In my conversations with Ferneyhough, he has clearly indicated his opposition to such tempo-based solutions to polyrhythmic composites. He maintained that polyrhythms conceived as modulations of speed cause a reorientation of the strong and weak beats that lend metric sense to a given passage. Meter, the relationship between strong beats and their polyrhythmic elaboration, is of prime importance in his music. Accordingly, I first viewed the strategy of changing speeds as a transitory stage in the learning process. I believed that ultimately I should be able hear rhythms in their original tempo. Now I am much less concerned with what I am is thinking and much more concerned with what the music actually *sounds* like. Making a test recording easily verifies whether a rhythmic passage is accurate and whether or not it conveys the appropriate metrical feeling.

The tempo-based solution to the nested rhythms does not solve all the problems in bar 2. Because the beginning and ending points of the polyrhythm between the upper and lower lines are offset, the least common multiple method used with success in bar 1 does not work at all in bar 2. The grid of subdivisions would be far too large to be practical. I was left with the situation of being sure of either one of the two lines but not both at the same time. One line would have to be approximated, but which?

This question is present in every polyrhythm. One of the lines must act as the primary voice into which secondary and tertiary lines are incorporated. (Take the simple example of 3:2: either one thinks in two and hears three against it or the reverse.) For me the primary line is usually the one with the greater amount of rhythmic information or the line that will sound more obviously right or wrong to a listener. In bar 2, I read the lower line as primary into which I folded the triplets of the upper line as precisely as I could. In short, I calculated the denser rhythmic information of the lower line and *guessed* where the more straightforward triplet music would fall.

Guessing is an underutilized strategy in solving difficult rhythmic problems. I chose to guess the triplets because I had reasonable trust in my reflexes to play accurate triplets. But as Ronald Reagan said, "Trust and verify." To verify the accuracy of my guesswork I recorded myself playing the lower line on a padded surface and played the right hand on instruments. In effect, I recorded only the line I was guessing. By listening to the recording I could easily tell how accurate my approximated triplets were. Through a series of trial recordings I simply fine-tuned them by playing slightly earlier or later as the situation required. This process recognizes that the ultimate judge of rhythmic accuracy is the ear. I could generate polyrhythmic graphs of least common multiples or use computer models if I wanted (I didn't), but in the end, human ears would judge the performance, so human ears should guide the learning process.

In bar 9 (see figure 3.6), a difficult four-part structure posed yet another problem by combining nested rhythms with offset starting and ending points. Here again, any least common multiple strategy would be unmanageably complicated. Since a thread of duple rhythm runs through bar 9, I began by calculating all rhythms in some relationship to a primary duple value. A method emerged of "flattening" the polyrhythmic structure into a single line by reading the entire passage as a filtered version of the primary 128th note subdivision. Opposing rhythms could then be considered as grace notes of different breadths against a primary pulse. In the polyrhythm 7:8, for example, the second eight could be heard as a grace note to the second seven, appearing at the distance of 1/7 of the subdivision (or 1/56 of the entire beat) before its "main note." Continuing this way, the 7:6 figure that starts exactly on the eighth sixteenth note of the 13/16 bar can be calculated relative to the 128th note subdivision of the pulse. The second note of the 7:6 figure arrives, for example, at 6.88 128th notes of beat eight. The third 7:6 note comes at 5.714 128th notes of

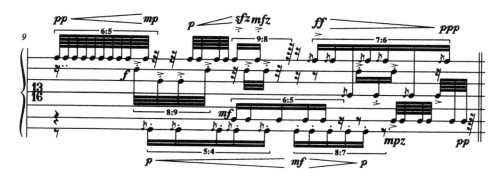

Figure 3.6. Brian Ferneyhough, *Bone Alphabet*, bar 9. Copyright © 1991 by Hinrichsen Edition, Peters Edition Limited, London. All rights reserved. Used by permission.

beat nine, and so on. Of course, no one can hear subdivisions of a thousandth of a 128th note. However, by mapping these calculations onto a grid as carefully as possible, I obtained a very useful (and accurate) graphic representation of the composite rhythm. I was able to learn the 7:6 notes as grace notes of varying speeds against the primary duple subdivision.

That unfortunately is the easy part. Flattening the rhythms of bar 9 into some variation of a 128th note can easily lead to a stale rhythmic composite instead of a living polyphonic structure. If we use the "grace note strategy," opposing rhythms risk degenerating into an unrelated series of points in orbit around a primary line. To enliven the rhythm it is necessary to import the particular sensibility, the aura if you will, of each line. I find that 7:6, for example, has a very different kind of rhythmic personality than does a duple subdivision at exactly the same speed. It's a question of feel. Distinctions of rhythmic coloration provide each polyrhythmic structure with a healthy internal friction. Such friction might easily go missing if all rhythms are construed as grace notes to a single primary pulse. To avoid this, separate lines must be colored carefully by the use of different mallets and striking techniques and must be projected as clearly distinct from the dominant subdivision. In many cases strategies used to solve rhythmic problems are related to broader questions of interpretation. After all, Ferneyhough describes localized rhythmic interactions as "comportment," a word with implications beyond the temporal plane. In *Bone Alphabet* rhythm is synonymous with behavior, gesture, and mood.

Figure 3.7. Brian Ferneyhough, *Bone Alphabet*, bars 5–6. Copyright © 1991 by Hinrichsen Edition, Peters Edition Limited, London. All rights reserved. Used by permission.

At times, forces of rhythmic continuity or discontinuity generate sensations of tension or repose that are not unlike the functions of dissonance and consonance in tonal harmony. Rhythmic consonance can be found in bars 5 and 6 (figure 3.7), where a continuous line of rhythm in 6:7 is expressed in both and 16th- and 32nd-note values. The result is a thread of rhythmic coherence that functions with the cohesive value of a tonic chord or perhaps pedal point in tonal music. It becomes the static value against which the 11:12 and the 11:8 material can sound as rhythmic dissonance. Eventually this tension is answered by a three-part contrapuntal structure of 5:4, 8:4, and 8:5 at the end of the bar. Harmonic rhythm, normally used to describe the progression of dissonant and consonant effects in tonal music, is supplanted by "rhythmic harmony," to use Ferneyhough's term.[3]

3. Ferneyhough and Boros, "Shattering the Vessels of Received Wisdom," 15.

Figure 3.8. Brian Ferneyhough, *Bone Alphabet*, bars 20–22. Copyright © 1991 by Hinrichsen Edition, Peters Edition Limited, London. All rights reserved. Used by permission.

Even the physical drama inherent in a performance of *Bone Alphabet* is articulated by Ferneyhough's rhythmic language. Here "comportment" refers to both the abstractions of musical behavior and to the palpable theater of performance. In bars 20–22, seen in figure 3.8, Ferneyhough composes a "practicing" motive. Very similar rhythmic material, in this case the triplets in the upper voice, is repeated at varying speeds in much the same way that someone might practice a passage, first slowly then faster, slower again to fix some problems and, at the end, in its entirety at tempo. Reconfiguring the nested polyrhythms as changes in tempo supports the sense of fractured line inherent in this passage. An accurate performance of this material should stutter; it must sound, feel, and look interrupted and incomplete.

To convey this sense, I first learned all of the material at the same speed, in essence equalizing the tempo of the sixteenth-note triplet. This was done so that all triplets would *feel* the same no matter what their final speed was. I then calculated the precise speed of the rhythmic material using the strategy of converting nested polyrhythms to tempo described above, and then cut the individual rhythms together as sudden and unpredictable changes in speed. The conversion of nested polyrhythms to tempo is easy at first: a simple sixteenth-note triplet at an eighth note equals M.M. 60. At the end of the bar, however, the rhythm becomes more difficult. The last four sixteenth notes are divided in seven parts and then a triplet is played over the first four of the seven. The arithmetic for calculating the speed of the new triplet is basic. The notation indicates that the triplet is to be played over the first 4/7 of the final quarter note (with the quarter note tempo at M.M. 30). The quarter note at M.M. 30 is therefore divided by 4/7 (or multiplied by 7/4) to give a new basic tempo to the nested triplet of 52.5. Similar calculations for subsequent triplets reveal tempi of M.M. 75, M.M. 44, and M.M. 79 respectively. This kind of wedge of temporal proportions starting from a value serving as a central axis and proceeding to longest and shortest extremes (M.M. 60, 52.5, 75, 44, and 79) is also an operating principal in macrostructural proportions.

At first it might seem overly optimistic to be able to remember and reproduce tempi like 46.3 or 52.5. In personal experience though, I have found that it is not difficult to train even a very finely calibrated tempo sense. I clearly remember listening to pop recordings often enough that I could count off the next track even if there was a long silence between tracks and the tempo relationship between the two was odd. Repeated listening allowed me to sense when the next song would begin. The same holds true for *Bone Alphabet*. Since each slight difference in tempo produces a different rhythmic "feel," we can learn tempo changes as bodily reflex. This was a powerful realization in the development of my interpretation of *Bone Alphabet*. I needed to *feel* the music. In spite of its considerable rhythmic challenges, a successful performance of *Bone Alphabet* requires a musician and not a computer. The same musical sensibilities of pacing, movement, and emotional engagement that I use when I listen to Patsy Cline or perform Bartók also function well in Ferneyhough.

Form

In *Bone Alphabet* distinctly different musical archetypes—again, differentiated by what the composer calls comportment—are cut together in a kaleidoscopic, highly interpenetrated formal scheme. Double bars separate one kind of music from another. Comportmental types are characterized by different tempi, by

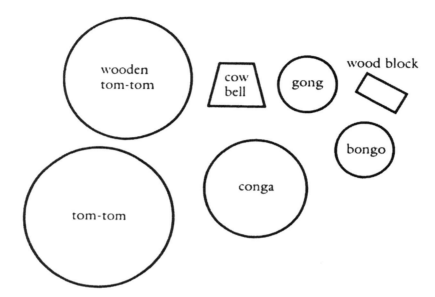

Figure 3.9. Brian Ferneyhough, *Bone Alphabet*, diagram of instruments. Drawing by Steven Schick.

the number of polyphonic lines from one to four, and by the presence or absence of ornamental figuration such as tremolos and mordents. Projecting the form in *Bone Alphabet* depends on the clarity with which each formal type can be rendered and on the performer's ability to switch among types with immediacy and authority. The psychology of narrative connection as it is understood in eighteenth- and nineteenth-century music is almost entirely absent in *Bone Alphabet*. Musical archetypes are discontinued in midthought, interrupted by other material, and then retrieved with the same suddenness with which they were abandoned.

Form in *Bone Alphabet* also means quite literally the form of the human figure in performance. The "form" of the work, then, means exactly that: the confluence of bodily movements, extruding limbs, the sudden muscularity of interruption and contradiction or silent tableaux of a freeze frame. Form is

Figure 3.10. Brian Ferneyhough, *Bone Alphabet*, "Soft triangles." Drawing by Steven Schick.

architecture, but is also the way that ultimately intelligence is packaged and expressed as action by a human body. When I started work on *Bone Alphabet*, this kind of physicality, the theatricality of the body, was the last thing I expected to find. I had thought that the so-called complexity composers were cerebral at the expense of physicality. In the case of Ferneyhough nothing could have been further from the truth.

The physical expression of ritual and drama in *Bone Alphabet* begins with the size and shape of the chosen instruments. I arrange my array of instruments in a quasi-keyboard fashion (figure 3.9), which compresses the overall distance from high to low. This is a practice that I use for most works of multiple-percussion. The arrangement is designed to minimize the overall size of the set-up and thereby to facilitate rapid horizontal movements. The rotating ball-and-socket joints of the shoulder and hip more easily negotiate the series of interlocking "soft" triangular shapes (figure 3.10) than those involving straight lines.

Bone Alphabet is a departure from enormous percussion set-ups of classic first-generation percussion works from the late 1950s and early 1960s. *Bone Alphabet* does not pretend to create a microcosm of the percussive universe. Instead, it takes a distinct sonic and therefore sculptural and choreographic point of view. The extremely limited instrumentation of *Bone Alphabet* produces a spare sound world, but the small set-up also serves to focus and sharpen the gestures of performance. Since the bare-bones set-up (hence the "bone" of *Bone Alphabet*) includes no sustaining instruments, every sound must be activated by a discrete physical action. There are no moments of repose while gongs ring or timpani resonate. This one-to-one relationship of movement to sound creates a choreography that mirrors the acoustical shapes of the work. An alphabet of gesture represents the music and telegraphs it meaningfully to the audience.

As a result, physical gesture in *Bone Alphabet* communicates very differently from gesture in earlier percussion pieces. There is a kind of grandeur about a stage filled with percussion instruments. The human performer, however, is often dwarfed by the sheer amount of stuff and is tempted to exaggerate movement simply to feel present among all of the instruments. The result is frequently something like playing *King Lear* in a stadium: in unbounded space even epic rage is likely to seem rather puny. The gestural world of *Bone Alphabet* functions by establishing parity between the size of the performer and the size of the instrumental stage upon which performance is enacted. In the context of a work for seven small instruments, even the subtlest movements are readable. Motions as small as the upstroke and attack arcs of mallets can import dramatic significance. Larger motions such as shifting body weight from leg to leg or the sudden torque of the torso are then positively balletic. In most percussion pieces gesture is read in gross terms: a sequence of generalized postures against which rapidly articulated pitch and rhythmic material acts as a primary means of expression. However, the gestural unit of meaning is calibrated finely enough in *Bone Alphabet* to articulate musical information at the same speed and with the same degree of eloquence as do the purely acoustical qualities of the piece. Because of the preponderance of very rapid rhythmic material, much of the choreography of *Bone Alphabet* is located in the hands and wrists. Most of the beauty and meaningfulness of the choreography therefore resides in the small movements. The rest of the body serves to position the mallets over the correct instruments but is effectively muted as a means of physical expression. The performer is pegged out over the set-up by the need to be in almost constant contact with every instrument in every bar. As a result, rapid-fire movement in the hands and arms of the player is answered by a strangely static stance in the legs and torso. The general

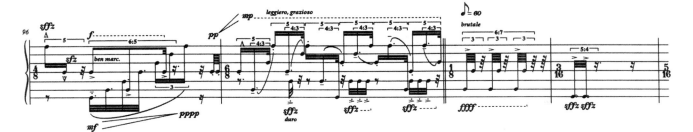

Figure 3.11. Brian Ferneyhough, *Bone Alphabet*, Big gestures, bars 96–99. Copyright © 1991 by Hinrichsen Edition, Peters Edition Limited, London. All rights reserved. Used by permission.

sense of stasis in the body sets the stage for rare instances in which longer passages feature a clear melodic trajectory. In these moments the trunk of the body is liberated from the necessity to stand guard over the center of the set-up and momentarily attains expressive agency. When the whole body finally moves, it does so powerfully and persuasively. Such moments engender an interesting musical/physical correspondence: the more strongly vectorial the melodic line becomes, the more the entire body becomes involved in its execution.

Significant points of musical arrival are announced by these globally unified gestural structures. In figure 3.11 the sudden filtering of the musical texture creates silences that, given the context of Ferneyhough's dense music, can only be called explosive. Conversely, in figure 3.12 rapid chords, sometimes involving all four mallets, saturate the acoustical space. On either end of the spectrum of density— that is to say with silence or saturation—the trunk of the body is released from its central position in the set-up and becomes involved in the generation of the striking motion. In these brief moments the figure of the player looms larger in the physical universe of the piece and signals a point of choreographic as well as musical arrival.

It is important to note that in no case are these gestures simple afterthoughts. An accurate performance of *Bone Alphabet* leaves no unused strength or concentration that can be spent for choreographic affectation. Meaningful gesture is the ultimate calibration of a committed performance, a kind of Richter measurement of the musical tectonic forces underlying the composition.

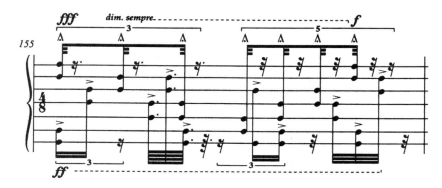

Figure 3.12. Brian Ferneyhough, *Bone Alphabet*, chords, bar 155. Copyright © 1991 by Hinrichsen Edition, Peters Edition Limited, London. All rights reserved. Used by permission.

A final observation: because of its highly inflected score and the intellectual demands it places on a performer, there is a widely held misapprehension that *Bone Alphabet* is a purely rational exercise. Some people feel that it is music for the brain alone. Both in the case of *Bone Alphabet* and with Ferneyhough's music in general, nothing could be further from the truth. To me, playing *Bone Alphabet* is a passionate experience, much like playing the timpani solo in Brahms's Fourth Symphony is, or what I imagine it must have been like to play with Miles Davis or Janis Joplin. For a performer *Bone Alphabet* poses an equation that forces the integration of the intellect with the senses. One sees this most clearly in the curious combination of a highly detailed and highly rationalized rhythmic language with performance instructions that border on the poetic. One is asked to execute a rhythm like 11:8 or 17:16 but to do so in *modo analitico* or *danzando* or as an *ostinato frustrato*. Organicity results. A persuasive performance of *Bone Alphabet* demands more than technical facility and intelligence; it requires a complete human being, one for whom thinking *and* doing are indistinguishable and interdependent.

By all accounts I should be finished with *Bone Alphabet*. I've learned it, performed it widely, recorded it, talked and written about it. The disorderly universe of learning should long have settled into the comfortable steady state of repertoire. But I often feel compelled to return to the uncertainties of my first attempts, to the cragginess of problems too formidable to be leaped with a single bound. With any luck

Bone Alphabet will settle into a kind of prolonged adolescence where the malleability of learning coexists with mature manifestations of performance.

I am grateful to Brian Ferneyhough for *Bone Alphabet*: for its invitation to reevaluate the basic tenets of the percussive art and for the life-changing experience of learning it. In the immortal words of Prince, "Thank you for a funky time."

The Affliction of Memory

Longtemps, je me suis couché de bonne heure . . .

—Marcel Proust, opening of *Remembrance of Things Past*

My earliest memory is of fishing with my father in the small creek that ran through our farm. He said we were fishing for bullheads. Later when we walked backed to the house through a field he told me to watch out for the bull. I remember wondering about bulls and bullheads. I remember being confused. My earliest musical memory comes from a few years later. On a northern lake spring becomes official on the day that the winter ice breaks up. A week of warm weather had turned the ice on Clear Lake dark and mushy and on that day warm southerly winds broke it into chunks and pushed them slowly towards the north shore. By dusk the winter ice was nothing more than thousands of small pieces of ice washing up against a stone beach. I sat in front of my grandparents' house on the lake and listened to the sound of a giant but almost inaudible ice chime.

The modern study of memory is full of stories like these. Like Proust's *madeleine*, something bewitches us and we remember. We examine our stories to understand ourselves. And as creatures who remember, we naturally also examine memory: how we encode, rehearse, and recall information and events. In short we are fascinated by how and what we remember.

In memory research every story is dutifully annotated with reminders about the unreliability and mutability of memory, especially of personal episodic memories such as childhood or eyewitness accounts. We remember, but we never know if these memories are accurate and true accounts of the facts. I might have fished for bullheads and dreamed of bulls, for example, and simply conflated the two. Undoubtedly the ice chime has become more beautiful in my mind's ear with every retelling of that story. (Never underestimate the corrupting effects on accuracy that attend the desire to please a listener with a good story.) More than a hundred years of research into practical memory has produced an avalanche of anecdotes and analysis. Indeed the research has also yielded an impressive number of insights into the formation and recollection of everyday memory. Unfortunately, the same hundred years of memory research has shed almost no light on the major issues of musical memory. The central questions to many performers—of how and why musicians memorize pieces of notated music—have never really been addressed.

Part of the problem is that memorizing music operates very differently from remembering almost anything else. The timeline seems to run in reverse. In everyday life, specific and discrete episodes are stored involuntarily for a protracted period to be recalled, again involuntarily, at an unknown point or points in the future. You remember—you do not have to try to remember—that Aunt Mary Lou burned the pie one Thanksgiving even if you did not know at the time when or even whether the recollection of this event might be relevant enough to be brought to the forefront of consciousness as "a memory." With music, instead of recalling a discrete event at a vague and unknowable point in the future, one *constructs* a memory over time for recall at a known (and often publicized) moment in the future. The moment when a memory becomes relevant is not a mystery in memorizing music. With everyday memory I can keep a charming story about a burned pie in my arsenal of other charming stories and deploy it as needed. If I forget, nothing serious happens. I will simply have to sit quietly by as others relate their hilarious pie stories. With music, one's memory of bar 22, for example, becomes intensely relevant precisely at the end of bar 21. And, of course, there are serious and well-known consequences to forgetting.

Memorizing notated music is essentially the voluntary verbatim recall of sequentially ordered information that is learned and rehearsed for maximally accurate recollection at fixed and given points in the future. A failure to remember has severe consequences. Everyday memory almost never conforms to these parameters. And since science often follows ubiquitous behavior, almost no scholarly attention has been paid to the formidable task of memorizing and delivering complex pieces of music in public concerts. Add to that the qualities that are unique to memorizing percussion music—the absence of a fixed instrument, the intensely physical nature of the practice, and with it the commensurately heavy reliance on kinetic memory—and institutional memory research has one message for us: we're on our own.

However neglected it may be in the cognitive sciences, memory stalks almost every important question involving the performance of contemporary percussion music. We performers deal daily with the magic and frailties of memory, yet the mechanics of our memory and its utility in learning and performance remain veiled and elusive. We memorize without quite knowing how, and when we perform, we recall or fail to recall in equally mysterious ways. Memory is alchemy, a hocus-pocus involving the senses and intellect. In one moment we can summon complex musical material with precision and accuracy, and in the very next instant we can be stunned by our inability simply to play the next note.

Musicians worship the mystery of memory with silence. We have an incomplete language to talk about, understand, and therefore improve upon our memory. And surrounding the greatest danger of performing music from memory—forgetting in public—there is a veritable taboo. Therefore the big issues of memory and memorizing—the techniques, worries, virtues, meanings, and processes—are dealt with privately, like an embarrassing affliction. My professional colleagues and students are more likely to discuss a nasty case of psoriasis with each other than their difficulties and fears in performing from memory.

The Twentieth Century Tries to Forget

Perhaps our uneasiness with memory has historical roots. The twentieth century was famously suspicious of memory, especially the way it was treated in tonal music of the eighteenth and nineteenth centuries. Listening to tonal music is a lot like reading a gothic novel. It's essentially an exercise in memory with lots of characters and plot twists to keep track of. Tonal music is a stage set for linear drama, a morality play where appearance, deception, and redemption are critical values. You have to recognize elements as they are introduced and then you must *remember* them as they disappear, return in disguise, and eventually soar in triumph (or fall chastened back to earth). Musical cues help light the way. A cymbal crash flares to freeze action at a particularly memorable moment. A deceptive cadence means we have been had: the story isn't over yet. (Think of Glenn Close rising from the bathtub at the end of *Fatal Attraction* as Hollywood's version of a I 6/4 chord.)

Not surprisingly, composers of the early twentieth century who sought to uncouple themselves from the past also disassociated themselves from the traditions of memory. To them, memory meant remembering how it had always been done. It meant shouldering the crushing weight of inherited wisdom: Is there a problem with orchestration? Solve it the way that Rimsky-Korsakov did. How does harmony function in the context of large-scale form? Look to Brahms or Mahler. To the new generation of musical experimentalists, memory was a repository of habitualized strategies to be thwarted at all costs. From European serialism to Cage's use of the *I Ching*, from the Bauhaus to the Surrealists, the goal was to short-circuit memory by creating rules and contexts that disallowed ingrained, historically remembered reflexes.

The motto of the experimentalists was to forget the past. Press on. The tide of censure against remembering crested in midcentury with special poignancy just at the moment when there was so much to forget.

German music from the early 1950s, represented best by the early Darmstadt School, is literally almost "unmemorable." Melodies and chords, the historical currency of memory, were declared extinct and replaced by serial systems that were as disciplined and unforgiving as any other twelve-step program. No heroic aspirations were allowed. No nostalgia. And most of all, no connection of any kind to the stench of the Nazi past. The past was cut off at its roots in an aesthetic referred to as *Kahlschlag* (literally the clear-cutting of a forest) and a new generation started over without the affliction of memory.

However, the rootlessness didn't last. Beginning in the 1970s a slender arm of experimentalism tentatively reconnected to memory as an underlying concern in creation. Soon everyone seemed to be remembering: postmodernism, neoromanticism, postcolonialism, and the new totalism. We became a culture of quotation where everything seemed to be defined somehow against a past (if not *the* past). The need to connect to a historical sensibility was arguably triggered as a response to the chaos surrounding the war in Vietnam and, in Europe, the spirit of 1968 (perhaps the last moment of social and political demarcation that was shared equally on both sides of the Atlantic). These movements, to my recollection in the United States at least, were superficially "memory-less," not rising in defiance of history as much as oblivious to it. They were conflagrations in real time—prefigurations of the instantaneous *Gesamtkunstwerk* of the Web—complete with a freshly minted soundtrack of rock music and delivered with near immediacy into our living rooms by the new medium of television. It was a crazy time and as the dust cleared so did our cultural amnesia.

The response was a new music of memory, of which the work of Morton Feldman is the most poetic. His achingly beautiful trio *Crippled Symmetry* (1983) for flute, piano/celeste, and percussion is structured in long arcing cycles that are just out of the range of memory. In *Crippled Symmetry* slight rhythmic variations among otherwise identical phrases leave us wondering at any given moment whether we are hearing repetition or modification. We can't quite tell. The question of what is new and what recycled becomes further complicated since each player plays his or her part independently of the others, and therefore points of arrival at major harmonic and textural changes are slightly staggered. Note in figure 4.1 that, while the bar lines themselves are aligned, each measure is of a different length, assuring that practically from the first beat of the piece, the players will follow their own independent rhythmic trajectories quite apart from one another. A score that is not enforced vertically—that is when the questions of who will be where and when they will arrive cannot be answered—necessarily smudges the boundaries between new and old ideas, the music seems to float forward in a perpetual state of balance between recollection and prefiguration. Listening to *Crippled Symmetry* evokes a forgotten vocabulary of memory: of foreshadowing and recollection, of being in and out of time. The vast landscapes of Feldman's late music are both unflinchingly contemporary and redolent of the past: his subtly shifting patterns sound like Schubert if Schubert had been

Figure 4.1. Morton Feldman, *Crippled Symmetry*, 4 bars from page 1. Copyright © 1983 by Universal Edition A.G., Vienna. All rights reserved. Used by permission of European American Music Distributors LLC, agent for Universal Edition A.G., Vienna.

a sound installation artist in the East Village. A listener is left perpetually grasping for what is and what was, and both are tantalizingly just out of reach.

Performers of the twentieth century dealt in their own way with memory. To them memory meant memorizing—standard practice for the nineteenth-century virtuoso. To memorize is to internalize; the goal is to *own* the music. However, with ownership comes privilege. Romantic performance ideals, plentifully documented by recording well into the twentieth century, granted license not simply to transmit, but also to embody and ultimately warp the music. The affectations of self-indulgent virtuosi were often more obscuring than enlightening. It is no wonder that more than one score from the early twentieth century contains a proviso against an overly personalized interpretation. Performers of contemporary music reacted by imposing purified and exacting standards of accuracy. Great performers of the late twentieth century from Claude Helffer to the members of Speculum Musicae were brainy types who traded romantic indulgence for a cooler sensibility of intellectual detachment. Their performances even looked different. Through performances with music stands and scores (an imposing group of objects standing guard as the composer's deputized representatives on stage), the music seemed clearly external to the performer and therefore immutable and credible.

For most performers of contemporary music who choose not to memorize, playing from score is a philosophical and not a practical decision. They do not avoid memorizing to save time or out of the fear of forgetting. At best their performances are as profound and deeply felt, as grounded in reflection, intuition, and indeed muscular memory as any Horowitz interpretation of Rachmaninov. No, theirs is a decision to store musical information on the stable medium of paper rather than in the human body with its notorious propensity to mold and warp. More importantly, the constant need to *look*—signaling the ever-present involvement of the brain as a cognitive intermediary—underscores the distinctly rational perspective most of these performers seek to bring to interpretation. In the newest music, the presence of the page on a music stand is also a kind of proof that the player is not simply inventing on the spot.

Helpful Hints to Aid in Memorizing

In trying to understand the practical side of learning and memorizing music, I have drawn widely on personal experience. For the past thirty years I have made a practice of learning all solo works from memory. My process involves memorizing as the very first step in the learning process. I never play a piece from the score and then gradually convert it to memory. I never sight-read ahead to see what things will sound like (in very complex music by Xenakis, Ferneyhough, and James Dillon, for example, sight-reading is not an option anyway). I memorize the first bar, then the second and third and so on until I have memorized the entire piece. I do not work backwards and rarely work out of order. (Some exceptions are noted below.) I find that by learning the piece in order, the natural dramatic flow of the music from beginning to end can be experienced in very slow motion during the learning process. Over the months of memorization, I prepare myself for the moment in performance when I will relive it all in the rush of real time.

My memorization strategies are personal and often idiosyncratic. In particular, my memory strategies rely heavily on physical memory. This is the very kind of memory that performers are often warned against. And indeed, rote repetition to build a muscular reflex is dangerous as the sole strategy of memorizing. At some point or another most performers have experienced the empty feeling of being on musical autopilot.

Very often this feeling immediately precedes a catastrophic memory error. However, in general I trust my bodily memory, especially if the physical reflexes of memory are well supported by appropriate mental structures. I have often thought that the sign for "remember" in American Sign Language closely resembles my methodology of high reliance on kinetic memory. Make two fists with your thumbs on top. Now touch the middle of your forehead with your right thumb and bring it down to meet the left thumb: remember. This act of connecting a thought to the hands is exactly what we do. It is good to be reminded that as practicing percussionists we are not remembering a random series of syllables; we are remembering music that has been translated into muscular movements. It is good to learn to trust the body.

I have preferred methods for memorizing. However, I do not assert that my methods are any better than anyone else's. I acknowledge that the comments below may not lend themselves to generalization and may therefore not be applicable to someone else's practice. My goal is simply to cross-reference my experiences, along with those I have had with my students, with evidence and terminology borrowed from more formal studies of memory.

The Long and Short of What We Know

Discussions of memory cleave neatly in half—on one side there are issues of great emotional depth but which resist easy analysis; on the other side there are a few things that can be described easily but turn out to be pretty banal. This division is reflected in the way memory has been studied. For more than two thousand years the *ars memorativa* were seen as an arm of philosophy, more precisely of ethics. Major treatises came from Cicero, Thomas of Aquinas, and Giordano Bruno. In the past hundred years or so, the study of memory has concerned itself with *tasks*—often how easily research subjects could memorize and retain lists of unrelated numbers, words, or abstract syllables. What we have learned in the modern study of memory began with Hermann Ebbinghaus and his book from 1885, *Über das Gedächtnis (On Memory)*.[1] Since the time of Ebbinghaus we have learned a lot about the behavioral and physiological basis of memory. But the short list of abstracted truths of memory—what we can say with certainty about how we create effective and usable memory and how we can learn to improve our memory—remains painfully basic.

---

1. Hermann Ebbinghaus, *Über das Gedächtnis: Untersuchungen zur experimentallen Psychologie* (Leipzig: Duncker & Humblot, 1885); trans. Henry A. Ruger and Clara E. Bussenius as *Memory: A Contribution to Experimental Psychology*, with a new intro. by Ernest R. Hilgard (New York: Dover, [1964]).

To illustrate what we know, let me pose four scenarios:

1. Your frail grandmother arrives at midnight by train at the station in the center of a dangerous city. She asks you to be on time to pick her up because she is afraid. You do not forget because there are serious negative consequences to forgetting.
2. You sit next to someone on an airplane. He introduces himself as Joseph Haydn. You can build on pre-existing knowledge to help form a mnemonic association.
3. You won the lottery yesterday. Your friend asks, "How's life?" You do not forget to mention the lottery because it is an extraordinary event in the context of everyday life.
4. You go to get cash at the ATM. Your code number is also your birthday, your wedding anniversary, and the code for your voice mail. You do not forget because this number is well rehearsed.

With these stories in mind, the best advice to any performer wishing to improve his or her memory is to imagine how horrible it would be to forget in public and then go back and practice harder. This effectively covers the four basic points in the scenarios. The likelihood of remembering increases: if there is a negative consequence to forgetting; if we can create a body of expertise or knowledge into which to fold new material; if what we wish to remember is extraordinary; if we rehearse. Unfortunately most of this is out of our control. We cannot control the consequences of forgetting. They exist whether we like it or not. Likewise the growth of an expertise that will allow for mnemonic associations is beyond our immediate control. This accrues over time as a natural consequence of consistent practice and performance. And for the most part we cannot control the "extraordinariness" of the music we wish to memorize. It seems safe to presume that we would not be interested in memorizing and performing music that we did not find to be extraordinary for one reason or another. In the final analysis, the only criterion of memory that we performers have consistent control over is rehearsal. We can shape the amount and quality of our practice.

Understanding the role of rehearsal in memorizing takes us back to Ebbinghaus and his experiments on the nature of episodic memory. (Episodic memory is the recollection of specific events unique to an individual; these memories are often personal and highly characterized by perception and use. Its partner, semantic memory, refers to a body of universal knowledge and is not dependent on the specific experiences of an individual. Episodic memory responds to the question, "Where were you when President Kennedy was assassinated?" Semantic memory answers the question, "When was John F. Kennedy assassinated?")

Using himself as a subject[2] Ebbinghaus tested the formation and durability of episodic memory by recording the conditions under which he could make two errorless readings of a given list of three letter nonsense syllables. By using nonsense syllables such as HOZ JAK GUB rather than COW SUN SIP, for example, Ebbinghaus was able to exclude preexisting knowledge and associations. As a result his findings do not need to be adjusted to account for the prior knowledge of the participant before they are applied as abstract data. After he learned the list initially, Ebbinghaus quantified the process of recall by remembering the list at intervals from minutes to days later. Once there had been appreciable decay of the original material he took note of the number of readings of the list necessary to restore it to memory.

Some obvious things emerged quickly. Ebbinghaus observed that syllables at the beginnings and ends of the list were easier to recall—thus establishing the memory-strengthening principles of *primacy* and *recency*. He also observed that, once learned, the list was easier to restore to memory the second and third times it was memorized. What is perhaps less obvious is the shape of the memory curve. Most of the memory loss took place early: he was able on average to retain 58% of a list after 20 minutes, 44% after one hour, 34% after 24 hours, and 21% after 31 days. The memory *savings*, or the amount of material retained between recollections, fell off dramatically between initial memorization and the first two recorded recollections, but stabilized over time. Seemingly, once information was converted to long-term usage it became relatively secure.

For a musician the key to a secure memory is likewise the ability to manage the conversion of information from short-term to long-term memory. In my own practice I distinguish three groupings along a spectrum from immediacy to reliability:

Very short-term memory—the immediate recall of a short phrase or fragment often consisting of nothing more than the physical reflex of repetition,

Working short-term memory—a usable store of memory, essentially long-term memory under construction, that is defined increasingly by rational processes, and

Usable long-term memory—a full-fledged piece or substantial portion thereof that can be recalled consistently and under pressure to form the foundation of a performance.

A few factors predictably affect the conversion of information from very short-term to usable long-term memory. Slow learning tends to make more indelible long-term memories and converts a greater percentage

2. As recounted in Steven Rose, *The Making of Memory* (New York: Anchor Books, 1993).

of initial short-term information to long-term memory. Distraction at the moment of remembering tends to retard the conversion process, and the resulting long-term memory is pockmarked with moments of fallibility. Finally, there is a fragile balance between familiarity and difference. Familiarity with the material, and by extension the extent to which it might be similar to a known vocabulary, speeds the process of transformation to long-term memory by creating links to mnemonic associations. However, too much similarity makes new material indistinguishable from old and therefore unremarkable and unmemorable. The problem exists in reverse as well. We remember remarkable and unusual events unless we are so barraged by novelty that everything is unusual in which case we lose our ability place new events into a context of the known. In short we remember what is remarkable as long as we have the preexisting mental architecture to make sense of it.

Chunks

Very short-term memory is essentially the intake mechanism for new information. Here complex material is broken down and bundled into manageable units. First described in the 1930s by Ian Hunter in his observations of mnemonist A. C. Aikens,[3] these units or "chunks" allow us to store a few seconds' worth of information in very short-term memory. The length of a chunk is a fixed physiological phenomenon that varies slightly from person to person. Scan the digit test below. It is easy to recall shorter groups of numbers by reading them just once. As the groupings get longer you will reach a point when you can no longer repeat a group without "studying" it or breaking it into subgroups. When you have to subdivide a group to remember it, you have reached the maximum length of your chunk. (If you read the digits aloud the chunk will be slightly longer since aural and visual means of intake collude to reinforce each other.)

8623
3035
16218
68125
972354
714371
8152623

3. See Alan Baddeley, *Your Memory: A User's Guide* (New York: Macmillan, 1982), 151.

4261783
51627349
16782826
647210384
819283465
0198374659
8176464945
15284673187
16253472983

To see how learning in chunks affects performance, think of your telephone number. (Note that in the United States telephone numbers are chunked into groups of three, three, and four digits.) Repeat your number aloud (thus making it a kind of performance). Now repeat your number starting on the second group of three digits and loop around to the beginning to finish where you started. Now start on the eighth digit and loop to the beginning. Now say it backwards. The ease with which you are able to repeat your telephone number as you learned it from beginning to end implies that the chunking mechanisms of learning and rehearsal reinforce the natural groupings in performance. As I test myself, everything else produces uncertainties and irregularities in recollection, since the chunks I used to learn and rehearse the number seem opposed to the way I "perform" it. Note the difficulty of saying the number backward without first visualizing it and then *reading* it backwards.

Like the recitation of telephone numbers, the memorization of music is most effective when performance is maximally aligned with the chunks used in learning. Alignment can be enhanced if the chunks reinforce the natural musical phrases or gestures in the piece. After all, why choose an arbitrary chunk length when many composers conveniently divide their music into chunk-length phrases? After identifying a chunk to be learned, the first goal of practice is to strengthen its integrity—to be able to remember it as different from other chunks and recall it with maximal immediacy and precision. The next step is to sequence the chunks and attach them to the temporal framework of a piece of music as a series of sequentially ordered, rhythmically charged surface units of memory.

A musical chunk often depends on the support mechanisms of physicality and gesture. When I memorized Iannis Xenakis's *Rebonds A*, I worked with passages of a few chunks in length—essentially the amount of music I could sing in one breath consisting of anywhere from two beats to an entire bar depending on my practice tempo. To reinforce the integrity of the chunk, I first played a passage at the instruments while looking at the music. Next I sang it in one breath with my eyes closed. Then I imagined it as vividly as possible while I stood away from the set-up. Finally I played it on instruments without looking at the score. In this way each chunk was reinforced through independent visual, aural, rational, and kinetic mechanisms. As the piece approached performance level, I tried to integrate these separate approaches into a single multilevel memory scheme by trying to see, hear, think, and move within the piece all at once.

Practicing this way became a kind of ritual of its own and captured some sense of the nexus of calculation, mystery, and physical intensity I hear in Xenakis's music. By learning *Rebonds* as a combination of mental discipline and physical repetition, my interpretation began to approach what I feel is the great polarity of Xenakis's percussion music—as a corporeal ritual suspended between the precision of thought and the ineffability of myth. My intention was to strengthen an interpretative point of view by cultivating an organic connection between the way I learned the piece and the way I ultimately wanted to play it. Along the way I discovered that if the mode of preparation blossoms in its own image as mature music, then performance becomes essentially the memory of learning. I know that I am not the first one to have noticed the similarity between mature forms and the way these forms were created and developed. Or, as more than one person on the family farm has noted, the chicken is roughly egg-shaped.

Finding Meaning

Ebbinghaus noted that meaningful material could be learned many times faster and retained much longer than meaningless material. It's simple. If I ask you to remember the nine letters "polar bear" you are likely to learn them more quickly and remember them longer than the letters "lupkj swrt." In musical practice it's less simple, given that "meaningfulness" is an elusive quality in music. Where do we look to find *meaning* in music? Not very far, as it turns out. In tonal music a theme stated in a key has meaning in the sense that any variation, modulation, or repetition thereof can be conceived as an inflection of its initial statement. The phrase "a bigger dog" means something because the words stand for ideas that we can remember and compare to commonly accepted standards. Similarly, motivic development or modulation can be considered meaningful because either can be calibrated as a deviation against the backdrop of an accepted given.

I hasten to add that I am not commenting in general about linguistics, semantics, or the cognitive sciences as these disciplines apply to musical perception. That is far beyond my range of competency and the scope of this book. But I do believe that the use of the word "meaning," applied specifically to memorizing, best describes how a lot of performers learn music. It would not be unusual to hear a performer say, "This part is like the first section only twice as fast." Or, "The end of this repetition leads into the key change." These are comments that reflect notions of category, comparison, and action that comprise core components of meaningfulness. As meaning aids memory, I assert that musical meaning aids musical memory.

Georges Aphergis's *Le Corps à Corps* (1982), a work for solo percussionist who vocalizes while playing *zarb*, provides an example of memorizing through meaning. In *Le Corps à Corps*, as elsewhere in his music, Aphergis often "retroconstructs" phrases by building them backwards. In other words he asks you to play the last note, then the last two notes, then the last three and so forth until he has built the entire phrase from back to front. In *Le Corps à Corps* this process is applied to three distinct musical entities: drum figures, imitations of drum sounds by means of onomatopoetic vocal syllables, and a text in French about a crash at a motorcycle race.

Note the use of retroconstruction as applied to the French text in the following passage:

coule

sang coule

le sang coule

son bras le sang coule

à son bras le sang coule

fraîche à son bras le sang coule

blessure fraîche à son bras le sang coule

de sa blessure fraîche à son bras le sang coule

The final line gives us the text in its entirety: ("Blood is flowing from the fresh wound on his arm"). Aperghis uses the same process to build other lines of text, and in the end he sequences those complete lines into a narrative. The same multiphase process of building-in-reverse produces the drum rhythms as well as the vocalized drum and motorcycle sounds. The final version of each phrase of music and text in *Le Corps à Corps*, in other words the presentation of that phrase in its entirety, comprises a platform of meaning in the piece. Each subphrase thereof can be understood and remembered as a version of the complete phrase—as an inflection of an original meaning in the same way that "bigger" is an inflection of "big." This greatly simplifies practice. One learns the handful of final phrases first and works in reverse.

A performer soon discovers that *Le Corps à Corps* is not so simple after all, since there are often several simultaneous and interpenetrated reverse processes working at any given moment in the piece. But encoding each subphrase with a meaningfulness that is related to a primary phrase allows us to generalize. Each variation of a basic material does not have to be remembered as a unique entity. Variation can be registered instead as a version of something more basic. In fact without the ability to generalize and categorize information, our memories would look like a huge junk heap of unrelated thoughts before long. The Borges story "Funes, the Memorious,"[4] is about a gifted mnemonist who could not generalize (to Funes a dog at 3:14, seen from the side, needed a different name from a dog at 3:15, seen from the front, since to him they were two separate things). The story ends with his death by congestion.

The ability to generalize also allows us to apply principles of the predictability and redundancy of language to the learning of music. Note how the rules of language imply a greater or lesser probability of correctly guessing the way the following sentences might be completed.

Fill in the blank:

1. "I . . ."
2. "I told him not to eat the pie. But he said he was hungry, and he was going to eat the pie whether I wanted him to or not. Sure thing, as soon as I turned my back, he went into the kitchen and ate the . . ."

Obviously the constraints of grammar and meaning in the second sentence steer us to a more predictable response than in the first sentence. Our ability to extract meaning from context enables us to limit the range of potential appropriate responses. Music works this way also. We know that the furious cadential figure at the end of the Beethoven "Eroica" Symphony will eventually land on an E-flat-major chord. Performers of this music do not need to "memorize" the fact that this chord includes a B flat rather than a B natural. The rules of musical grammar leave no other choice. When the goal is memorizing *Le Corps à Corps*, the rules of musical meaning also allow us to limit the range of options for what comes next and accordingly raise the probability that we will remember accurately in the heat of performance.

---

4. Jorge Luis Borges, "Funes, the Memorious," in Borges, *Fictions*, ed. with an intro. by Anthony Kerrigan (London: Calder & Boyars, 1974).

Microdistribution and Practice

We know from experience that as we practice a piece our learning curve improves. Just as putting the last few pieces of a puzzle together is easier and quicker than placing the first pieces, each new note we learn in a piece of music establishes an increasingly complete framework that affords more support and leaves fewer options for what we will learn next. With memorization, the more we learn the faster it comes.

Alan Baddeley documented this principle in his study of British postal workers who learned to type.[5] A change in mail-sorting technology made it necessary for a large number of postal workers to learn a special typing technique. The workers were separated into three groups that studied the new technique for one, two, and four hours per day respectively. The total number of hours of study was the same for all groups. In other words the group that studied four hours a day worked fewer days. The results of the study demonstrated convincingly that those workers who studied fewer hours per day over a greater number of total days learned most effectively.

One can infer from Baddeley's work that it is not the overall number of hours spent studying but their division into the number of work sessions that is critical. I know from my own practice that the rate of intake of new information must be pinned to a coherent framework of understanding that is built from a series of microprocesses that involve the *intake*, *rehearsal*, and successful *testing* of new material. *Intake* is obviously the first attempt at learning a passage—the initial mapping of information in the domain of very short-term memory. *Rehearsal* and *testing* are processes by which conversion to workable short-term and long-term memory is effected.

A key element in the conversion to long-term memory is testing. For me a successful test means being able to play a passage accurately on the first try and being able to repeat the section accurately numerous times. Testing verifies the accuracy of new information and closes a stage of memorization by confirming that the new material has been successfully logged into usable long-term memory. A practice strategy involving numerous shorter work sessions rather then fewer longer ones results in more frequent testing. As a result the final performance is more densely packed with points of confirmation—moments where you can say, "I know that this is right and I know what comes next."

One of the biggest problems in memorizing complex music is the problem of juggling passages at different stages of development. You learn a passage and test it before moving ahead, but as you learn the next

5. Baddeley, *Your Memory*, 27.

section, the first one begins to decay. You start to forget it. The more you learn, the more you have to juggle. I try to solve this problem by distributing the intake/rehearsal/testing cycle over what I think of as a practice rotation—a period of time from four to six consecutive practice days. This process is most applicable to sequential learning where one starts from the beginning of a piece and works bar by bar to the end. A typical rotation is a macroversion of the intake/rehearsal/testing cycle that leans more heavily on intake and rehearsal at the beginning and is more engaged with testing at the end. A typical cycle looks like this:

Day 1 Material A: intake
         Material A—rehearsal
         Material B—intake
         Material B—rehearsal
         Material A—rehearsal
         Material A—testing

Day 2 Material A: rehearsal
         Material A—testing
         Material B—rehearsal
         Material B—testing
         Material C—intake
         Material C—rehearsal
         Material A—testing

Day 3 Material B: rehearsal
         Material A—rehearsal
         Material C—rehearsal
         Material D—intake
         Material D—rehearsal
         Material A—testing
         Material B—testing
         Material C—testing

Day 4 Material D: rehearsal
         Material D—testing

Material C—rehearsal
Material C—testing
Material A–C—testing
Material E—intake
Material E—rehearsal

Forgetting

The length of Material A or B depends on the difficulty of the music, but it is likely to be just a few chunks long (recall that the chunk is the length of very short memory, the "intake" unit). "Material A" becomes what I think of as a "memory packet," perhaps a few bars long in a piece like the first movement of Kaija Saariaho's *Six Japanese Gardens*; probably just an eighth note in *Bone Alphabet*. I learn a piece by adding memory subdivisions together from small to large: chunks combine to make memory packets; packets are combined to produce phrases. Phrases are combined to form larger formal subdivisions and ultimately an entire piece. The piece in its entirety then is a series of overlaid memory subdivisions of varying lengths, each of which is rehearsed and tested independently to create an interlocking support structure that resists forgetting.

Central to this structure is the role of the memory packet. Packets are kept purposely small enough—just a few chunks in length—so that if I forget a packet I can move to the next without missing too much music. Memory packets are loaded with kinetic information, each consisting of trained and reliable physical reflexes that are initiated by a mental cue. The packets are then lined up consecutively and triggered in order. How a packet is fired is what I actually *remember* in performance. The triggering mechanism is usually the initiating physical pattern of a packet: I must remember at precisely the right moment that a packet begins with a certain left-hand motion, for example. I then depend on kinetic reflex to fill in the rest of the material.

This is pure management strategy. I am delegating. Every component of the process is carefully profiled for maximum efficiency. The brain as the triggering mechanism is relatively inactive, but what it is asked to do is crucial. By keeping the brain calm, performance becomes meditative and the body is not impeded. I do not have to *think* every note (imagine the cerebral electrical storm that would accompany thinking every note of Roger Reynolds' *Watershed*, for example.) The body is subservient to the dictates of the brain and fills in the rest of the packet as a kinetic response. The body, however, is ultimately where the music comes from: for its obedience to the brain it is rewarded with the true complexity of music. (As Whitman wrote, "if the body is not the soul, then what is the soul?")

One of my earliest experiments in memorization sought to reinforce the strength and identity of the memory packet. I divided James Wood's *Rogosanti* into 3-to-5-bar phrases, each containing several packets. I pasted the phrases onto flashcards and practiced playing phrases out of order by choosing cards at random. Ultimately I was able to shuffle the deck and play the phrases in any order. The goal was to strengthen the rapport between the mental function of triggering and the kinetic response that produced the remainder of the packet. In case of a memory lapse in performance I wanted to be able to trigger any packet at any time in any order.

As the kinetic response became increasingly reliable, I found that all I had to remember were the triggers. Eventually I could practice *Rogosanti* effectively away from the instruments by mentally walking along a triggering path consisting of roughly seventy-five phrases each with four or five triggers—a relatively small task considering the enormous complexity of the piece. If I forgot a trigger, the worst thing that could happen was that an individual packet was lost. In that event I simply moved ahead to the next one with only a small bump in the music. Interestingly in more than fifty performances of *Rogosanti*, I would occasionally forget a trigger, but once triggered, my muscular/kinetic memory *never* failed to accurately perform the rest of the packet.

Learning (and occasionally forgetting) *Rogosanti* taught me that forgetting is an activity. We often think that forgetting is the *absence* of something. We do *not* remember. Information is missing. But in fact forgetting is *something*: it is what we are doing instead of remembering. We can avoid forgetting by viewing it as undesirable behavior that we replace via practice with the more desirable behavior of remembering. We are accustomed to behavior modification as a part of practice. This is the same strategy we use if we rush triplets; we practice in order to construct a new behavior that does not rush triplets.

What kind of behavior typifies forgetting? A simple answer is that forgetting is the name we use to describe memories that fail on account of the insufficiency in the domains of *accuracy of input* or *reliability of recall*. Obviously if we recall something with complete accuracy, but that thing was wrong to begin with, then the accuracy of our memory clearly loses value. If you get the time wrong for an important job interview and arrive an hour late, I would advise against arguing that you did not really forget but just arrived on time according to falsely encoded information. No, by anyone's standards you have *forgotten*. Presuming that we learn a score accurately in the first place, the sole concern of a performing musician is then accuracy of recall (although anyone who misreads a note and has to relearn it will attest to the difficulty of corrections to the memory stream). In the realm of recall we see two potential problems: resisting the natural degradation of memorized information, and avoiding interference at the moment of recollection. The latter is the simpler problem to solve.

Interference is a part of musical performance. We are sometimes nervous; we see our parents in the audience and we worry that they will regret financing our musical education once they have seen our performance of Vinko Globokar's *?Corporel*. Our nervousness makes us rush or think of other things. We play faster than information can be funneled from brain to body. We forget. But, interference is easily dealt with. We begin by accepting that we will get nervous. (I contend that we *wish* to get nervous—it enhances the sense of occasion surrounding a concert and is the surest barometer of the importance we attach to a performance.) One strategy to deal with nervousness is to address the symptoms of nervousness rather than nervousness itself. We might become nervous, but we can learn not to rush difficult passages. We can learn to control breathing in order to minimize wandering thoughts and sweaty palms. (Try playing fast material a little slower and slow music a little faster in problematic passages, as Artur Rubinstein once advised. The disruption of ingrained behavior alone enlivens the mind.)

The deterioration of information stored in memory is a more complex problem. One obvious solution (recall here my contention that almost everything to be said about memory and memorizing is painfully basic) involves returning frequently to the score in practice. This allows for the constant calibration of the accuracy of memory. But the inevitable deterioration of information forces us to admit that our memories are malleable. We may feel sure that what we are remembering is accurate, but images and information change gradually over time. In my memory of fishing with my father, the creek on our farm is roughly as wide as the Colorado River in flood season; a single bullhead could feed the five thousand. The accuracy of these stories has not suffered because I failed to rehearse them. It is precisely because I have rehearsed them via retelling with such frequency that they have changed. Each repetition of the story featured slight embellishments that were then rewritten as fact in the next retelling.

With pieces of music, something similar happens in spite of having a score to help enforce accuracy. After more than five hundred performances of Iannis Xenakis's *Psappha* I can return to the score as often as I wish, the piece is not on the page anymore; it is in my body. My memory has changed the piece. I may play the notes as accurately as I ever did, but I have reformulated the weighting of internal voices and dynamic shapes and included subtle shifts of tempo (as well as some not so subtle ones). These changes are now part of the piece to me. Playing from memory not only allows but also privileges these kinds of changes. My performance of *Psappha* is less a liberal interpretation of Xenakis's text than it is a conservative, slowly evolving, consistently repeatable version of the text I have created from his score.

La Coupure (2000)

James Dillon

When we use our bodies to store memorized musical information we also invite the evolutionary forces of the body to commingle with the music. Because we change, the music will change with us over time. By far the most sophisticated piece of solo percussion music to explore the ragged boundaries between memory and kinetic plasticity is James Dillon's masterful *La Coupure*. *La Coupure* ("The Cut," or in this case more accurately translated as "The Divide") is a work of about sixty-five minutes in length, scored for percussion soloist with real-time audio and video technology. The work is the central movement of the composer's massive *Nine Rivers* suite of pieces. James told me that he thinks of *La Coupure* itself as a river. And as all rivers do, it divides—the conscious from the unconscious, the rational from the intuitive, the remembered from the forgotten.

La Coupure was commissioned by IRCAM and I premiered it in Paris on March 11, 2000. The piece consists of nineteen small movements (called "modules" in the score since their order is variable) ranging from two to five minutes in length. One module is scored for marimba solo, another four for vibraphone solo. The remaining modules feature small multiple percussion arrangements. A representative moment from *La Coupure* is seen in figure 4.2.

Figure 4.2. James Dillon, *La Coupure*, 12 bars from page 1. Copyright © 2000 by Hinrichsen Edition, Peters Edition Limited, London. All rights reserved. Used by permission.

I knew from the outset that I would memorize *La Coupure*. This was necessary in the first place because of the presence of a live video component in the piece. Music stands scattered across the stage would disrupt the shots of the many minicameras mounted on instruments. Furthermore, at several moments in the piece I was asked to combine brief passages chosen from among the nineteen movements into spontaneously assembled collages (the "cuts" of *La Coupure*). The collages were not to be improvised cadenzas; I was asked to reproduce composed material exactly. Neither were they to be worked out in advance. They were to be chosen in the moment—assembled on the spot by cutting and pasting together passages of a few bars in length. I could reorchestrate if I wished—playing drum music on vibraphone or a rack of metallic noise instruments, for example—but the basic material in terms of rhythms and dynamics could not be changed. Playing from memory was the only possible way to extract musical material for these "insta-collages" from many different places in the score in rapid succession—passages that furthermore were intended to be played on set-ups scattered across the stage.

If learning more than sixty minutes of complex music from memory was not a sufficient challenge, the entire score arrived quite late, leaving me about thirty days for the task.[6] With just a month of work ahead of me, I made two early decisions that proved valuable. First, I decided the order in which I would learn the movements and grouped them into three work phases of ten days each. Each work phase included a broad spectrum of instruments; I did not learn all of the drumming modules at once, for example. While it might seem at first glance to be more efficient to learn all of the drum music at once since a single set-up could accommodate all sections, I knew that the similarity of the material would prove to be anesthetizing. Anything that fatigued the mind would only slow the process of memorization. Each work phase also included movements of varying difficulty from relatively simple to very complex music. That meant that each day's practice was designed to contain a consistent mixture of difficult and simple music. (Learning all of the difficult music at once would have ground progress to a halt.) This allowed the work to proceed at a relatively even pace and took full advantage of my regular practice rotation of intake, rehearsal, and testing described above.

Second, I decided that even if I fell frighteningly behind schedule, I would learn the piece as though I had as much time as I needed. I knew that the learning curve would start to work in my favor as I progressed. The more I learned, the more complete the framework of the piece became. As I assembled an

---

6. To be fair, James finished the piece in a timely fashion, but inexplicably the score remained with the publisher for weeks before being sent to me.

architecture of meaning in *La Coupure*—working in much the same way as I did in *Le Corps à Corps*—I was able to accelerate the rate of input of new material. But this would happen only if I *really* learned. Shortcut strategies—moving too quickly or approximating difficult passages—fail to lock information into a level of corporeal awareness on a level that is deep enough to form a framework of meaning.

Among the many daunting practical problems involved in memorizing *La Coupure*, the most forbidding, and not coincidentally the most interesting, were ones of global organization. As we have seen, *La Coupure* is a work of more than hour consisting of nineteen modules of notated music and several "insta-collages." There are moments for electronic sounds alone, as well as playfully interactive moments where the soloist engages the computational elements of the piece in game-like constructions. There are also silences where video images are featured elements. The considerable energy of a work of this length and complexity is organized as a minisociety where decisions must be made, questions of priority answered, and frictions resolved. *La Coupure* is a true *fourmillante cité*, to cite Baudelaire's description of the teeming chaos of nineteenth-century Paris as a swarming city, literally a "city of ants."

The need for memory in *La Coupure* functions with a dual imperative: first, it is a means to organize the work on a global level, and second, it serves to control a moment-to-moment series of tasks in the piece. The former aligns itself with the ancient view of the *ars memorativa* as a mechanism to create formal order in a complex society and, as a result, to link the ethical and moral qualities of the individual to the needs of the group. The latter, more modern view sees memory as fundamentally horizontal in nature—as the tensile force of narrative structure. In the modern world, memory answers practical questions: What do I do next? How does it relate to what I just did and how will it lead to events in the future? In the historical view of Cicero and Quintillian, memory often serves vertically as the core of a hierarchical system in order to recollect and enforce rules that govern the interplay of simultaneously unfolding structures. In the modern view a person who memorizes demonstrates a skill; in the ancient point of view that person reveals an ethical and intellectual orientation.

The ancient world considered memory to be the critical element of a moral worldview. To Cicero memory was a branch of "prudence" and as such one of the "virtues." Roman stoics saw memory as a crucial quality in the moral force needed to control fantasy. Earlier still, Greek society saw memory as key to social organization. In Aristotle's view, memory was the arena where the raw input of the senses could be transformed into material suitable for manipulation by the intellect and action by the body.

The early Church linked memory with ethics as a critical component in recollection and therefore distinction between good and evil. And indeed, we in the immediate postcolonial world do not need to look as far back as ancient Greece or even the early Christian Church to see that when memory fails, chaos ensues.

Above all in the ancient world, memory set the stage where ideas were connected to deeds and where moral force could be translated into meaningful action. This mutually dependent relationship between the ethereal and the concrete was established and widely understood as early as the first century BC. According to classical rules, memories are to be stored as a series of changeable images (*images*) stored in fixed places (*loci*). We start with the concrete by first establishing a fixed and reusable place. Quintillian urges us to imagine a building. It should be spacious with a varied internal architecture. We then translate the ideas we wish to remember into images loaded with meaning and place them in well-lighted areas at regular intervals within our imagined place. Recollecting the memories involves walking along a predetermined path through our imaginary place and collecting the images as we go. As we wish to memorize more or different things we simply wipe away the images and store new images in the same and reusable places.

Classical notions of memory are thoroughly documented in scholarly literature, especially well in Frances Yates's excellent book *The Art of Memory*.[7] The contemporary percussionist might well be inclined to doubt the effectiveness of such strategies in memorizing music. However, students at the University of California, San Diego, were able to recall a list of ten objects stored in *loci* of their choice with absolute accuracy for as long as ten weeks. Furthermore, this strategy worked exceptionally well with *La Coupure*.

The stage set-up for *La Coupure* is large and intricate. Furthermore, a complex pathway of movements through the sequence of modules, collages and passages of electronic music means that the monumental scope of *La Coupure* is actually the result of many small, discrete moments played in sequence. Two adjacent sections are rarely played at the same set-up, and the path between any two stations is never repeated. This means that even though there are several drum passages that use the same set-up, this set-up is never approached from the same direction twice. In this way each small section of *La Coupure* has a unique musical ideation and is uniquely positioned in space. Approaching each set-up triggers the memory of both the specific musical materials to be played as well as their emotional tenor. In exactly the same way as Cicero collected images placed at critically positioned *loci*, the performer of *La Coupure* collects musical material along a carefully predetermined path.

The performance of the "insta-collages" was among the most bewildering memory challenges that I have ever dealt with. Recall that the collages are to be assembled from passages chosen spontaneously from

7. Frances A. Yates, *The Art of Memory* (New York and London: Routledge, 1999).

any of the notated modules. My usual memory strategies rely on a carefully ingrained sequence of events. Disconnecting a musical phrase from its temporal context—from what normally precedes or follows it—thwarts that sequential quality. I practice expressly so that I will always *automatically* go on to whatever comes next. Playing things out of order disenabled the automatic quality of the memory sequence. I could do it, but I had to think. Normally my memory is more physical than mental—that is, a memory packet is mostly an automatic physical response triggered by a quick mental impulse. This ratio was reversed in the collages. Most of the effort was mental; very little kinetic memory was used.

I used much of the rehearsal time in the days leading to the performance to smooth the bumps in the collages, in essence to recreate the smoothness of physical response I had cultivated in the original material. Material in the collages needed to flow seamlessly, not as a series of highly differentiated bits with strong references to their modules of origin, but in a gentle way that seemed to recall the entire piece at once. The plan was that *La Coupure* as a whole would breathe as the focus of memory alternated between the specific material of the modules—detailed and located in pinpoint space—and the more diffuse orientation of the collages that belonged to all modules and all points in space at once.

Memorizing *La Coupure* was a galvanizing experience for me. The overlapping strategies of practical memory along with a strong dose of the universalizing force of memory as it was used in the ancient world conspired to bring strongly to mind a new sense of *why* we memorize. Or at least it reinforced to me why I memorize. I memorize as a sign of emotional commitment to a musical project. I memorize to bring the music as close to my body as possible. And I memorize to create a sense order in myself. The forces of complexity in any worthy piece of music can be frightening. Questions abound. Can we understand and manage those forces? Can they be sufficiently channeled at the moment of performance to allow listeners to share the precious weightlessness we feel as we are suspended just above the turbulence of real music? I memorize in order to answer these questions.

I memorize because memory is fundamentally a moral quality. Memorizing demands that we take our responsibility to the score and a composer's wishes very seriously. Any lapses there and we will be left standing on stage without any idea what to do next. Memory highlights process. It focuses not just on the final product of performance but also on *how* we get there. When we memorize, we not only have to have the right answer; we have to show our work. And because the work of memorization involves a lengthy and involved process, thanks to memory our contact with music is prolonged, intense, and meaningful. Intense and meaningful contact with music: that's why I memorize.

Face the Music
A Look at Percussion Playing

One of my favorite photographs of myself playing was taken in the late 1970s. Every summer my wife, Wendy, taught in a program for deaf and hearing-impaired children. And, every summer, for reasons that now escape me, I thought it was a good idea to play a concert of contemporary percussion music for the kids. The photo shows me in midperformance of Karlheinz Stockhausen's *Zyklus*. I am coiled like a discus-thrower to deliver a fierce backhand stroke to a gong. All of my weight is on one leg; hair is flying. In the front row of children a deaf boy has his fingers in his ears. He will not hear the sound, but he still knows that it's going to be really loud and reacts accordingly. Physicality and gesture in percussion music are powerful tools of communication.

Anyone who has ever attended a percussion concert can tell you that the experience of percussion music involves the eyes as well as the ears. In the first place the instruments themselves are significant objects. They may be intriguing or monstrous or captivating or distracting to look at. As architecture, percussion instruments articulate a performance space into habitable and nonhabitable domains. As sculpture they provide a cueing system for aesthetic and cultural concerns that helps translate the purely acoustical qualities of performance: Are there railroad ties and oxygen tanks? Listen for an edgy, urban approach. A Javanese gong and *teponastli* (a wood drum of indigenous cultures of Mexico and Central America)? Maybe associations with world traditions are at play. Certainly the instrument as sculpture is not a new idea in world percussion traditions. The physical beauty of the gamelan with its carved wooden stands and shimmering banks of metal instruments, or the totemic carvings on African or Native American drums signify the powerful force these objects exert on the performance and appreciation of music. Since such instruments are meant to outlive their practitioners they also convey historical sense. They serve as repositories for communal memory and provide a linkage to antecedent and future practice.

In the western canon however, the multiple percussion set-up is usually neither beautiful nor permanent. The many percussion pieces in the tradition of John Cage's *First Construction (in Metal)* attest to our continuing love affair with the crude constructions of percussive junk and, implicitly, the impermanent relationship between an object and its uses. After all, instruments like brake drums, flowerpots, and mixing bowls are by nature objects whose original utility has been reassigned. But nearly every contemporary percussion set-up, with or without junk, is transitory and expendable. A set-up is normally designed for a single piece, after which it is dismantled and the individual instruments cannibalized for use in other pieces. (A set-up for *Zyklus* that would be kept intact and handed down over generations would certainly be rare.[1]) In fact a good part of the provocation of contemporary western percussion music—its very modern-ness— derives precisely from the impermanence of its physical architecture. In an increasingly peripatetic society, we have become accustomed to the nagging sense of dislocation that accompanies travel and relocation. (How resonant with the air of a bygone age are the opening hundred pages of *Grapes of Wrath* as Steinbeck describes the spiritual paralysis of people who have lost the farms on which their parents, grandparents, and great-grandparents were born.) Likewise a contemporary performer who must negotiate the endlessly mutable instrumental topography of percussion music is also deprived of the stabilizing forces of place.

However physically provocative percussive structures might be, they achieve expressive agency in performance primarily through the gestures of percussionists. The instruments serve as a frame, a stage for the disposition of dramatic action. Looking at percussion in effect gauges the fluid forces of performers in motion against an immovable background of percussion set-ups and their constituent instruments. The way a percussionist looks and moves on stage is among the most important and highly personal aspects of percussion playing. For percussionists the goals of individuality, complexity and coherence are as important in the world of gesture as they are in the sonic and interpretive aspects of performance. The task is not an easy one. One of the contradictions of contemporary percussion music is that, although percussion set-ups are endlessly variable, individual instruments that comprise the set-ups have become increasingly uniform. If every marimba is identical, if all drum stands are of uniform height and each tray table equally large, then the gestures that result as a performer moves among these objects also accrue distressing uniformity. Standardization has many advantages of course: replacement parts are easy to find and percussionists generally know what to expect when they borrow instruments while on tour in Estonia or Bakersfield. But standardized gesture in response to standardized instruments can often mute the expressive force of physical presence. Imagine the homogenizing

---

1. For years a set-up for *Zyklus* was kept in a special practice room in the percussion department at the University of Illinois. At the time of this writing there is a permanent *Rogosanti* set-up at Yale University.

effect in the world of acting if every actor, no matter what his or her size or shape, and regardless of the role or genre involved, had to play on exactly the same set of couches, paintings, and armoires.

Looking closely at gesture and its relationship to percussion music requires an examination of how human bodies move in performing on percussion instruments. We humans are combinations of more or less straight bones that are connected to our torsos by rotating ball-and-socket joints. We position ourselves over percussion instruments by means of gross movements involving the legs and torso and then strike the instruments with motions initiated by the arm, wrist, or hand. As a result, most percussive gesture consists of two concurrent bodily tempi that are typified by two very different types of motion: fast movements necessary to play individual notes are usually angular motions, but slower preparatory movements involving ball-and-socket joints are often curving. Multiple percussion set-ups are best designed accordingly. The most efficient arrangements do not impede the small angular gestures of striking—groups of instruments are set at the same height and positioned as close as possible to accommodate short strokes. But the entire set-up is often rounded as a reflection of the rotating motion of shoulders and hips as they position the body to strike. See the diagram of instruments for Stockhausen's *Zyklus* in chapter 6 (figure 6.1, p. 186) or the soft interlocking triangles of my suggested *Bone Alphabet* set-up in figure 3.9 (p. 114) as examples. Serious technical problems result if these functions are confused. In a set-up where a performer has to reach out and over several ranks of instruments (think of leaning over a vibraphone and row of cymbals to play a set of temple blocks, for example) the body loses its ability to prepare and support the stroke. Instead the player bends forward, and the arms and hands must both position the stroke as well as execute it. The lack of support from the torso reduces sound density, causes fatigue, and, not least of all, looks awkward. On the other side of the spectrum, a beginning marimbist who takes five or six steps to play a one-octave scale is essentially playing individual notes with his or her legs.

A performer who obeys the dual rules of preparation and stroke by constructing compact, well-organized set-ups curates efficiency. With efficiency comes organicity and ease of performance. It sounds like a good idea, but some of the most beautiful looking percussion music defies just this kind of efficiency. Harry Partch strung gourds, light bulbs, and shell casings out on wickedly irregular eucalyptus branches. His most exciting percussion music is also balletic because of the need to stretch, stoop, and spin to play his instruments. Performances on the Partch instruments outline the mutually informative rapport between the size and shape of set-ups and the expressive potential of the gestures used to engage them. Because the Partch instruments are complex and intriguing physical objects they prompt complex and expressive performance gestures. Conversely, complex and expressive performance gesture is required if the performer is to be visible against the bewitching sculptural qualities of the instruments. The potency of gesture therefore derives from its readability, in other words from the relationship between the size and nature of movements and a context outlined by the architecture of instruments.

Readable Gestures

Gesture as expression requires two essential qualities: gestures must be *readable* and they must be *meaningful*. These twin concerns—readability (the visibility of bodily shape and movement relative to a given background) and meaningfulness (the way that these shapes and movements connect with the expressive intent of a piece of music)—comprise an important component of percussion playing that is almost entirely within the control of the performer via interpretation rather than the province of the composer via the score.

The first requirement of a readable gesture is that it must be large enough to be visible. A viola fingerboard, for example, serves as the stage for fascinating actions, but because of its small size and the fact that in many orchestras and string quartets it faces away from the listener, these actions are generally not easily visible. Percussive gesture is very often visible for the simple reason that percussionists very often play large instruments. However, the relation between a gesture and its context remains important. A *forte* bass drum stroke, for example—this gesture might involve an arm motion of around two feet—looks small on a stage full of large and complex percussion instruments. It is essentially unreadable against its background. (The same two-foot arm gesture by a violist in a string quartet would be eminently readable, not to mention a cause for general concern.) For this reason, percussive gesture as an identifiable component of interpretation began with the more compact set-ups of the second generation of percussion solos (see the discussion of first- and second-generation works in chapter 1). Early percussionists may have moved beautifully and persuasively, but expressivity was limited to the large motions of stroke preparation—the small, angular motions of striking were simply less appreciable against the background of the large and complex set-ups of first-generation pieces. Set-ups in the second generation are roughly human sized and thus have humanized the relationship between a performer and his or her set-up. The resulting parity between movement and context allows for readability.

Parsons' Piece (1968)

William Hibbard

William Hibbard's elegant *Parsons' Piece* is one of the earliest of the second-generation works for percussion. Recall that second-generation works sought to constrain the enormous sonic possibilities of percussion by using smaller arrangements of instruments; the notion was that through limitation come focus and detail. Some second-generation composers pursued limitation by extracting the sonic substance of first-generation works and then refining it into a personal and coherent language. David Lang, for example, took his favorite guiro moments from *Zyklus* and distilled them into *Scraping Song* (1997/2001). William Hibbard built *Parsons' Piece* from the twelve most resonant instruments of Charles Wuorinen's *Janissary Music*—a dozen instruments being a convenient enough number for a composer interested in extending twelve-tone technique into the domain of rhythm and mallet choice.

Hibbard's choice of very resonant instruments (these are by implication often also large instruments) created not just the sonic but also the gestural profile of the work. Large and resonant instruments have a dual function in the visual sphere: their size assures large, visible gestures, and their resonance means that the sound of a note continues long past the actual moment of its attack. Resonance implies that a great quantity of sustaining sound can be produced with relatively few attacks, and since resonant sounds often require careful preparation and a weighted stroke emanating from deep musculature, the sonic construction of *Parsons' Piece* foregrounds the larger gestures of preparation and positioning rather the smaller motions of striking. With fewer attacks but a greater need for the deep, rotary motions of preparation, *Parsons' Piece* approached the aesthetic of dance to a degree that was unprecedented in percussion music at that time.

With its combination of beautiful metallic sounds and heightened visual sensibility, it comes as no surprise then that *Parsons' Piece* turns out to be an excellent training ground in the relationship between gesture and instrumental color. The work was composed for William Parsons, who was the resident percussionist with the Center for New Music at the University of Iowa while I was an undergraduate student there. Parsons moves beautifully. With economic movements, he stresses a narrative sense in even the most complex music by literally pointing the listener towards the next important sound or event. In one of my first experiences with important percussion music, his interpretation of Stockhausen's *Kontakte* was as close to an aria as any performance I have seen by a percussionist.

The key to negotiating the rapport between the sonic and gestural elements of *Parsons' Piece* lies in understanding the physical architecture of its set-up (see figure 5.1). Whereas most percussion set-ups are arrayed as horizontal constructions with instruments that are placed next to each other, *Parsons' Piece* is a set-up turned on its head. The vertical arrangement of three tam-tams, three *almglocken* (tuned cowbells), three cymbals and three low drums (the metal instruments are mounted on a single large rack) means that every instrument is clearly visible to the audience. It also means that *Parsons' Piece* is virtually "weightless." Gravity is a principal means of stroke generation on the horizontal surfaces of drums and keyboard percussion instruments (I often tell my students to let the mallet *fall* as much as possible). However, the normally salutary force of gravity is rendered all but useless on suspended instruments like tam-tams and *almglocken*. The goal in *Parsons' Piece* is to simulate the effect of gravity in the tam-tam and *almglocken* strokes. The mallet has to fall sideways, in other words. This is especially important in the work's many lyrical moments. Hand and arm muscles can generate mallet speed, of course, but unless muscle tension on the stick can be released at the moment of impact, the sound will inevitably be too thin and harsh to sustain the resonance required for lyricism.

On a technical level, a zero gravity performance strategy requires centering the body on an instrument and then shifting the weight of the legs and torso considerably forward so that the direction of the stroke

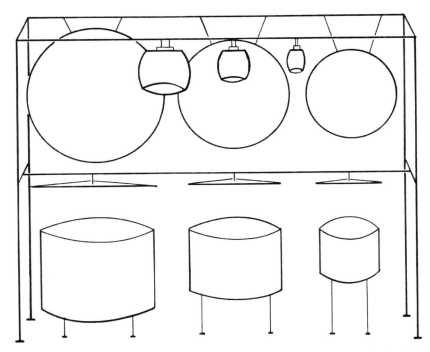

Figure 5.1. William Hibbard, *Parsons' Piece*, instrument diagram from score. Copyright © 1976 by Ione Press, a division of ECS Publishing, Boston, MA. Used by permission.

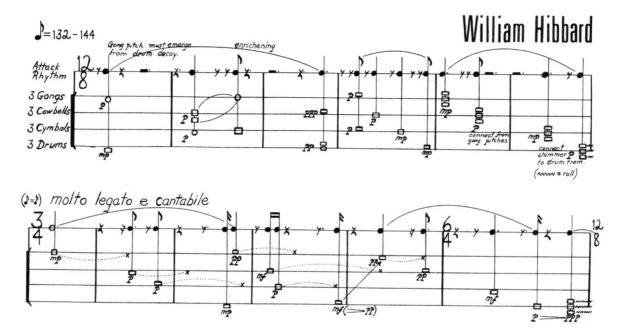

Figure 5.2. William Hibbard, *Parsons' Piece*, bars 1–12. Copyright © 1976 by Ione Press, a division of ECS Publishing, Boston, MA. Used by permission.

is absolutely perpendicular to the face of the instrument. By releasing all tension from the mallet exactly at the moment of impact, the weightlessness of falling can be simulated. Furthermore, the need to center the body as completely as possible before each stroke means that there is an almost constant level of microshifting in the legs and torso and very little reaching with the arms. The resulting fluidity in the upper body and arms means that a performer of *Parsons Piece* can almost literally embody the music (see figure 5.2).

Parsons' Piece exposes two fundamental components of readability: *parity* and *correspondence*. Parity describes an environment of maximum readability that results from equivalence in size or physical intensity between the set-up (or performance space) and the performance gestures. *Parsons' Piece* works well in this regard since the set-up is about human sized: instruments on either side of the arrangement can be reached with outstretched arms if necessary. Furthermore, the vertical distance between the bass drum (occupying the lowest physical position in the set-up) and the tam-tam (in the highest position) is not excessive. In very large set-ups as parity is challenged so is a performer's sense of balance. The first thing to go is the grounding function of the lower body and the stability of the centerline. If a player attempts to fill a too-large space, he or she begins to move to instruments by walking rather than shifting weight. As the feet become more active, the center of gravity rises and the player loses the feeling of being centered. Of course, percussionists step or even walk while playing large set-ups. The challenge is to keep a low center of gravity and maintain stability along the centerline of the body while stepping. Practice this by lowering your weight slightly; now shift 100 percent of your weight to one foot, lift the weightless foot and use the rotating ball-and-socket joint of the hip to reposition it without destabilizing your upper body. With 100 percent of your weight on one foot, you are in the position of maximum mobility. The other end of the spectrum, when your weight is equally balanced on both feet, produces immobility. With your weight evenly balanced, you can't move; with 100 percent of your weight on one foot, you must move. Keeping a low center of gravity and maintaining centerline stability is so important to my approach to large multiple percussion pieces like *Zyklus* or Morton Feldman's *The King of Denmark*, that if time is short before a concert I will often walk through a piece, rehearsing *only* the sequence of foot positions.

On the opposite side of the spectrum of gestural parity, very small set-ups often mean that, however engaging the acoustical music may be, performance actions are too small to be of expressive significance. It is always possible to exaggerate performance gestures on small instruments of course, but I have found that movements extraneous to the requirements of sound production usually seem false if not pretentious. In one elegant solution to this problem, Toshio Hosokawa notates extremely large preparatory motions for short cellular phrases in his *Sen VI* (1993).

"Sen" means "line" in Japanese; in particular Hosokawa evokes the lines of classical Japanese script. The Zen view of calligraphy holds that meaning is found in the pregnant silence just before the actual stroke of the brush. In *Sen VI*, Hosokawa amplifies the aura of "nothingness before the stroke" through intense and concentrated motions of preparation that are many times longer than the phrases they lead to. In other strategies designed to deal with imbalances between gesture and its context, popular music, and even orchestras in some cases have amplified the physical presence of performers through live video projections on giant screens. Add pyrotechnics, lasers, and a battalion of dancers and it is possible to import the intimacy and physical intensity of performance in a small space into an arena.

In one ingenious example of gestural amplification, Erik Griswold's *Strings Attached* (1999) for six snare drummers magnifies the small performance gestures normally associated with that instrument by means of an inventive system of attached strings that enables an audience almost literally to see the music. A small hole is drilled near the tip of each snare drum stick and threaded with a bright white nylon rope. Four of the drummers are stationed at each of the four corners of the stage and are connected by strings to the top of a central pole (a standard theatrical lighting pole usually does the trick). Two more drummers are positioned at opposite sides of the stage. Their sticks are tethered to each other rather than to the pole. In each case the rope is cut just long enough to play—when the stick hits the drum, the rope is taught. Every time a drummer who is tethered to the pole plays a note, a physical wave of reverberation runs up the string. Tremolos produce a series of small waves. The players who are tied to each other produce more complex shapes since their strings lack the stabilizing effects of the immovable central pole. If the strings are brightly illuminated against a black background, the effect is not of rope, but of waves of white light that exactly mirror the sounds of the piece.

Because the waveforms on the ropes correspond precisely to the actions of the drummers, Griswold's strings not only represent just individual sounds, but also reflect the larger forces of form. In a passage where the players begin in unison, then go out of phase with each other and return to unison, the visual shapes respond accordingly to signal the relative orderliness or disorderliness of the music. On opposite sides of the order/disorder spectrum, moments of rhythmic stability or extreme agitation look calm. In unison passages the ropes move together—order is created because one thing is happening rather than many things. In some performance spaces the ropes of the downstage players can obscure those of the upstage players since their shapes are so similar. Again, unity results. On the other hand, highly differentiated complex rhythms create small and chaotic waveshapes on the ropes. As a result, distinction of shape is impeded. The most palpable results come in moments of real dissonance—where one player departs significantly from the language of the group. Dissonance, the force of otherness in music and the antivenom against inertia in life, imports friction and therefore impetus to the visual as well as acoustical domain of music.

The importance of visual dissonance in *Strings Attached* is especially apparent in structures that cause the ropes to move in rotating patterns around the pole. In these passages hairpin crescendo and decrescendo figures are passed around the circle of players. From the perspective of the audience, these circulating sonic structures might easily be heard as global shifts of intensity rather than motions in space. (To realize the full impact of spatialization one needs to be *inside* the circle.) However, the clearly visible motion of the ropes reinforces the movement of sound in space by means of the *correspondence* between an action and its sonic result. Correspondence strengthens both the integrity of gesture and the force of the sound. Of course this is the secret to the impact of live performance. When we *see* music as well as hear it, the acoustical qualities of music resonate with greater clarity through the emotional and interpretive cues of gesture. It's the old rule: when you have something important to say, it's best to say it in person. (Imagine the emotionally eviscerating experience of listening to *Hamlet* on the telephone or receiving a proposal of marriage by e-mail.)

Toucher (1973)

Vinko Globokar

Correspondence resonates on many levels in Vinko Globokar's *Toucher* (1973). The piece consists of six scenes excerpted from Berthold Brecht's play *Leben des Galilei* (1939/1942). The scenes have been translated into French, and a percussionist is asked to find seven instruments that correspond to the colors and tonal qualities of seven vowel sounds. The piece begins with what Globokar refers to as the *Ankündigung*, a brief tutorial for both the player and audience that demonstrates the vocal sounds and their corresponding instruments. The text taken from Brecht follows; a single percussionist is asked to speak lines from the play—representing thirteen characters in total—and play along on the instruments. Brief instrumental interludes separate the scenes. Each time the text contains one of the vocal sounds listed in the *Ankündigung*, the percussionist strikes the instrument associated with that sound. Regular note heads imitate the sounds of accented or principal vowels; "x" indicates an attached or secondary vowel sound and should be played by changing the striking area on the instrument or dampening the sound. However one realizes the sounds, the goal is to make the instruments "speak" in imitation of the text by touching them. No sticks or mallets are allowed. Thus we have the title, *Toucher*. In the outermost scenes (1 and 6), Globokar allows the percussionist to speak in full voice (see figure 5.3). Scenes 2 and 5 are to be performed almost inaudibly, and scenes 3 and 4, central in so many ways to *Toucher*, are mute. The percussionist may only mouth the words.

> Ankündigung:
> Vortrag eines Theaterstücks durch einen einzigen Darsteller.—Sieben verschiedene Schlaginstrumente wählen, mit denen die Klangfarbe der angegebenen Vokale nachgeahmt werden kann. Der angehängte Vokal wird durch andere Anschlagsart oder durch Abdämpfen auf dem gleichen Instrument erzeugt. Der Hauptvokal ist mit ♩, der angehängte Vokal mit ♪ notiert.—Nur mit Fingernägeln, Fingern, Fäusten, Handballen oder Händen

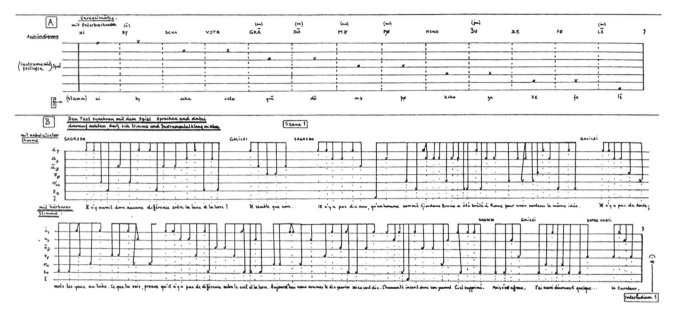

Figure 5.3. Vinko Globokar, *Toucher*, Ankündigung and page 1 of scene 1. Copyright © 1978 by Henry Litolff's Verlag, Frankfurt. All rights reserved. Used by permission.

spielen, also ohne Schlägel oder andere Hilfsmittel.—In Teil A die Silbe mit lauter Stimme vortragen, dann die gleiche Klangfarbe und die gleiche Artikulation auf dem Instrument nachahmen. In Teil B mit unbeteiligter Stimme die Person nennen, die sprechen wird (Galilei, Sagredo usw. . . .) und ebenso die szenischen Anweisungen vorlesen (Une fenêtre s'ouvre et une usw.).—Darauf die gesprochenen Texte auf den Instrumenten "spielen," als ob man sie rezitieren würde, indem man die Instrumente mit den Händen zum "sprechen" bringt.—Nach jeder Szene des Teils B ein Interludium spielen. Die Reihenfolge der Interludien ist frei.—Die Ausführung muß sehr präzis sein. Die Texte stammen aus "Galileo Galilei" von Bertolt Brecht.

(The presentation of a theatrical piece by a single performer—choose seven different percussion instruments with which to imitate the colors of the given vocal sounds. Mute final vowels are to be produced by dampening the sound or by changing the manner of playing the instrument in question. A primary syllable is indicated by a note head, a concluding or silent syllable by an X fixed to the stem of an eighth note. Play only with fingernails, fists, the balls of the hand or the hands, in other words without sticks, mallets or other artificial devices. In Part A, perform the syllables in full voice and then imitate the vocal tone colors and articulations on the instruments. In Part B, use the voice alone when naming the person who will speak [Galilei, Sagredo, etc.] and stage instructions [Une fenêtre s'ouvre et une, etc.]. While reciting the text proper "play" the words on the instruments as if to make the instruments "speak." After each scene in Part B, play an interlude. The order of the interludes is free. The performance must be very precise. The text comes from *Galileo Galilei* by Berthold Brecht.)

Text:

SAGREDO: Il n'y aurait donc aucune différence entre la lune et la terre?—GALILEI: Il semble que non.—SAGREDO: Il n'y a pas dix ans, qu'un homme nommé Giordano Bruno a été brûlé à Rome pour avoir soutenu la même idée.—GALILEI: Il n'y a pas de doute; mets les yeux au tube. Ce que tu vois, prouve qu'il n'y a pas de différence entre le ciel et la terre. Aujourd'hui nous sommes le dix janvier seize cent dix. L'humanité inscrit dans son journal: Ciel supprimé.—SAGREDO: Mais s'est affreux.—GALILEI: J'ai aussi découvert quelque . . . [Entre Sarti] le curateur.

(SAGREDO: So there would be no difference between the moon and the Earth?—GALILEI: It seems not.—SAGREDO: It was not ten years ago that a man named Giordano Bruno was burned in Rome for having supported the same idea.—GALILEI: There is no doubt; look through the tube. What you see prooves that there is no difference between the sky and the Earth. Today is January 10, 1610. Humanity writes in its journal: Heaven is abolished.—SAGREDO: But that's frightful.—GALILEI: I have also discovered that . . . [Enter Sarti] the guardian.)

Toucher establishes a one-to-one correspondence between vocal sounds and physical gestures. Every time a word contains the sounds "i" or "ü" (as pronounced in the French words "il" or "tube") the percussionist plays the first of the seven instruments as a resonant or dampened sound respectively. Each of the remaining six instruments correlates in similar fashion with specific vocal sounds. Since these instruments also occupy positions in space, each vocal sound also produces a unique gesture. In my arrangement "i" and "ü" are played on a small cowbell to my front and right. The sounds of "ay" or "ou" (as in the "é" of "passé" or the "ou" of "prouve" respectively) are played on two instruments to my far left. The relationship between sound and space is enormously useful in memorizing the piece. Since each sound is assigned a discrete gesture, the piece is grounded in physical memory on a technical level, and by a distinct choreographic sense on an aesthetic level. Gesture also provides an important feedback mechanism for the nonnative French speaker. For example, Americans often confuse subtle distinctions between the pronunciations of "ou" and "ü" as seen in the words "vous" and "vu" in the following sentence: "Avez-vous vu ma femme de ménage?" Playing *Toucher* enforces this distinction ("vu" is pronounced closer to the front of the mouth) because the two sounds are to be played on two different instruments. Although the playing is usually too fast to enable a listener to see the correspondence between individual sounds and gestures, generalized movement that outlines grammatical sense can often be discerned. Importantly, the sound "é," when it comes at the end of a verb, indicates an action in the past. Since, in my set-up at least, this sound requires a noticeable movement to my left, text set in the past tense is visually as well as sonically distinguished. Sagredo's frantic warning to Galileo in scene 1 that Giordano Bruno had already been burned at the stake for heresy ("Il n'y a pas dix ans, qu'un homme nommé Giordano Bruno a été brûlé à Rome pour avoir soutenu la même idée.") is unmistakably profiled by jabbing left-handed gestures that accompany the phrase "had been burned" ("a été brûlé").

I had been interested in *Toucher* for many years before I actually learned it. I had one big problem to solve: I couldn't speak French. I knew that I could learn the text phonetically without actually knowing the language, but what interested me in *Toucher* were not just its sounds, but also its social and personal relevance. So, on one hand I learned *Toucher* quite quickly—it took just under a month once I had chosen the instruments. On the other hand I spent about two years preparing for the piece by studying French in my spare time. (A brush with college-level French didn't go very far with the complex implications of the Brecht text.)

I found again in *Toucher*, as I had experienced with other pieces, that a varispeed learning process brought complexity to the final product of performance. Since the playing was learned quickly, the instrumental music was organized around an air of spontaneity. Even now, after having played the piece for more than ten years, I find that I can easily change techniques, striking areas and even instruments within the set-up as the need arises. My interpretation of the text was rooted in a much longer period of study. My delivery of the scenes can also change from performance to performance, but the primacy of the voice, and by extension the multiple levels of meaning and relevance, is deeply embedded.

Toucher seems relevant for a number of reasons. Its historically telescoped view of individualism starts with Galileo Galilei as he confronts the orthodox Aristotelian vision of the earth at the center of the universe as held by the Roman Catholic Church and attempts to replace it with the sun-as-center science-based view of Copernicus. Implications fast-forward to Brecht, who, writing *Leben des Galilei* at the apex of Nazi power in Europe, undoubtedly saw Galileo as a sympathetic character—the individual voice of truth in a world of despots. Globokar's 1973 treatment of the theme arguably responded to the almost anarchic celebration of individualism that attended demonstrations in Paris and other large European cities in May of 1968. The theme of "otherness" is also invoked. Scene 5 of *Toucher* describes the clashes between Galileo's neighbors and the soldiers who sought to cordon off infected areas of Florence during the Black Death. What Globokar does not treat here, but which Brecht underlines quite carefully, is that Galileo's neighbors suspect him of bringing the plague to their doorsteps. With his strange life and unconventional ideas, he, Galileo, is to blame. He deserves to die; we don't. When I first learned *Toucher* in the late 1980s, there was a lot of similar talk about the culpability of the gay population—about the way they brought the plague of AIDS on themselves.

Running through *Toucher* are also themes of naïveté and the role of the intermediary. There are in fact just two people in the piece whose desire to tell the truth transcends concern for their own well-being: Galileo and Andrea, the nine-year-old son of Galileo's housekeeper. In a scene of central importance both for Brecht and Globokar, Galileo has given Andrea an apple that he used to demonstrate Copernicus's heliocentric view of the universe. When Galileo later finds that Andrea has not eaten the apple, but is using it to show his friends how the heavens really work, he is both angry and fearful. Andrea's response to Galileo's insistence that their private conversations should not be shared is positively piercing: "Pourqoui pas? . . . mais c'est pourtant la vérité" ("But why not? . . . it *is* the truth"). The response is made more poignant since it comes in one of the voiceless scenes of *Toucher*. Like Galileo, the percussionist is effectively muted; only the instruments with their perhaps purer voice are allowed to speak. The innocence of truth spoken by a child may be an iconic commonplace in the literature of ethical dilemmas, but as Charles Wuorinen once told me ironically in response to a questionable idea I had for interpreting his *Percussion Duo*, the great thing about cheap tricks is that they always work. Galileo is justly accused and he knows it. His response is a weak: "Oui, mais ils l'interdisent. Nous autres, nous ne pouvons pas prouver ce que nous considérons comme juste" ("Yes, but they forbid it. The rest of us cannot prove what we believe to be right").

In this critical moment of dialogue, Galileo reveals himself to be a character of ambiguous integrity. As the inventor of the first working telescope, he was uniquely in a position to prove Copernicus's abstract speculation that the sun and not the earth was at the center of the solar system. Even Brecht could not quite decide whether or not to cast Galileo as a hero. He posits multiple views of the astronomer: as worthy protagonist, victim and coward. Whatever Galileo may have been, we know for sure that the sun-in-the-middle idea was not his. He was unfortunately just the intermediary: the one person in the world who could prove it and pass it along to mainstream scientific thought. Galileo started by developing the telescope to impress Cosmo [Cosimo] de' Medici in order to enhance his already comfortable position in the Medici court, and he ended up being caught in the middle between the nobility of science and a heretic's fate on the burning stake. *Sic transit gloria mundi*, as any messenger bearing bad news knows all too well.

The Theater of Meaning

As messengers in our own way, performers know that an intermediary balances illusion and risk: on the most basic level we're part cardshark and part trapeze artist. In the guise of smooth expert we package a composer's vision in maximally consumable form, but if something goes wrong we take the fall. This is the performer's lot. (It wasn't my idea to play a three-part polyrhythm on a low gong with soft mallets, but there I am on stage fully committed to demonstrating the superiority of this conception over all others.) But if we percussionists seek to expand the notion of performance beyond its narrowest definition as "execution," we will need to leverage not just our sonic but also our theatrical potential. We must be able to create a theater for the transfer of meaning by engaging action across a wide spectrum of granularity from activating single notes, to curating global theatrical forces within a given piece, to contextualizing the relationship of a performance to its setting.

But what constitutes "a theater of meaning" for percussionists, given that percussion music *always* involves the naturally theatrical qualities of movement on a provocative stage of instruments? And how does this kind of theatricality differ from "theater music," that distinct if somewhat dated genre in the world of contemporary music? A percussion piece is "theatrical" in my mind if it relies on a mutually informative rapport between gesture and meaning. That is to say that the actions of playing must develop within a context that lends sense to an audience's experience of the music, and that in many cases an audience's experience of the music in turn informs the player's actions. The pieces themselves may or may not include the traditionally theatrical elements of text in the manner of *Toucher* or *To the Earth*, or "staging" along the lines of Mauricio Kagel's *Dressur* or "*Schlag!*"—Roland Auzet's provocative combination of circus and percussion music based on the circus scenes of Günter Grass's revelatory *The Tin Drum*. However, the action of playing must be an intrinsic and inextricable agent of understanding. In short, a sense of theater relies on physical presence to telegraph intent and curate meaning on a variety of levels. Is a note on or off the beat? The quality of a preparatory gesture can help tell you which. (See below [p. 173] for strategies to represent unattached grace notes in *The King of Denmark*.) Are oppositional instrumental groups beginning to act in concert? Uniting them by means of an increasingly shared gestural vocabulary can sharpen a sense of transformation. (See the discussion of merging metallic and skin music in Roger Reynolds' *Watershed* in chapter 6.) How does a given audience understand a performance? The broadest reading of theater reveals that the way a piece of music looks to an audience has a lot to do with the way that audience looks at music.

Three works for solo percussion articulate the theater of percussion in relation to contextual, compositional and gestural concerns respectively: Stuart Smith's . . . *And Points North* (1988), Kenneth Gaburo's *Antiphony VIII: (Revolution)* (1984), and Vinko Globokar's *?Corporel* (1985).

Theater and the Meaning of Place

. . . And Points North (1989)

Stuart Smith

Stuart Smith wrote . . . *And Points North* for me, and I premiered it at the summer percussion course in Bydgoszcz, Poland where I taught from 1988 to 1990. I gave many subsequent performances including one at the Internationale Ferienkurse für Neue Musik in Darmstadt, Germany, and in 1990 on my last recital as a faculty member at Fresno State University. These three performances of . . . *And Points North* stick in my memory because of their real associations with the imaginary places in the piece, and because of the way they highlighted the intrinsic theatrical qualities of each concert setting.

Stuart Smith relates that when he was a child in the state of Maine, a sign near the on-ramp to the Maine Turnpike captivated him: "Maine and points north." To him "points north" meant leaving the manicured life of small-town America and moving towards distant and unexplored spaces. Likewise, the three movements of . . . *And Points North* progress along a path from an urban setting to unbounded wilderness. The first movement, scored for tuned pipes, small cymbals, wood block, and an overturned metal bucket, consists of the residue of modern America. A perfectly workable set-up could be assembled with a little imagination and a couple of hours spent in any junkyard in the country. The music is complex, featuring Stuart's rhythmic trademark of overlaid quintuple and septuple subdivisions, and relies on conventional concert rhetoric (see figure 5.4). An introductory text is flanked by a tight instrumental accompaniment. Likewise a lengthy passage of melodies played on the tuned pipes and wordless singing on the same pitches effectively restricts the percussionist to traditional roles of performance. Gesture follows suit. The playing is distributed evenly over the small set-up. That, along with the need to face the audience while singing in order to balance the voice with the music of the pipes, means that the percussionist is effectively motionless: action is limited to the small motions of striking. My preference is to sit with the instruments arranged neatly on a table in order to minimize my physical presence and thereby strike the pose of a "classical musician."

The second movement leaves restrictive urban postures for more loosely constructed passages of text and music and an instrumentation that is much less binding (see figure 5.5). The sounding objects are in most cases not even instrumental: the second movement is scored for two trees that are shaken and struck

Figure 5.4. Stuart Saunders Smith, . . . *And Points North*, from second page of first movement. Copyright © 1992 by Sonic Arts Editions. Used by permission of Smith Publications, 2617 Gwynndale Ave., Baltimore, MD 21207, USA.

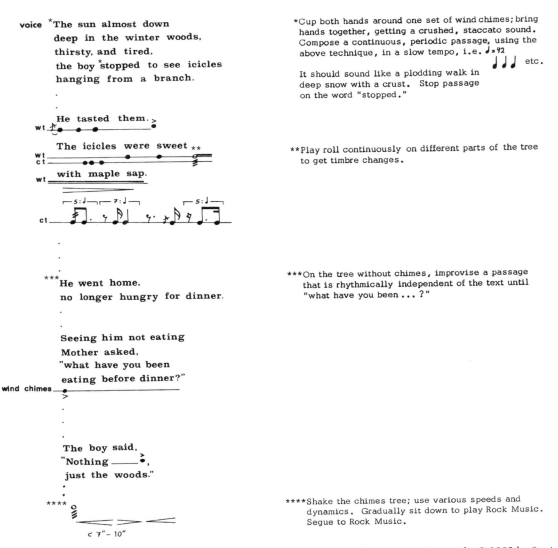

voice *The sun almost down
deep in the winter woods,
thirsty, and tired,
the boy *stopped to see icicles
hanging from a branch.

He tasted them.
wt

The icicles were sweet **
wt
ct

with maple sap.
wt

ct

He went home,
no longer hungry for dinner.

Seeing him not eating
Mother asked,
"what have you been
eating before dinner?"
wind chimes

The boy said,
"Nothing ____ ,
just the woods."

****

*Cup both hands around one set of wind chimes; bring hands together, getting a crushed, staccato sound. Compose a continuous, periodic passage, using the above technique, in a slow tempo, i.e. ♩=72

It should sound like a plodding walk in deep snow with a crust. Stop passage on the word "stopped."

**Play roll continuously on different parts of the tree to get timbre changes.

***On the tree without chimes, improvise a passage that is rhythmically independent of the text until "what have you been ... ?"

****Shake the chimes tree; use various speeds and dynamics. Gradually sit down to play Rock Music. Segue to Rock Music.

Figure 5.5. Stuart Saunders Smith, . . . *And Points North*, text from second movement. Copyright © 1992 by Sonic Arts Editions. Used by permission of Smith Publications, 2617 Gwynndale Ave., Baltimore, MD 21207, USA.

(one of the trees is strung with a dozen sets of glass wind chimes) plus a set of resonant rocks and logs. The sounds enjoin the everyday actions of standing, walking, shaking, stooping, and kneeling. These vivid motions are played against, and sometimes disappear behind the trees. The actions here are large and significant—readable as musical expression in other words—but in the context of trees and rocks, the percussionist appears to be less a musician and more an average person in the forest.

By the third movement, the "percussionist as musician" has completely disappeared along with the last vestiges of conventional musical constructions. This time the text is in Passomoquady, a Native American language still spoken by a very small group of people in Maine. The music moves fluidly between the sounds of the voice and the "instrumental" sounds of birdcalls and footfalls along a twenty-foot-long path of dried leaves. In the final moments of the piece the percussionist follows the path of leaves upstage into darkness and disappears into the far reaches of "points north" (see figure 5.6).

I like . . . And Points North, partly because Stuart wrote it for me as a gesture of friendship, and to a very large extent because I admire the courage of its aesthetic. It has never been easy for a composer of "serious music" to address simple issues like the uneasy relationship between humankind and nature. In the late 1980s, even a harmless flirtation with New Age ideals such as these was a provocation. (Rzewski dodges this bullet in his environmentally minded To the Earth by grounding it in the unassailable virtues of a Homeric hymn.) If eyebrows were sometimes raised by Stuart Smith's plainly idealistic reading of humans in nature, they were arched to gothic proportions by my performance of . . . And Points North in the insular, modernist world of the Darmstadt Summer Course.

Darmstadt was and continues to be a lively outpost for young composers and performers. However, in the 1980s and early 1990s at least, any acknowledgement of life outside the mind was immediately suspicious. The watchwords were thinking, music, and thinking about music. As one small but important example, there was always a lot of griping in Darmstadt about the plain and horrible food in the cantina at the Georg-Büchner Schule where the courses were held. (I still feel that only malnutrition could account for some of the concerts I heard in those days.) But complaints were always dismissed with a supercilious air: certainly we were interested in more important things than what we ate. But if eating well was frivolous, then . . . And Points North and its evocation of the mysticism of nature was incomprehensible. (This reaction was all the more surprising to me since Darmstadt is within shouting distance of the home of Goethe and the pantheistic reverence that nineteenth-century Germany had for nature in its many forms. But then again the Darmstadt course, for all of its provocative music-making and the lifelong friendships I made there, was always somewhat of an opaque experience.)

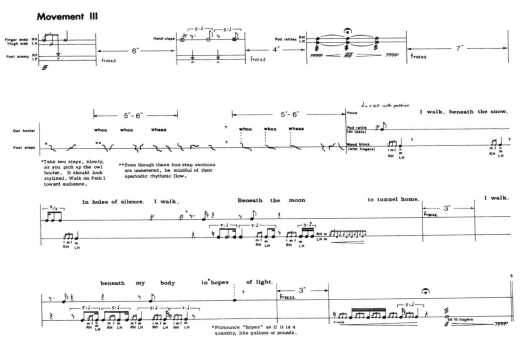

Figure 5.6. Stuart Saunders Smith, . . . *And Points North*, page 1 of third movement. Copyright © 1992 by Sonic Arts Editions. Used by permission of Smith Publications, 2617 Gwynndale Ave., Baltimore, MD 21207, USA.

The response to my Darmstadt performance of . . . *And Points North* was unfailingly polite. There were a lot of insightful comments about the first movement and its integration of text and singing with the pitch and noise vocabulary of the instruments. Many people also responded positively to the overt virtuosity of the movement, cued to no small extent by its intensely focused physical language. And they took Stuart seriously, because he is after all a gifted composer. There was no real criticism of the second and third movements, because for many listeners they simply did not qualify as music. The audience in Darmstadt regarded all of the tree shaking and leaf walking the way a cat watches television—they looked directly at it but didn't actually see anything. All of this reveals the obvious: that the sonic and gestural attributes of a piece of music are made meaningful in large part through and within specific performance contexts. As further evidence of the substantial contextualizing forces exerted by *place* on musical communication, at the time of this writing I am in Geneva where I recently conducted a performance of *Ballet Mécanique* in the context of a world-music percussion festival. That performance produced a similar kind of bewilderment in the audience. It was the right piece but the wrong party.

In contrast to Darmstadt, I don't think I have ever felt more comfortable in a place than when I lived in Fresno, California, and taught at Fresno State University from 1983 to 1990. Its agricultural setting eased my homesickness for Iowa, but Fresno, with its small group of interesting artists, was more than just a country town. The poetry scene especially, with writers of national reputation like Philip Levine and Peter Everwine, was vital and deeply rooted in Fresno's multiethnic, working-class values. Whereas Darmstadt was full to the brim with concerts and seminars, Fresno's great advantage lay in precisely the opposite: not much was going on. That meant that when something did happen, it was automatically an event with profile. The notion that readability is action noticeable against its background clearly extends to concert programming and even to the concerts themselves.

Fresno always treated me well, and my final concerts there—a series of three recitals—were crowded and friendly affairs. People came with the desire to like what they heard, and they responded favorably to . . . *And Points North*. But it was clear that the second movement spoke to them most persuasively. In this music there is a small amount of remarkable action against a relatively stable background—not unlike the arts scene in Fresno itself—and it steered a middle course between the confusing complexity of the first movement and the more free-form sonic environment of the third movement. I have lived most of my life in small towns. Even San Diego, where I live currently, with easily over a million inhabitants, is not really very urban; it's more like a little midwestern city with really bad traffic. These places have always seemed to define themselves as what they want to avoid: they are caught between the fear of urban chaos and discomfort with the wide-open spaces of the country. I don't think I ever understood Fresno better than when I saw the ease with which Fresnans greeted the controlled action and stable frame of the second movement of . . . *And Points North*.

The Polish students at the Bydgoszcz summer percussion institute responded very well, as you might have guessed by now, to the third movement of . . . *And Points North* when I premiered it there in June of 1990. I suppose that is predictable given that Bydgoszcz is situated in the very middle of a northern forest. But the reaction was a lot more personal than that. In 1990 the political situation in Poland was in maximum flux. The labor union Solidarity was on the verge of gaining real power, and everywhere in Eastern Europe that summer there was the feeling that big changes were on the way, and soon. One day towards the middle of the course someone drove up from Warsaw with a load of "Solidarnösz" visors, and the teenage drummers in the course used the occasion to stage an impromptu parade through the streets of the city. They would have been rousted by the police the year before (the following year they would have been part of mainstream politics), but in 1990 they marched with a mixture of swagger and risk. Even the language seemed to be changing. The Polish word "dobrze" (for "fine" or "good") had always carried with it an air of resignation, implying that things were far from fine or good. But in 1990, "dobrze" meant just that. You need a four-channel playback system, or timpani have to be carried up three flights of stairs for a rehearsal? *Dobrze.* It was in this environment of reconsideration and fearlessness that . . . *And Points North* was first heard. The end of the piece simply mesmerized the Polish students. The idea of walking out forever into unbounded space carried with it such extreme poetic and practical implications that I realized that they were seeing things in the music that I would never really understand. The fact that the Passamaquoddy text was unintelligible to them only added to their appreciation: it was clear to them that a New World requires a new language.

Political Movement

Antiphony VIII: (Revolution) (1984)

Kenneth Gaburo

Kenneth Gaburo's *Antiphony VIII: (Revolution)* also relies to a great extent on the contextualizing forces of the performance setting and, given its politically charged agenda, it relies on the pressures of its historical and political backdrop as well. For two years, in 1983 and 1984, at the height of the American buildup of midrange nuclear weapons in Europe, Kenneth Gaburo traveled across the United States speaking, protesting, and collecting what he called "testimony." He would arrive in a town and invite people to testify on video about "what it felt like to be expendable," again in his words. The raw video material is an amazing collection of frank and moving responses. He excerpted some of these responses and knitted them together as the basis for a four-channel tape that also included the sounds of a camera shutter (a snapshot to announce the testimony), clangs, moans, and other noises. The solo percussionist performs on a very large set-up, and over the course of the piece moves through several psychological states from indifference through distraction, bombardment, confrontation, and, finally, exhaustion and change. The piece is classic Gaburo: political, provocative, at times a little sloppy, and ultimately very moving. But what fascinates me about *Antiphony VIII: (Revolution)* is not the application of theater to a specific (and necessarily short-lived) political milieu, but to the way theatrical energy in the piece supports more durable issues of internal compositional coherence.

Kenneth, realizing perhaps that Ronald Reagan would not be President forever, did not ask the question, "What do you think of the current administration's reckless disregard for the future of the planet as it prepares to annihilate the population of the earth hundreds of times over?" Popular musicians addressed the situation in just this specific way. Sting's "The Russians Love Their Children Too" comes to mind—a fine song, but would the average teenage consumer of pop music today even know what the song was about? By posing a much more general question about human expendability, Gaburo extended the life of his piece by years. Importantly in the context of this discussion, he was also able to route his considerable energy internally, towards the workings of musical composition, rather than externally through the rapidly changing and uncertain discourse of politics and protest.

The theater of *Antiphony VIII: (Revolution)* proceeds along a path of expanding sonic materials as the performer gradually explores the large number of instruments, and is related by gesture to the growing potency of the material on the tape. The piece opens as the percussionist walks on stage clicking his or her mallets and casually "discovers" a very large percussion set-up. The pointed testimony on the tape is sparse enough to be ignored. ("What does it feel like to be expendable?" "I think maybe the question is so absurd that I don't have an answer for it.") Accordingly the percussionist responds with indifference to the tape, and slowly explores the set-up as a musician might do in the early stages of learning a piece. The score is not metered, but rhythmic relationships and phrase trajectories are carefully indicated by small and large accents.

As the tape material becomes more emotionally provocative, the sonic exploration also grows in intensity. ("How does it feel to be expendable?" "I feel helpless. I feel empty. My life may be too small. Insignificant.") In the next section the percussionist begins to join phrases from instruments on opposite sides of a kidney-shaped arrangement. Under growing distractions from the tape, the player is suddenly indecisive and can't quite choose which side of the set of instruments to perform on. The noticeable increase of gestural torque involving large and rapid side-to-side movements makes the percussionist suddenly appear much larger against the set-up. The next passage (section C in the score), "bombardment," involves the length of the set-up as well as its breadth. Here the tape can no longer be ignored. ("It's scary and if I think about it, I get outraged.") The percussionist races from one end of the set-up to the other: the large number of instruments, which had once signified opportunity, now seems more like a trap. Gestural and sonic vigor grows in response to the provocations in the text throughout the sections that are marked "fire with fire" and "revolution/transition." The voices on the tape have the player's full attention by now. ("If we all blow ourselves up, I guess there's nothing lost.") The fight is on; the noises of the percussionist rise in confrontation.

Finally the percussionist is convinced that a course of action that seeks to meet force with force is fundamentally unwise. "Change," the final section of *Antiphony VIII: (Revolution)* means calm and not acquiescence. ("I hope that it never happens, because I like looking towards the future, making plans.") The player runs out of combative energy, first dropping one stick and then the other out of exhaustion, and

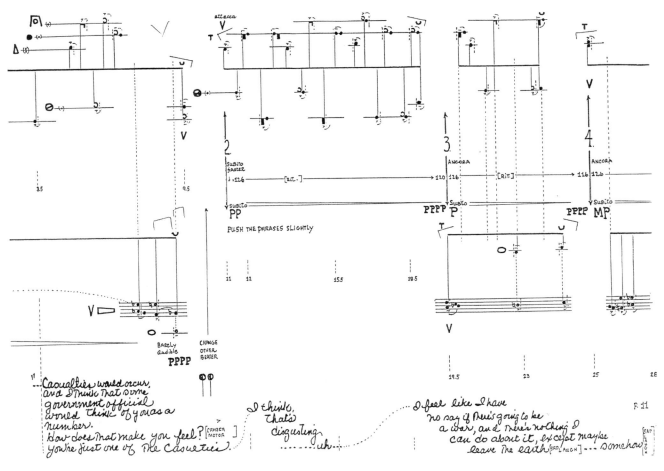

Figure 5.7. Kenneth Gaburo, *Antiphony VIII: (Revolution)*, opening of page 11. Used by permission.

finally finishes peacefully with a new sense of resolve. The final phrases of *Antiphony VIII: (Revolution)* are played on a hand drum stationed far outside the constricting circle of instruments—the percussionist finally escaping all of those drums and cymbals with their traditions in military history. The piece ends simply with skin on skin. Kenneth never ran short of metaphors.

The strength of *Antiphony VIII: (Revolution)* lies in the connections between its gestural world and the changing psychological state of the performer. This is especially convincing in the early moments of discovery of the instruments and in the performer's dawning awareness of the tape material. My interpretive weaknesses, from my initial rehearsals with Kenneth to the work's CalArts Festival premiere in 1984, and up to my last performance of it just months before Kenneth died in 1993, were theatrical. I had difficulty controlling the intensity of the frenetic moments of confrontation and ultimately the phase of exhaustion that leads to dropping the sticks. "Drop them by accident, as though you can't hold on to them any longer," Kenneth told me repeatedly. But I have always been a very bad actor. To me the theater of percussion always meant that actions were related to sounds: I just could not feign exhaustion since, well, I wasn't exhausted, and there wasn't anything in the music to cause it. I ran into David Harrington at the hotel on the morning of the premiere—the Kronos Quartet had played at CalArts the night before—and he asked me what I was doing on the festival. I responded, "mostly learning to drop my sticks." I don't know if I ever really got the exhaustion part right, but Kenneth never gave up. He asked me to move the instruments farther and farther apart so that the piece would be more tiring to play. Just before a 1986 performance in Melbourne he asked me to play without my glasses: that would make it more fatiguing, right? Once I caught him on stage just before a concert moving the instruments around to make reaches more awkward. Kenneth was the genuine article, an honest-to-God true believer. Ask him a simple question about a choice of sticks and then brace yourself for half an hour on the stick as relic of the military history of percussion, on the stick as emblem of encroaching capitalism, on the stick as gun, on the stick as phallus. I miss him a lot even if he could drive you crazy sometimes. The piece functions as a slightly stuttering poem that can surprise you at almost any turn with flashes of pure brilliance.

A Map of the Body

?Corporel (1985)

Vinko Globokar

While the overtly political agenda of *Antiphony VIII: (Revolution)* meant that it was essentially an individual's view of a communal concerns, the very personal nature of Vinko Globokar's *?Corporel* makes that piece a community's view of the individual. In particular *?Corporel* is a look at the body, at the seminude body of a performer on stage, and, in the best performances, of that image reflected as imagined corporeal awareness onto the bodies of the listeners. With the body as its point of departure *?Corporel* is both a piece of music in a very conventional sense and philosophical provocateur of substantial power.

The body as a theme in percussion music did not start with *?Corporel*. In many ways percussion music has always been about the body. We see the relationship between percussion and the body in the traditional association between percussion and dance that can be found in almost every culture. We see the body in the historical roots of European percussion as an instrument of war, that is to say as a tool of physical force rather than of the intellect. The tenacious view of the percussionist as inherently corporeal rather than intellectual comes to us from Dionysus via Descartes: to many people we continue to represent the forces of brutishness and energy, of the palpable, visceral, and erotic rather than the refined and rational. (Much of the early enthusiasm for Edgard Varèse's *Ionisation* was the misguided assessment that it was the first truly intelligent piece of percussion music. The brain had ousted the body, or so some people thought, and percussion music had thereby finally satisfied a necessary prerequisite for entry into the pantheon of high art.) We can see the ongoing role of the body through the intense physicality of contemporary virtuosity and through the persistent maleness of our art. Even as women comprise an ever-larger percentage of percussionists, for many people it continues to be the body of a man that comes to mind with the word drummer.

The intertwining paths of historical and cultural development that inform a view of percussion as an art of the body lead to the same paradoxical place. Our bodies are at the same time universalizing—we all have one and we all need one—and they are distinguishing—no two bodies are alike. Bodies are the source of vitality and identity, but they are equally the source of neurosis and fragility. It is upon this murkiness that *?Corporel* seeks to shed a little light. In point of fact though, *?Corporel* begins in the dark. The lights come up on a shirtless percussionist seated cross-legged on stage. The opening sounds are exploratory and halting: hands cover the eyes and begin slowly to grope the face; movement is accompanied by the sounds of breathing and vocal sound effects. The score tells you what to do but necessarily what sound should be produced. Ultimately, the sounds in *?Corporel* are unpredictable since everybody and every body is different.

Since the body of the performer is also the instrument in *?Corporel*, the piece functions on an onto-logical level like no other. The performer both generates and receives the actions of playing—every stroke is both an act of interpretation and very often a source of pain. (How might a player interpret Xenakis, one is tempted to ask, if every note were felt as intensely as it was played?) And since the player is also the only

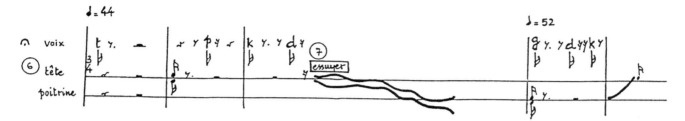

Figure 5.8. Vinko Globokar, *?Corporel*, opening of page 2. Copyright © 1989 by Henry Litolff's Verlag, Frankfurt. All rights reserved. Used by permission.

instrument, that means that there are no other instruments to hide behind. The performer may be shirtless on stage, but he or she is naked in much more profound ways.

The nakedness of *?Corporel* disenables a lot of habitualized concert behavior. The instrument as an external object is simply not there: there is nothing to adjust, tune, or muffle between entrances. There are no pages to turn or sticks to change. There is nothing to express distance between the player and the instrument—no moments where you play a note and then stand back to admire it as it resonates. There is no moment of appraisal at the end of the piece where the sound decays and the performers remain. In short the comforting barrier of instruments is gone. I began to learn *?Corporel* with the fear that the limited sounds of body percussion would be insufficient to support an entire piece; I finished by realizing that without the demarcation and limitation of instruments, the piece was problematized by offering too many, rather than too few possibilities.

One way to find a handhold in *?Corporel* is to approach its theatrical moments like music and its musical moments like theater. A performer might easily fall into the trap of thinking that, since *?Corporel* is "theater music," theatrical elements must be foregrounded at all times. However, cross-wiring the theatrical to the musical in a mutually reinforcing combination prevents a monodimensional reading of the piece as pure genre. (In the same vein, the French director François Truffaut once claimed that one secret to Alfred Hitchcock's success was that he filmed his love scenes like murder scenes and his murder scenes like love scenes.)

?Corporel opens with a series of fragments that present "theater" and "music" as oppositional orientations. Theater is represented by moments whose meaning is transmitted primarily through the agency of gesture rather than sound. Theatrical moments are organized on a timeline where one centimeter equals a

second. They consist largely of everyday motions with strong extramusical associations: groping, wiping, caressing, and clapping among others. Vocal elements are effects based on the sounds of breathing (various degrees of resistance to the breath are caused by the increasingly constricted sounds of "h," "s," and "f" and produce varying degrees of noisiness). Finding theater in *?Corporel* is straightforward, after all there you are half-naked on stage caressing, rubbing, and hissing. Coaxing music takes a bit more effort. Musical passages in *?Corporel* are notated in conventional ways as rhythms in tempi. Body sounds consist of the conventional percussion techniques of striking and slapping—filled note heads indicate striking on bony surfaces and unfilled ones on the soft surfaces of the body. Musical passages feature syllables, voiced on inhalations, rather than sound effects.

Globokar seems to be presenting us with an equation: since neither the musical nor the theatrical material seems complete by itself, a strategy of reapprochement between the two might lead to some kind of organicity. Language, for example, might result if the short inhaled syllables of the musical passages could be combined with the connective material of the breath taken from the theatrical material. A real musician might appear if the totemic rhythms of the notated music could import expressive sense from the emotionally charged gestures of the theatrical passages. If we could find a way of adding the two sides together we might find a complete person. Globokar's first strategy for unification seeks to bridge the musical/theatrical gap by osmosis, that is to say, by quick alternations between musical and theatrical moments which, by their proximity, encourage the development of shared behavior. A defining section of the piece, seen in figure 5.9, presents a series of episodes that cut between the musical and theatrical material. The passage starts with a long musical section, here face-slapping in precise rhythms and vocal trilling sounds. A short theatrical moment of hair rubbing and a kissing sound follows. In successive phrases, the musical passages get shorter and the theatrical ones become longer as the performer toggles between the two states.

When osmosis by proximity proves to be insufficiently catalytic, Globokar ups the ante and combines theatrical and musical elements within the same passage. The performer gradually reclines from a seated to a prone position, while the accompanying material consists of syllables *and* sound effects, striking *and* rubbing. This synthesis precedes three critical moments of theatrical and musical unity where the percussionist emerges as a complete entity. In the first of these, a moment of repose is marked by a fermata—a purely musical notation. But the silence is soon interrupted by snoring, the most overtly theatrical gesture that Globokar has required to this point in the piece. Synthesis can also be found in the frenetic fight scene that concludes *?Corporel*. The self-inflicted violence might mean that the partnership of musical and theatrical considerations is perhaps not an easy one. However, the most telling moment of organicity comes in the

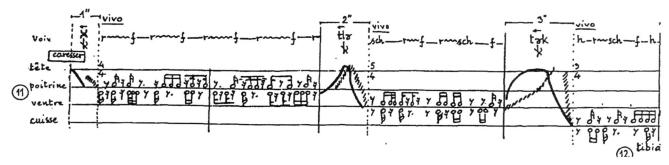

Figure 5.9. Vinko Globokar, *?Corporel*, alternating episodes of musical and theatrical material on page 2. Copyright © 1989 by Henry Litolff's Verlag, Frankfurt. All rights reserved. Used by permission.

only real language in the piece. For an instant the player is still, freed finally from the tasks of music and the tics of theater, faces the audience and says: *"J'ai lu récemment cette phrase. L'histoire des hommes est la longue succession des synonymes pour le même vocable. Y contredire est un devoir."* (I recently read the following remark. The history of humankind is the long succession of synonyms for the same word. It is our duty to disprove this.)

This moment is so stunning, seemingly so full of "meaning" that important questions inevitably occur. What precisely is our *duty* in *?Corporel*? Are we presenting a fable with its concomitant need for explicitness and resolution, or is the piece something much more general and evocative? And, why, as long as we're at it, is there a question mark in the title?

Globokar, both as a person and as a composer, resists any attempt to generalize his music, to package it in a *prêt-à-porter*, conveniently ready-to-wear pattern. Globokar's music is always intensely personal, and accordingly, to whatever extent I have developed a philosophical point of departure for the piece, it is also a personal one. I cannot recommend a concept for the piece to anyone else, but I can recommend that every performer find one. A percussionist who seeks to learn *?Corporel* as a series of unrelated takes will fail to embrace the rich world of contradictions that drive the events of the piece, their sequence, and ultimately their consequence. A performance of *?Corporel* reveals a recursive set of paradoxes. It reveals the body as a principal source of continuity and connection. (However different our thoughts or beliefs might be, we use our bodies in remarkably similar ways: we all eat, we walk, we touch, we hold.) Likewise the body is revealed as the force of uniqueness. (No matter how closely we might be linked by a shared physiology, each of us irreproducible and singular.) In *?Corporel* the forces of theater with their roots in quotidian gestures are universalizing. (We can all recognize ourselves in the everyday gestures of snapping, rubbing, and scratching.) However, music as the refinement of abstraction and reflection is individualizing. ("Humankind is the long succession of synonyms for the same word. It is our duty to disprove this.") With one foot on either side of the Cartesian mind/body divide, *?Corporel* demonstrates that bodily expression is inherent and constructed, natural and divined. But as it pulls us apart, almost literally limb from limb, *?Corporel* also points us towards organicity. Through fleeting moments of theatrical and musical synergy, Globokar shows us that percussion music at least, as the concrete substance of the body translated momentarily into the ineffability of sound, is simultaneously musical and theatrical. As a synergy of actions and sounds, the physical and the musical, *?Corporel* reminds us that the word *melos*, Greek for arm or limb, also gives us our word melody.

?Corporel also outlines the risks and uncertainties of performance. It is admittedly a risky proposition for many musicians to perform shirtless. For women these issues are compounded. Whether or not a female percussionist chooses to play the piece shirtless—I have witnessed riveting performances both ways—our willingness as a culture to objectify the female body invariably threatens to rob female physicality of its complex connection to the spirit. (What is the corollary of disembody . . . dis-emsoul?) But for all percussionists the risks and contradictions implied by *?Corporel* are real. For many percussionists, percussion music is about finding just the right instrument and curating just the right sound, but *?Corporel* is a percussion piece without instruments and instrumental sounds. For many percussionists, percussion is about mastering technique, but *?Corporel* is almost entirely devoid of percussion techniques. Where does that leave us? *?Corporel* may have given us a map of the percussionist's body, but the question mark shows us that, in fact, we still do not know exactly where we are.

Organicity

The King of Denmark (1964)

Morton Feldman

In many ways Morton Feldman's *The King of Denmark* is an antipercussion piece. Where much percussion music is loud and noisy, *The King of Denmark* is to be played as softly as possible using only the fingers and hands. Where much percussion music privileges rhythm, sometimes even in its most basic guise as pulse,

The King of Denmark seems to float along in timeless ether. In fact *The King of Denmark* was born as an antipiece—as a rebuttal to Karlheinz Stockhausen's *Zyklus* composed five years earlier. Both works involve large set-ups, a novel notational scheme, and a score that gives the performer great interpretative latitude. But Stockhausen's piece is loud, rhythmic, and formally forceful. *Zyklus* leads the performer along a path of decision making where one choice informs and leads to the next until, even in sections where the performer has considerable freedom, a sense of carefully scripted forward momentum and inevitability results. *The King of Denmark*, on the other hand, often sounds as if it's going nowhere. Sounds simply drift. According to Feldman's indications the sounds should not only be as soft as possible, they should be equal. Equal in volume? Equal in importance? If all sounds are equal and no one sound is more important than any other is, there can be no forward momentum sweeping towards the next important event. Since "a goal" is a locally privileged event, the absence of greater importance for one point over another means that there can be no large-scale direction. It's beautiful idea, but many performers find that decision making in *The King of Denmark* is difficult for just this reason. If you don't know where you are going, how do you know what to do next? Indeed, one of the biggest pitfalls for a performer of *The King of Denmark* is a version of the piece that might be called aimless exploration. (First I'll do this, then maybe I'll see what this sounds like, then I'll do this again, then how about . . . no, wait.) In the absence of structural propulsion, I was determined to construct an interpretation of the piece which, while embracing Feldman's temporal aesthetic, still sounded deliberate. It was not an easy task, but fortunately the score is clear and helpful.

The score itself is a graph (see figure 5.10), divided on the horizontal axis into units of time at M.M. 66–92 and on the vertical axis into three rows of high, medium and low sounds. Numerals represent the number of sounds to be played in each unit of time. Thick vertical lines denote clusters consisting of different instruments if possible (the score says thick horizontal lines, but this is a mistake). Roman numerals represent simultaneous sounds. Large numbers encompassing high, middle, and low registers indicate single sounds to be played in any register. Broken horizontal lines indicate sustained sounds. The vibraphone is to be played without motor. Additionally Feldman calls for some specific instruments and techniques: bell and skin sounds, cymbal, gong(s), timpani, vibraphone, a G-sharp crotale, gong, and timpani rolls. A frequent point of confusion is the propriety of hand-struck instruments like tambourine and wind chimes. A purist's view—strangely I find myself on this side of the argument—is that, while these instruments are played by hand, the actual sounds result from objects striking one another. I feel that tambourine jingles or wind chime tubes effectively constitute surrogate mallets and should not be used in the piece. I have heard many versions of *The King of Denmark* with these sounds but never where they did not sound obviously out of place—

louder, more percussive, and as a result, more important. These instruments may technically fulfill the requirement of hand percussion, but they certainly break the rule requiring equality of sounds.

In any piece that incorporates a large degree of freedom—*The King of Denmark* is clearly no exception—a performer might start by detailing those elements that are controlled by the score and those that are left to the performer. Since Feldman dictates the number of notes per unit of time and indicates whether these notes are to be played on high, medium, or low instruments, *The King of Denmark* effectively controls density and register. Density, or literally the number of things happening at any given moment, carries with it implications of verticality and ultimately harmony; register controls the sense of the horizontal, of linearity with implications of melody. On the other hand, color in its various manifestations—from the choice

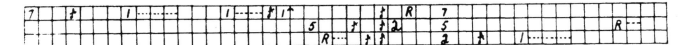

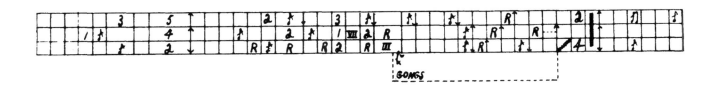

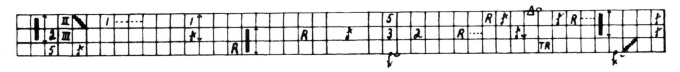

Figure 5.10. Morton Feldman, *The King of Denmark*, page 1, showing graph. Copyright © 1965 by C. F. Peters, New York. All rights reserved. Used by permission.

of instruments, to the way they are arranged, to the performance gestures required to play them—is largely the province of the performer.

The first challenge in any interpretation of *The King of Denmark* is to develop a workable set-up. My set-up began as an experiment: I wished to develop a correlation, on the finest level of detail possible, between the structure of the piece, particularly the critical issues of density and register, and performance gesture. Part of the reason for this choice was musical. A few years earlier I had discovered the sensual pleasure of gesture in William Hibbard's *Parsons' Piece*. Choreography clearly operated as an expressive and supple element in the work, but it seemed secondary to the actual composition of the piece. I wondered if gesture could be relocated and attached to the deep structures of music. On a personal level, by the mid-1980s, when I first learned *The King of Denmark*, I had begun practicing T'ai Chi in earnest, attracted at first by its fluid curving movements and its superficial similarity to the movements of dance and percussion performance. In fact a large part of the way I understand movement in multiple percussion—the engagement of deep rotating motions and control over the shifting of weight—came from my early study of T'ai Chi. An important lesson of T'ai Chi, however, was that coherent movement develops power only if it is anchored to the deep energetic structures within the body. In T'ai Chi the surface is beautiful only if it is tied to what lies beneath.

I began my experiments in performance choreography by linking the personally expressive medium of gesture to the two elements directly controlled by the score, register and density. First I constructed a set-up by arranging a large number of instruments into two concentric circles. The inner circle consists of dry sounds and the outer circle of resonant sounds. At the zero-degree and 180-degree points on the circle (zero degrees is the point closest to the audience; 180 degrees the farthest) I place the highest, therefore the smallest, instruments. (Note: I do not consider the vibraphone to be a large instrument, but rather each of the thirty-seven bars to be a single small instrument. Accordingly the vibraphone is placed at 180 degrees.) At the 90-degree and 270-degree points on the circle I place the lowest, therefore the largest, instruments. Therefore when I play the high instruments I am facing either directly toward or directly away from the audience. In either event the combination of small movements used to play the small instruments and my orientation relative to the audience minimizes the size of the performance gestures. To play the large instruments on the sides of the set-up I am forced to reach out, and by expanding my lateral visibility to the audience, I create large and readable gestures. As a result, gesture relates to register in a very simple and direct way: the lower the sound the larger the movement, and vice versa.

The representation of musical density via gesture creates thornier problems. For starters, Feldman engages three quite different strategies for engineering density in *The King of Denmark*. For most of the piece Feldman treats density as a *linear* phenomenon: a succession of individual events or small clusters that accrete to form clumps of dense material or thin out to create single lines. (See again the first line of the piece in figure 5.10.) In a second type of construction, four occasions—three "big 5" gestures and one big gesture of seven notes—contain events in any register are to be placed freely over the course of three to nine units of time. In these structures Feldman releases his otherwise firm control over density. The performer may group the notes together to create a sudden surge of activity surrounded by silence, or he or she may spread the notes out over the entire available time to produce expansive linear moments. In either event these passages have a *peripheral* function; they alter the psychology of the piece by resetting the performer's inner clock to much slower increments of tempo. A final passage that calls for "as many sounds as possible" to be played within five units of time fills the musical space to *saturation*.

Each density type—linear, peripheral, and saturation—requires in turn an individualized approach to performance gesture. In an example of linear gesture, note how the passage in figure 5.10 forms a wedge of register, starting with high notes, expanding to fill all registers, and then contracting again towards the middle. I realize this passage by playing the opening seven notes on small instruments near the zero degree point in the circle. Instruments in this part of the set-up are not only small; they are also on the far upstage side of the set-up. I play them with my back to the audience, effectively shielding the small movements from view. As the material increases in density and register by including lower instruments, performance gesture becomes more complex. Lateral expansion to play low instruments must be balanced by quick retreats to the centerline of the set-up to address the high instruments. The representation of density by means of choreographic gesture can then be read as gestural simplicity in sparse monoregistral passages and greater complexity in response to greater density across multiple registers. Physical movement also serves to indicate the relative coherence of a phrase. Uninterrupted motions outline the first real phrase of the piece linking the second sustained high note (on the fifteenth beat of the piece) to the single grace note on a low instrument near the end of the line. On the contrary, the opening three events—the seven-note gesture, the isolated grace note, and the first high sustained sound—are treated separately. To separate these events as music, I separate them in space via gesture by returning to a neutral position after each event. (For me this is a posture of minimal readability: weight on both legs, facing away from the audience, hands in front of my body and shielded from view.)

This kind of gestural cueing provides a workable solution for interpreting the many detached grace notes in the piece. We normally think of a grace note as being secondary or ornamental to some other, primary note. But Feldman often strands grace notes without an obvious point of reference. I perform the freestanding grace notes by stopping in a neutral posture before going ahead to the next event; grace notes that are clearly linked to primary events are connected to those events by uninterrupted motions.

The four peripheral events seen in figure 5.11, three "big 5" and the single "big 7" passages, stand outside the normal flow of time and serve as pivotal junctures in the piece. These are not really phrases, but points in space that suddenly illuminate the "frame" of the piece. Almost every other passage isolates a portion of the circular set-up; here we see the outline of its farthest reaches. The peripheral music is peculiar, a constellation of events unified by the breadth of its compass and atomized by the pointillism of its geometry. In order to translate this quality into gesture, I choose instruments spaced at equidistant intervals around the circumference of the set-up. In these moments gesture is expanded to its maximum range by the need to reach, but by choosing instruments that are spread evenly around the circle, the body is forced to pass through the neutral center of the set-up between each attack. The result is at once expansive and directionless, encompassing and disconnected.

The moment of saturation at the end of the piece is marked "as many different sounds as possible." The phrase "as . . . as possible" is a consistently problematic direction whether the indication is "as fast as possible," "as many as possible," or in *Toucher* even "as slow as possible." As always this phrase poses the question: What is *possible*? Generally I convert the phrase "as possible" to "as necessary"; at the end of *The King of Denmark* I play "as many sounds as necessary" to create a moment of noticeably greater density. Since I want this phrase to be both musically dense and gesturally differentiated, I make a single rotation within the circle of instruments at a rate calculated to produce one revolution within the five time units allotted in the score. For the first and only time in the piece the hands move at a constant speed, a kind of fast typing motion, while the rest of the body steps slowly around the circle. This phrase is an improvised tour of the set-up—I do not calculate which instruments I will play. This moment is naive and exploratory,

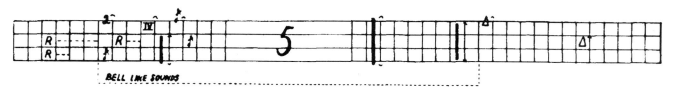

Figure 5.11. Morton Feldman, *The King of Denmark*, peripheral event, page 3, line 1. Copyright © 1965 by C. F. Peters, New York. All rights reserved. Used by permission.

a strange twist coming at the end of an interpretation marked by careful cultivation of sonority and, commensurately, a strongly deliberate choreographic sense.

In order to link gesture more closely to sound, each of these movement strategies, linear, peripheral, and saturation, is further associated with a particular harmonic orientation. Dealing with harmony in *The King of Denmark* is tricky since harmony automatically evokes notions of hierarchy. But clearly if each note is to be equal, no note can be more important than any other note is. Therefore the presence of a "tonic" function is antithetical to Feldman's aesthetic in *The King of Denmark*. On the other hand, Feldman clearly has deep roots in German romanticism, and furthermore his late pieces—arguably his own realizations of what might have continued to be graph pieces—are deeply conscious of harmonic structure. My solution was to avoid explicit tonality—this would have been too strong in the context of a piece of only six minutes in length—but to cultivate evocative harmonic fields by foregrounding pitch, even among "non-pitched" instruments like temple blocks, flowerpots, and even cymbals.

The root of harmonic sense and likewise the source of musical line, in my interpretation of *The King of Denmark*, can be found in an extended mode that rings the circumference of the circular set-up. The complete source mode consists of:

Low F (vibraphone),
G quarter-tone flat, E quarter-tone sharp, and B quarter-tone sharp (resonant aluminum tubing),
A major triad (four temple bowls),
D natural (fire alarm bell),
A flat, C, and D (flowerpots),
E flat (Thai gong),
A quarter-tone flat (temple block),
A quarter-tone sharp (small cowbell),
G-sharp octaves (*almglocken* and crotale),
B quarter-tone flat (dowel rod),
B natural (mixing bowl)

Any sense of line in a musical interpretation curates similarity and coherence among points on that line. In a multitimbral instrumental construction like the set-up of *The King of Denmark*, cultivating linearity is a challenge since changes of instrumental color often tend to disrupt the sense of connection and forward momentum along the horizontal path. Consistent use of the source mode described above creates harmonic continuity—a useful tool to develop linear coherence in spite of coloristic interruptions that are inevitable in a large percussion set-up. To develop maximal connectivity within a line, a group of consonant tones is chosen (F, A flat, C, and E flat, for example). Lines that are fractured might use less consonant pitch arrangements. (A, A flat, E flat, G sharp, B quarter-tone flat, and B, for example.) In order to reinforce harmonic coherence through fluid movements I place consonant or triadic pitch arrangements within easy reach of each other. Fractured phrases feature both greater dissonance and employ more disjunct movements. The resulting correspondence between the quality of music and its means of expression via gesture allow an audience member to track unfolding phrases with considerable subtlety. In fact since the gestures of preparation are in many ways more visible than the movements of actual performance, a listener/viewer who uses both his or her ears and eyes will see what kind of music is coming *before* it is actually played.

Likewise, the peripheral music stands apart in harmonic as well as gestural terms. Here the sense of stasis, of stepping outside the flow of the piece, is reinforced through pitch unisons. For each of the five-note figures I use three A naturals (temple bowl, low Javanese gong, and Thai gong). A noise instrument like a cymbal or wind gong allows the tones to mix. (Memories of endless Thanksgiving casseroles where everything was held together with the ubiquitous can of mushroom soup seem strangely relevant here.) The fifth note in the series is a chime pitch other than A, which serves to announce the harmonic field that follows. Peripheral events are pivot points in the harmonic scheme. Pitch unison renders them harmonically neutral until the chime note signals a change in harmonic direction. The moment of saturation, where as many instruments as possible are played in a short time, is harmonically flat in its own way. Both pitch unison and saturation rob the harmonic field of profile, in the latter instance by suddenly cluttering the pitch field with dissonance so that no single harmonic sense gains ascendancy. This strategy recalls Schoenberg's surrogate tonicity at the end of *Erwartung*, where consonance is expressed not as a triadic marker but as the complete saturation of musical space.

My interpretation of *The King of Denmark* strives for organicity, that is to say for a maximally coherent and interpenetrated relationship among elements of gesture, color, musical line, and harmony. But the closer a performer comes to a unified vision of the piece, the more apparent are its contradictions. *The King of Denmark* is timeless, almost rhythmless, but in my view at least, a successful interpretation must be deliberate and forwardmoving. Feldman does not deal with pitch until the final two events of the work, yet in my view again, *The King of Denmark* requires an approach that foregrounds relationships of pitch and harmony. The set-up is large and varied, but the instruments are robbed of their weight and importance; a large gong and a small bell are equals. No matter how considered the interpretation, the piece pulses with illusion. Is the gong soft, or is it far away? Like the vibrating but rhythmically directionless canvases of Mark Rothko, the surface of *The King of Denmark* is a mirage: sounds appear, they float outward in no particular direction, and then they evaporate again into music. I started learning *The King of Denmark* by looking for certainty through the rapport between gesture and sound, and in the end I finished by staring directly in the face of uncertainty, contradiction, and, ultimately, poetry. This is why I cannot escape the pull of *The King of Denmark*, why I return again and again to rethink my version of it. In the end the softest piece in our repertoire produces the loudest echo. In the end the antipiece has become the touchstone. Samuel Beckett, writing in 1975, many years after the creation of *The King of Denmark* and with no particular thought towards Feldman, comes closest to the soul of the piece:

only dust and not a sound only what was it it said come and gone was that it something like that come and gone come and gone no one come and gone in no time gone in no time.[2]

2. Samuel Beckett, *That Time*, in Beckett, *Collected Shorter Plays* (New York: Grove Press, 1984), 235.

This Is Not a Drum
Manipulating the Material of Percussion Music

What does the material of contemporary percussion music consist of? More than one composer has posed this question, usually in the benign guise of inquiring what sound a certain mallet makes on a given instrument or whether crotales sound at the notated pitch. Occasionally there is the more naked demand to demonstrate the special effects of an instrument or its "extended techniques." This latter question in particular reveals the depth of a composer's difficulty with the material of percussion since it presumes the existence of a body of known and accepted sounds against which a category like special effects or extended techniques makes sense.

I have often found that conversations about percussion with composers, especially with younger composers, end with things being less rather than more clear. Of course there are many things that can be said with certainty. We percussionists can demonstrate a spectrum of sounds on various instruments. We can show how changing mallets produces variations of tone color. We can review the repertoire of performance techniques applicable to given percussion instruments. But in the end we will have demonstrated little more than a list of individual cases when what the composer really wants to learn is the *language* of percussion.

The problem is that the capacity for inflection—the systematic modification of a universally accepted basis to produce multiple variations of specific meaning—is a critical component of language. This is precisely what is difficult to find in percussion. Let's say for the purposes of discussion that there are ten thousand possible percussion sounds. Viewed as an equation, percussive material could be described as 10,000 times "n" where n equals 1. Ten thousand individual cases in other words. A composer, adopting the model of most other instruments, expects the equation to read 1 times n, where n equals 10,000. Ten thousand possible flowers related to the same set of roots, so to speak. With an instrument like the cello, for example, sonic richness comes from applying a broad range of techniques to a single complex object. With percussion, richness comes from adding more objects.

Single instruments like the cello or flute apply a unifying force and with it a musical coherence to their repertoire. The cello repertoire has a *sound* and over the several centuries of its existence has developed some rules governing its use. Composers know that there are some things that will work and others that will not. Being a well-trained composer means obeying the rules; an experimentalist will usually try to break some of them in an interesting way. In any event the rules are still there and you have to deal with them in one way or another. A composer looking for a similar set of rules for the "percussion instrument" will come away disappointed. In the end, the contemporary percussion repertoire, like the sounds themselves, is a series of special cases. Each piece has a unique instrumentation, a unique set of performance problems, and a unique musical and emotional profile as a result.

This chapter proposes to lead to an understanding of the material of percussion by examining important works from the repertoire. We must acknowledge that any conclusions based on the examination of selected pieces will necessarily be incomplete. The most we can hope for are portraits of pieces—personal ones at that since I have chosen the pieces—that present some of the many provocative ways composers have engaged the material of percussion for their purposes. We will not find a rulebook, but we can sketch a map of interesting paths.

Far from feeling discouraged by the absence of universalizing rules in percussion music, however, composers should take heart. Look to the pieces detailed below. The necessary involvement of the composer with very basic issues of sound and technique when writing for percussion etches his or her musical aesthetic and emotional choices into the fine print of the music. Percussion music at its best reveals and amplifies something fundamental about the composers and performers who engage it. Am I wrong in thinking that we see Iannis Xenakis and James Wood most clearly through their percussion music? Or that Roger Reynolds and William Hibbard achieved among their most compelling and passionate solo music in their works for percussion?

Material as Exploration

You can read in almost any music history textbook that one of the defining vectors of twentieth-century music was the "liberation of timbre." The texts further inform us that percussive timbre was liberated from its historically secondary function in support of harmony and melody and found a starring role in the noise constructions of Varèse and Cage. With so many percussion instruments to liberate, you might expect a sizable repertoire that sought simply to explore percussion sounds solely for their inherent, sensuous qualities. You would be wrong, because when you look at sound, you are inevitably looking at rhythm, texture, shape, and metaphor. Indeed one of the critical components of the definition of percussive material is that sound itself is not enough. I define the material of percussion music as sound leveraged over time. Percussion sounds can certainly be enormously appealing in and of themselves—I can be distracted for an hour or more by the amazing sound of the very low Javanese gamelan gong that sits in my studio. However, as inviting as any given percussion sound might be to the ear, in my opinion it does not become material until it is activated in the temporal domain as rhythm, texture, or shape.

Having Never Written a Note for Percussion (1971)

James Tenney

Two fascinating solo works for single percussion instruments demonstrate this keenly. James Tenney's *Having Never Written a Note for Percussion*, scored for a single solo percussion instrument and usually performed on a large tam-tam, is a single crescendo and decrescendo of about ten minutes in duration. If any piece of music were the unadulterated celebration of pure percussion sound, this would be it. Tenney's piece, however, is much less about the purity of sound than it is about rhythm, trajectory, and shape. Like other examples of Tenney's slow process-oriented music—his beautiful *Critical Band* (1988) for example—incremental change in *Having Never Written a Note for Percussion* produces a global sense of slowly unfolding structure but a local sensation of enormous and intense activity.

Imagine performing this piece as a tam-tam solo. You start with the softest possible tremolo at the center of the tam-tam. Only the lowest fundamental tones of the instrument are produced. As you slowly begin to play louder the sound level increases, brightening as more and more high harmonics are excited. At a certain point the performance space begins to reinforce pitched bands of vibrations. Louder still. Pitched humming sounds appear frequently now and seem to move around the room. You do not know which pitches will be activated or how they will move since every instrument and every performance space is different. Wave patterns alternately surge and abate as they are reinforced or canceled by the acoustical properties of the hall. You play even louder and the sound becomes noisier. The entire range of vibrations is in play now. Bands of pitch appear and disappear with great speed, beating against each other in conflicting vibrations like out-of-tune notes. Shimmering swatches of high-end noise spin upward only to dive back into the noise floor and reappear elsewhere in space as hints of pitch. Super-low combination tones percolate in the background. Near its peak volume the sound loses its particularity. The tam-tam sonority becomes molten and plasmic as individual sounds fuse into a solid undifferentiated wall of noise. At the absolute top, every bit of your energy is going into the tam-tam and it is pushing back at you just as hard. You hold this maximum for just an instant and then begin a controlled descent back through the warren of conflicting tones and noises. Ten minutes after you began, the tam-tam settles back into the lowest, softest fundamental tones and finally disappears altogether.

A simple portrait of pure percussion sound? Hardly! *Having Never Written a Note for Percussion* is as crowded as a Dickens novel. Furthermore it is crowded not just with a variety of sounds, but also with the rub of rhythm and texture. The sonic material here is more than just sound; it is about context and function as well. It is about the turbulent voyage of sound through time.

Silver Streetcar for the Orchestra (1988)

Alvin Lucier

Perhaps an even more primary example of sonic exploration is Alvin Lucier's *Silver Streetcar for the Orchestra* (1988) for amplified triangle. Lucier's piece is more primary than Tenney's because the instrument itself is. The triangle after all is simply a bent piece of metal without the enormous sonic richness of the tam-tam. The title is extracted from Luis Buñuel's evocative surrealist treatise on orchestration written in 1926. In addition to describing the triangle as the "silver street car of the orchestra," the treatise characterizes timpani as "skins filled with olives," the xylophone as "a child's game. Wood of water. Princesses knitting in the garden, moonbeams." Cymbals are "light shattered into fragments." And the snare drum is described as "little toy thunder. 'Somewhat' menacing." With these and other views of orchestration, Buñuel in effect filters the pure sound of an instrument through its own "id." He is more directly interested in what an instrument *is* or *does* than what it sounds like.

As a piece of music, *Silver Streetcar* also gets at what a triangle really *is* by traversing its sound. Lucier asks a percussionist to isolate qualities of speed, loudness, striking location, and amount of resonance and to explore each independently over the twenty-minute maximum duration of the work. The score gives starting reference levels for each parameter: the dynamic is *mezzo piano*; tempo equals M.M. 340; the striking area is the normal spot for orchestral playing; resonance is half-dampened between thumb and forefinger. Then the percussionist chooses just one of the parameters at a time and changes it as slowly and imperceptibly as possible over twenty or thirty seconds until a palpable change is noticeable. The dynamic might increase from *mezzo piano* to *mezzo forte*, for example. Another parameter is chosen and changed, and then another and another until the sonic possibilities of the triangle have been exhausted. The piece is to be amplified so that the subtle changes of sound can be made clearly audible.

Two elements are critical to a successful performance of *Silver Streetcar*. You must change only one parameter at a time and change it slowly enough that the manipulation of sound is almost imperceptible. These twin demands make the piece much harder to play than one might think. Performers are generally conditioned to make expressive changes as a consortium of actions. We habitually reinforce the diminuendo at the end of a phrase, for example, by also getting a little slower and making the sound perhaps a bit more resonant. But *Silver Streetcar* is not about expressive reflexes (or at least not overtly so). The preconditioned habits of expression must be unplugged in order for pure sonic exploration to take center stage.

Silver Streetcar may be about more than simple expression, but it is also about more than simple sound. The greatest difficulty of the piece, and as a result its poetry, lies in the necessity to channel the force of sound and the considerable intensity of performance through the smallest possible portal. Try making a long acceleration from M.M. 340 to M.M. 360 at *fortissimo* or, at the other end of the spectrum, move the striking area to the very corner of the triangle at *pianississimo* with absolute stillness in all other areas of sound production. You will soon see how much heat *Silver Streetcar* can generate. These kinds of performance problems mean that the piece is not just about sound but also about the production of sound. *Silver Streetcar*, seen as performance, is a telling evaluation of contemporary percussion performance traditions. A single instrument, especially a simple one like the triangle, is often lost in the context of large multiple percussion arrangements. In large pieces the movements of the player are necessarily geared towards large sweeping gestures. The triangle is often played by reaching over other instruments or picked up with the flick of wrist between the attacks of larger—one is tempted to say more important—instruments. We are so accustomed to hearing and playing it as a small part of a large piece—a side of fries in the grand buffet of percussion music—that we often do not really hear it at all. I can think of very few instances in the multiple percussion repertoire where a triangle stroke receives the undivided physical and mental energy of a player. (The *col legno* notes in the Bartók Sonata, the opening of Stravinsky's "Ragtime" from *L'Histoire du soldat*, or the triangle pages of Karlheinz Stockhausen's *Nr. 9 Zyklus* come to mind.) But in *Silver Streetcar for the Orchestra* the triangle enjoys the complete and undivided attention of the player. We can curate the sound of the triangle with its full range of nuance without compromise. The triangle repays the favor by returning us to sound. The slow changes in *Silver Streetcar*—modestly revealing one sonic layer at a time—show us that we are not dealing with a single, simple sound, but in reality a complex of many sounds. At first the listener is not quite sure if anything is happening—the music sounds vaguely like an annoying and endless *ding ding ding ding ding*. But any notion that the piece is a still life for triangle is quickly disabused. It's as though Heisenberg is whispering in our ear: the closer we look the more things seem to be uncertain and changeable. If you can completely inhabit the sound world then things really begin to move. In just the right hall with the right amplification, the sound of the triangle literally begins to disintegrate before your ears. You hear the hum of the instrument's fundamental; you hear high partials start to shimmer and the pinging of the metal beater as it bounces off the walls. *Silver Streetcar* enables us to look inside the living material of percussion music and see the crosscurrents of rhythm and texture that comprise the inner workings of sound itself.

Material as Shape

Nr. 9 Zyklus (1959)

Karlheinz Stockhausen

Karlheinz Stockhausen's *Nr. 9 Zyklus* (1959) was the first major percussion solo written for a particular set of percussion instruments. Cage's *27'10.554"* predates it by several years, but the scoring of the Cage work is not specified. Stockhausen was the first important composer to contend with the details of percussive material in a composition for percussion solo. *Zyklus* was also a first for me. Since it was the first major solo piece I learned, I remain grateful that my considerable naïveté at the time allowed me to simply attack the piece in the practice room without worrying too much about how to understand it first. (*Zyklus* means "cycle," with dual implications of circular shape and universality, as in a song or life cycle—a tall order for the first day on the job.)

Stockhausen's view of material is derived from his notions of shape and process. In his analytical essay about *Zyklus* published in "Texte" he describes the piece as "eine zyklische gekrümmte Form" ("a closed circular form").[1] The work in fact consists of numerous mutually reinforcing circular structures. From an analytical perspective the work is a kind of sphere—circular no matter where you look and without a useful handhold in sight. The piece is arranged so that nine different cycles of accelerating and decelerating music, each focusing around an individual instrumental sound, are overlaid out of phase with each other.

1. Karlheinz Stockhausen, *Texte zur Musik*. vol. 2, Aufsätze 1952–1962 zur musikalischen Praxis (1964) (Cologne: M. DuMont Schauberg, 1963–98).

While one instrument is at the maximally dense moment of its acceleration phase an instrument on exactly the opposite side of the circle is at its least dense moment.

The performer stands in the middle of a circular arrangement of instruments (almost always facing whichever instrument is at the peak of its acceleration phase) and gradually works around the set-up until he or she comes full circle (see figure 6.1). The player chooses a starting (and by implication ending) point anywhere on the circle as well as the direction he or she wishes to proceed around the circle. To change directions simply turn the score over; it works that way too. Even the score is circular in its way: it consists of sixteen unnumbered pages bound on a spiral. There is no first page and no sense of which side is up. These are choices to be made by the interpreter.

A coherent version of *Zyklus* depends on clearly understanding and answering—in this order—two basic questions posed by the piece: 1) To what extent should the performance have a clear dramatic shape; and 2) How fast should the piece be played? Beware of seemingly simple questions. When I refer to *dramatic shape* in *Zyklus* I do not mean the exercise of traditional displays of theatrical virtuosity. In this sense I explicitly do not equate dramatic with theatrical. Instead, drama in *Zyklus* results from the relative strength of traditional narrative constructions whereby a natural sense of beginning, climax, and ending

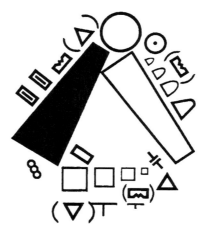

Figure 6.1. Karlheinz Stockhausen, *Zyklus*, diagram of instruments from score. London: Universal Edition Ltd., © 1960. Copyright renewed. All rights reserved. Used by permission of European American Music Distribution LLC, agent for Universal Edition (London) Ltd., London.

sharpens the event profile of the piece at the expense of its circularity. In fact, the very idea of dramatic profile at first seems to contradict the circular nature of the piece. After all, a circle consists of points equally distant from a center; a circle has no beginning or end and cannot have dramatic high or low points. If you can say what part of a circle you like best then it is not really a circle.

The first problem with Stockhausen's description of *Zyklus* as a circle is that the piece is not really round. The circular set-up includes instruments with substantial differences in power, immediacy, and memorability. A dramatic profile inevitably appears in the piece because the snare drum and tom-tom music is generally more potent and memorable than the gong and the cowbell music, for example. This is partly due to the fact that there is greater punch and rhythmic incisiveness in the sound of the snare drum than there is with the sound of the cowbell. But Stockhausen himself undoes his own circle by giving the drums loud and generally remarkable music to play. *Zyklus* might look like a circle but it rolls forward in fits and starts like a tire that has been unevenly balanced.

In retrospect I see that my interpretation of *Zyklus* highlights a dramatic orientation. I certainly did not intend to take an approach that openly contradicted the composer's stated intentions. I would have happily done what the composer wanted me to if only I had understood in 1975 what that was. I simply thought (and continue to think) that the snare drum and tom-tom rim shot music is more interesting than the gong and cowbell music—or maybe I just understood it better as a former rock drummer. In any event, I started with the snare drum/rim shot page and oriented the set-up so the drums were clearly visible to the audience. In my set-up there are no instruments hanging above the drums to obscure sight lines.

Inadvertently I had combined the most potent music of the piece with the most visually (and therefore theatrically) privileged point on the circle. If I start by playing the intense drum page, I am facing the audience. As I move around the circle, gradually turning my back, the less potent sounds of the cowbells, gongs, and triangle are further weakened by the absence of supporting physical energy in performance. A particularly interesting passage alternating between vibraphone and marimba coincidentally takes place at about the 180-degree point in the circle. Its location, exactly opposite the drums, means that this is the only other part of the circle that is completely unblocked by mounted or hanging instruments. Again, the persuasive force of choreography reinforces a moment of musical interest.

Coming around the circle as the piece moves to its conclusion, the snare drum notes and rim shots increase in density and importance. The strokes come faster and faster, each attack played with a gesture that points towards the place where the circle will be joined (not coincidentally also reaching out to the audience) as though to mark the greater importance of that one point on the circle. The circle closes with the rearticulation of the snare drum rim shot that began the piece, an event which by this time has attained a sense of dramatic homecoming worthy of a Mahler Symphony.

Stockhausen himself implies the importance of the snare drum page by referring to it as Period #1 in his own analysis of the score. This page contains two systems (thus allowing seventeen periods to be bound together in a spiral without having a blank page). By orienting the page so that the spiral is on the left and tom-tom rim shot and snare drum roll begins the lower of the two systems, the player moves around the circle in a counterclockwise direction. This page is the most compositionally controlled music of the piece. It features among the loudest, most rhythmic, and most memorable music in the piece. It the default starting point for most of the interpretations of *Zyklus* that I know, including my own. It turns out to be an excellent point from which to experience one of the primary compositional strategies of the piece: the movement from determined to undetermined structures and back.

Period #1, shown in figure 6.2 is completely determined. Every note is on or attached to a time line that runs consistently throughout the piece. Dynamics are clearly indicated by the size of the note head (or graphic rendering if the sound sustains as is the case with rolls, tremolos, and guiro strokes). By moving in either direction on the circle the music becomes increasingly less determined. The composer exercises less and less control, and as a result the performer has more and more freedom. Note that the second page (going in a counterclockwise direction around the circle) features structures that require the performer to make choices. Here the performer plays only one of the bracketed staves. On the third page the three elements in the

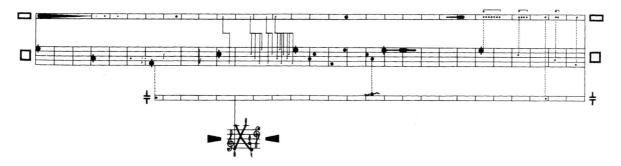

Figure 6.2. Karlheinz Stockhausen, *Zyklus*, Period #1, snare drum page. London: Universal Edition Ltd., © 1960. Copyright renewed. All rights reserved. Used by permission of European American Music Distribution LLC, agent for Universal Edition (London) Ltd., London.

triangular structure are to be played, one at each of the three points of attachment to the timeline. Most of the middle of the page is taken up with bracketed staves. On the next page a rectangular structure is added to the bracketed staves and triangle that we have already seen. The four elements in the rectangle may be played at any time during the span of the timeline occupied by the rectangle.

It is not difficult to see that with each successive page the number of structures that involve performer choice increases by one. Furthermore, each new kind of structure allows more freedom than the previous ones (see figure 6.3). The choice among bracketed staves is the least open choice—a staff once chosen must

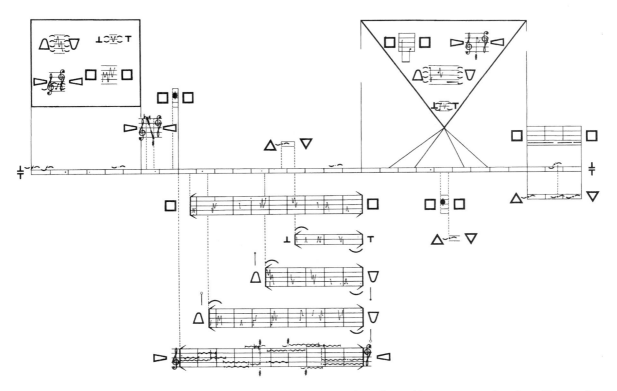

Figure 6.3. Karlheinz Stockhausen, *Zyklus*, Period #4, examples of variable structures. London: Universal Edition Ltd., © 1960. Copyright renewed. All rights reserved. Used by permission of European American Music Distribution LLC, agent for Universal Edition (London) Ltd., London.

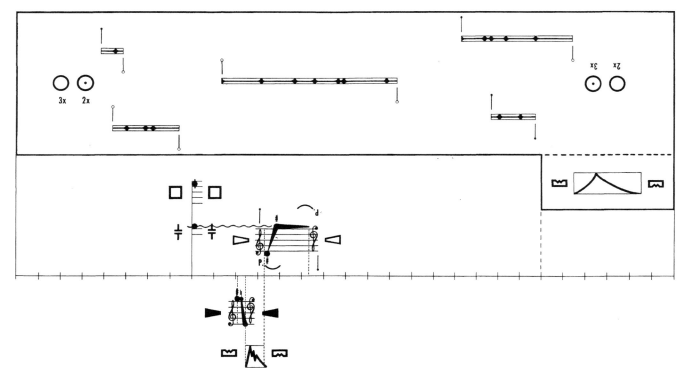

Figure 6.4. Karlheinz Stockhausen, *Zyklus*, Period #9, midpoint. London: Universal Edition Ltd., ©1960. Copyright renewed. All rights reserved. Used by permission of European American Music Distribution LLC, agent for Universal Edition (London) Ltd., London.

be played exactly. The triangular structure allows the choice of order of elements but only at given points along the time line. The rectangle allows the performer to choose both the order of elements as well as their placement in time.

Clearly the composer is gradually relinquishing control as the piece progresses. Look ahead to the midpoint of the piece (in my interpretation) where almost all of the material is contained in one of the variable structures with very few notes affixed to the time line (see figure 6.4). The cross-fade of control has been effected and the performer is now doing a lot of the composing.

Can this shift of control from composer to performer be communicated in performance? Can material be performed in such a way as to indicate its origin and intent? If so, might this not also serve to heighten a sense of dramatic momentum in the piece?

One is tempted to answer quickly that there is no way to tell in a performance of complex music like *Zyklus* whether the specific timing of a given triangle note or drum stroke was determined by the composer or assigned to the judgment of the performer. Stockhausen, however, does give a hint for how material determined by the performer might be distinguished from predetermined material when he suggests that performers try to create clusters, simultaneous events, or other unlikely timbral constructions. Given that Stockhausen's determined music follows a consistent and generally linear temporal distribution, one could imagine a "performer's music" that piles up in clusters or other unique constructions. If the long cross-fade between determined and undetermined music can be made perceptible, then a process of consequence may be established: each section will sound like the result of the one that precedes it and the cause of the one that follows. The music would be clearly in motion towards a goal, and dramatic intent naturally would ensue. The performer must decide to what extent the naturally dramatic cause and effect relationships are important in *Zyklus*. A version that begins with Period #1 and highlights the dynamic and charged relationship between determined and indeterminate music accomplishes this; alternate versions might easily mute the work's dramatic potential.

The ambiguity of cause and effect resides largely in the performer's domain and establishes *Zyklus* as a pivotal link in Stockhausen's evolution toward an increasingly intuitive music. *Zyklus* connects Stockhausen's roots as a serial composer—where the order of events, one leading to the next, is of primary if not axiomatic importance—with later Moment Form pieces like *Kontakte* (1960) where the sequence of sections is explicitly unimportant—no dramatic sense of cause and effect is intended. (Although just as *Zyklus* is not really a circle, *Kontakte* is not really Moment Form. Stockhausen looked at his original version for *Kontakte* and decided it needed a better beginning, so he composed introductory music. This clearly undermines his notion that there is no sense of cause and effect in the piece.) Beyond that, the first stages of a more active role for the performer, expressed in *Zyklus* as the freedom to maneuver blocks of composed music, looks ahead to the completely intuitive music of *Aus den sieben Tagen* (1968).

Stockhausen's view of percussive material is inherent in his choice of instruments for *Zyklus*. The circle of instruments reveals essentially a rounded triangle, each side representing a basic family of instruments: skins, woods, and metals. Stockhausen further formulates each group along a scale from tone to noise.

Among the metal instruments for example, the scale starts with the (relatively) pure tone of the gong, continues through the increasingly noisy sounds of the cowbells, tam-tam, triangle, and suspended cymbal to finish with the nearly absolute noise of the closed hi-hat. The tone to noise spectrum allows Stockhausen enormous freedom in the combination of sounds. Sounds close to each other in the tone/noise spectrum allow for compatibility and connection, whereas ones farther apart will be heard as contrasting colors. A phrase containing cowbells and gong will likely be heard as a line; one with gong and hi-hat will probably seem polyphonic. Combining instruments of similar tone to noise ratio across families allows the meaningful cross-fertilization of instrumental material. A phrase using tom-toms, log drum and cowbell blends well because, in spite of their differing materials, the instruments occupy a similar position towards the middle of the tone/noise spectrum.

By composing for a large and varied group of instruments, Stockhausen affords the performer an enormous variety of coloristic combinations within the indeterminate structures. Material within the structures is completely composed in detail, so the performer is asked essentially to sequence prefabricated materials. One of the main questions for any performer learning *Zyklus* is therefore compositional: How do I decide what event to play next and what implications do these decisions have? Embedded in decisions of sound combination lies the key to the question of how fast to play the piece. The tempo of *Zyklus* is variable as long as the increments along the timeline—the measures in effect—remain roughly equal. I have heard versions of the piece as long as twenty and as short as nine minutes.

Every percussionist who has played a large tam-tam or a piccolo wood block knows that tempo and sound are intimately linked: resonant sounds need time to bloom and decay and tend towards slower tempi while secco sounds disappear quickly and prompt the player to move ahead more quickly. Therefore at least one factor in the tempo of *Zyklus* has to do with the degree of natural resonance present in any given instrumental set-up. My preference in multiple percussion arrangements has always been for small dry sounds. This is partly as the practical consequence of frequent touring where small instruments are simply easier to transport, and partly out of my love for slightly junky, culturally transparent sounds. I normally opt for the "least Asian" sounding gong or the least sonorous log drums, for example. These acoustically impoverished instruments, to borrow Cage's term, tend to be lighter and smaller than their more traditional counterparts. Therefore my performances of *Zyklus* and many other pieces tend towards the faster end of the tempo spectrum.

The combination of sonic materials has even deeper impact on tempo in light of the choices involved in Stockhausen's indeterminate structures. Examine the first triangular structure in figure 6.5. Two events

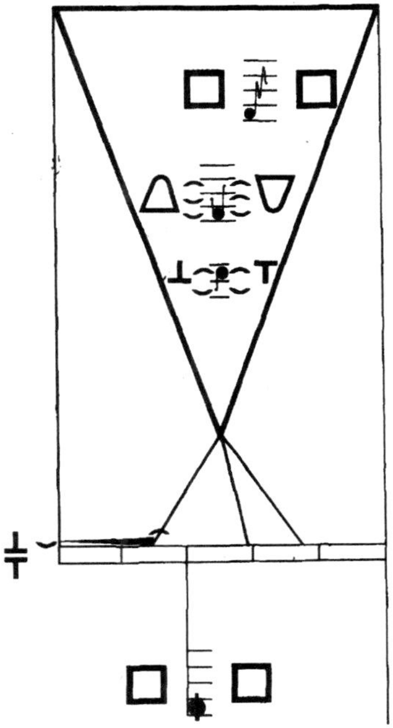

Figure 6.5. Karlheinz Stockhausen, *Zyklus*, Period #2, triangular structure. London: Universal Edition Ltd., © 1960. Copyright renewed. All rights reserved. Used by permission of European American Music Distribution LLC, agent for Universal Edition (London) Ltd., London.

have been placed on the timeline: an open hi-hat tremolo that crescendos for about a beat and a half, and a rim shot on the lowest tom-tom coming directly on beat three of the page. Three events in the triangular structure must be folded into the time line: the first at the very end of the hi-hat crescendo and the last two at precise points after the tom-tom stroke. What are the options for combination? One can either match colors by appending the suspended cymbal notes to the end of the hi-hat tremolo and following the tom-tom rim shot with the five-note tom-tom phrase. Or one could construct a phrase of contrasting colors by reversing those choices.

A sequence of similar colors is likely to be read as a line—an updated version of Schoenberg's *Klangenfarbenmelodie*. Contrasting colors might be understood as polyphony or at the very least as interruption. In either event the smoother timbral path resulting from matched colors can be navigated more rapidly than an uneven one. Or seen in reverse, time is required to establish and perceive a change of color. Either way, the key to a faster version is the linear sequencing of like colors into melodic constructions.

This is especially true around the "corners" of *Zyklus*, where the greatest accumulations of sonically diverse instruments are to be found. Refer again to the diagram of instruments for the piece (figure 6.1, p. 186), where the drums at zero degrees and the gong music at 180 degrees comprise the most homogeneous material. These pages afford the fewest combinatorial options. The structures leading up to and following these pages, however, are full of options. Here the question of tempo as it is reflected in the relative smoothness of a timbral path is critical. If your goal is to play a fast relatively linear version of *Zyklus*, I advise you to match instrumental colors whenever you have the chance. A slower, polyphonically rich interpretation would benefit by a maximally contrasted and interpenetrated color scheme.

Tempo and color are also related through the issue of mallet change. In a slower version of *Zyklus* a performer may have time to change mallets more frequently, using specialized mallets that cultivate maximum coloristic differentiation among the instruments. In turn the variety of color applies even more pressure for a slower version. A faster interpretation that requires a performer to retain a single set of "compromise" mallets for large portions of the piece tends to flatten distinctions of color and creates an even greater sense of linearity—and as a result produces even more speed.

These closely interrelated issues are the real driving forces behind *Zyklus*. You think you are making a simple choice—where to start, which direction to go, what stick to use, how fast to play—and you soon find yourself peering into the endlessly recursive cosmology of Karlheinz Stockhausen.

Material in Motion

Psappha

Iannis Xenakis

I know that I am not alone among percussionists specializing in contemporary music to acknowledge a great debt to Iannis Xenakis. Many of us learned to play percussion by playing his music. From the perspective of an early twenty-first-century percussionist who can find a plentiful and growing repertoire for solo percussion without having to look too hard, it is simply impossible to imagine the situation in the late 1960s and early 1970s when there was just a bare handful of important pieces. So in the mid-1970s, when we heard about Xenakis's new piece *Psappha*, it seemed as if everything changed overnight. I made the trip from Iowa to New York to hear Donald Knaack's Carnegie Hall performance, arriving at Penn Station almost literally right off the farm. That day I fell in love with New York City, walking nearly the length of Manhattan from the Upper West Side to Edgard Varèse's Sullivan Street apartment. That night I heard *Psappha* for the first time. It was one of the most purely happy days of my life.

It was a happy day with a dramatic twist. *Psappha*, as we now know, is savage and frightening. The sheer loudness of it, the naked rhythms, the brutal mechanics of composition—the implications were staggering. Until that point, contemporary percussion music seemed no different from other music; familiar ideas were simply scored for percussion. I could understand everything in the contemporary percussion repertoire, including the complexities of *Zyklus*, by applying the notions of phrasing, form and expression that I had learned by studying Brahms or *Pierrot Lunaire*. Trying to understand *Psappha* using those models was like going to a church social and discovering that someone had spiked the punch—you got something a lot stronger than you expected.

Psappha still packs a punch, but by now it is a part of our lives. It has been so widely played, taught, and discussed that it is very nearly a piece of classical music. There are even schools of thought about interpretative approaches: there is Sylvio Gualda's version as *urtext*; or what James Wood, Christian Dierstein, Roland Auzet, and many others have done with it since. *Psappha* has become a principal model with which to compare all other percussion solos. It changed *everything* about how we listened to and played percussion music from *Zyklus* onward. In spite of differences among interpretive approaches and teaching strategies, understanding the material of *Psappha* remains a simple (if not easy) matter.

However, any discussion of percussive material in *Psappha* is immediately complicated by the fact that Xenakis did not compose for specific percussion sounds. The piece is scored for six groups of instruments, A through F. Each group contains three instruments except group E, which contains a single instrument. The sixteen sounds (or sound groups, since many players double or triple the instrumentation to achieve variety) that comprise the sonic architecture of *Psappha* are to be chosen by the performer. Xenakis's indications in the score give some general guidelines to help in the choice of instruments. Groups A through C should be skin or wooden instruments; groups D through F should be metallic instruments. This is helpful. Nevertheless for a composer whose ideas about sonic material are as well defined as Xenakis's, *Psappha* contains a remarkable amount of freedom for the performer. This freedom was unprecedented in the percussion repertoire of the mid-1970s. The instrumentation of Cage's 27′10.554″, composed in 1956, may have been open, but one could expect that from the composer of 4′33″ and *Imaginary Landscapes*. Certainly the malleability—in effect the impermanence—of basic materials of construction coming from the architect of the Phillips Pavilion at the Brussels World's Fair and the composer of *Metastasis* was another story.

The openness of sonic material in *Psappha* is not its only ambiguity. There are many uncertainties in notation as well. Rhythms are indicated as notes that fall either directly on the beat or on the half beat (see the excerpt in figure 6.6). The only exception to the duple metric orientation in the score comes in the second line with a 5:4 rhythm. Tempi are indicated as minimums; the opening is marked greater than or equal to M.M. 152, for example. Most notably absent are metric groupings. The accents at the opening might be downbeats in a mixed sequence of meters—3+3+2+2, for example—or they could indicate syncopation in an unchanging meter like 4/4. Xenakis's score does not help us much in deciding which.

Questions of interpretation in Xenakis always contain both a conceptual and a practical component. The conceptual aspect of *Psappha* deals with Xenakis's long preoccupation with plurality: How many things are happening at any given moment in the piece? And, if the answer is more than one, how are those things related? And a practical follow-up: How can *any* interpretation of *Psappha* retain its integrity and subtlety in the heat and engagement of Xenakis's musical environment without devolving into base brutality? This dual aspiration, to embrace plurality and avoid brutality, illuminates three basic concerns facing any player wishing to learn *Psappha*. They deal with the choice of instruments, the speed of the music (given that tempi are expressed as open-ended minimums), and how (or even whether) to construct a sense of meter in the absence of metrical indications in the score. These are complex and interrelated questions, but inevitably instrumentation takes precedence. Solving the problems of tempo and phrasing requires at the very least having something to play.

The thorny questions of instrumentation in *Psappha* begin early. At the end of the first line of the score, Xenakis adds a brief phrase of A instruments to the continuous B line (seen in figure 6.6). What is the nature of the interaction between the two groups at this moment? Does A elaborate and ornament B, or act more as interruption and counterpoint? In short, how might instruments be chosen to produce a desired musical effect?

Imagine three potential scenarios of instrumentation and their impact on the opening moments of *Psappha*:

1. *Atomized*: sixteen separate and distinct instruments are chosen; they comprise sixteen groups of one instrument each, in other words. This approach seeks to minimize the presence of groups in the piece and locates the identity of material as individual instrumental sounds. This approach requires maximum

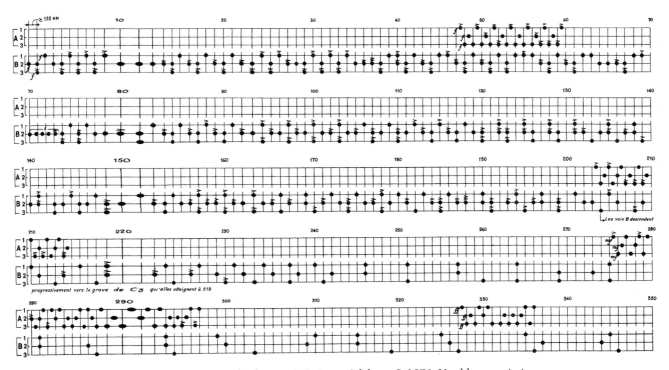

Figure 6.6. Iannis Xenakis, *Psappha*, bars 1–350. Paris: Salabert, © 1976. Used by permission.

differentiation of sound by means of a diversified choice of instruments and the specialized mallets that are required to serve them. The interaction between groups A and B at the end of the first line is not significant because the groups themselves are not significant. The passage sounds like a momentary increase in density and energy.

2. *Unified*: two distinct groups are identified. These groups might include an arrangement of skin instruments for A through C and an array of metal instruments for D through F. Global similarity of timbre tends to organize instruments as a scale from high to low and, as a result, foregrounds a melodic point of view. Maximally unified materials allow the performer to use the same mallets for several groups. Since group A is a higher version of group B—following Sylvio Gualda's model, both would be drums—

group A would serve to elaborate and imitate group B at twice its speed in the passage at the end of the first line.

3. *Modular*: the six groups of instruments, A through F, are maximally distinguished from each other via instrumental color. Each group would probably require a separate mallet type to reinforce its identity as distinct from other groups. Since groups A and B are internally coherent but distinct from each other, their interaction at the end of the first line would probably sound oppositional and polyphonic. This approach suggests that the piece consists of contrasting forces that engage each other on the level of the group and will necessarily require some kind of resolution over the course of the piece.

Let's follow the implications of the models presented above as they extend into other areas of the piece.

The *atomized* model is the approach least popular among today's percussionists. Mixing instruments *within* the major instrumental groups—especially if this is done unsystematically—tends to minimize the utility of using color as a means to outline form. Sounds are robbed of a global timbral framework. They don't belong to groups so they cannot be heard as natural completions of or oppositions to each other. The piece exists as a series of localized sonic events with limited capacity to generate large-scale interactions.

In general an atomized model requires slower tempi because it takes time for a listener to register and understand highly heterogeneous sound sources. (See the discussion of the relationship between sonic diversity and tempo with respect to *Zyklus* above). The practical difficulty of wielding and changing a larger assortment of mallets also implies slower speeds. In spite of some obvious liabilities in the atomized approach, it does have a few important advantages. With a greater number and variety of instruments, the momentary surface of the music will obviously be more colorful. This might help enliven the relative simplicity of Xenakis's rhythmic language. A performer may change instruments in order to address a particular moment, to highlight the high A voice in the grand silences at bar 984, for example, without worrying much how such a decision will affect the larger formal design of the piece.

The *unified* model is the most common approach to *Psappha*, thanks to the advocacy of Sylvio Gualda, who premiered the work and has championed it for nearly thirty years. It has become rare to hear a version of the piece, especially in Europe, that does not consist of some version of Gualda's set-up—an extended scale of drums covering groups A to C along with a collection of compatible but noisy metallic instruments for groups D to F. By minimizing sonic differences among groups A through C, the unified approach cultivates a sense of similarity in the opening pages of the piece. The music seems incantatory and unrelenting, as though it would express something if only it could be repeated often enough.

In the unified model, the piece divides neatly into two halves on either side of the large silences following bar 984, seen in figure 6.7. Before the silences the piece consists of drums; afterwards of drums and metals. However, the neatness of the formal division, along with the fact that it serves to introduce a radically different group of sounds at a relatively late point in the piece, is problematic. Since the unified approach creates minimal tension among the materials in the first half of the piece—among groups A through C—one wonders where the fuel for such a radical change comes from. Wouldn't there need to be a *reason* that the piece suddenly screeches to a halt, then continues in a series of abrupt and disturbing silences only to recommence with the inclusion of a brand new group of instrumental sounds? Doesn't the unproblematic relationship among groups A through C invoke a law of musical inertia whereby a frictionless path continues as before?

If a weakness of the unified approach lies in its inability to account for dramatic change in the piece, one of its great strengths lies in the way it reinforces the forward momentum of narrative sense. After all, the name *Psappha* itself refers to the poetess Sappho. Xenakis uses metrical structures from her poetry—and by extension the strength of narration—as a basic building block for *Psappha*. In the right hands the approach of unifying material comes close to reflecting the power and singularity of the human voice as it might have been heard intoning the work of Sappho. When I last heard Sylvio Gualda play the work (the percussion group Kroumata hosted him in Stockholm for the Stockholm International Percussion

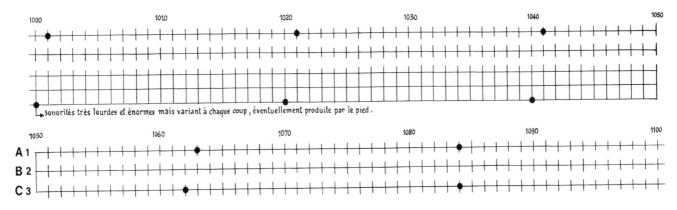

Figure 6.7. Iannis Xenakis, *Psappha*, the silences, bars 1000–1100. Paris: Salabert, © 1976. Used by permission.

Event in 1998), he maximized the incantatory qualities in the music in a performance was both majestic and tragic.

The *modular* approach to *Psappha* relies on locating the identity of material as the integrity of the six basic sound groups, each internally coherent and maximally distinguished from one another. Since the *group* is the primary source of identity, it must be both stable and recognizable. This suggests a middle ground between the unified view of *Psappha*, where the similarity of material produces timbral stability, and the atomized approach, where vivid colors are instantly recognizable. The modular approach must have both: the group must be stable in its construction—instrumentation may not change over the course of the piece, and recognizable in its usage—a group must be sonically vivid and assert an identifying pattern of behavior. Group B, for example, must always be heard as group B whether in the relatively stable music of the opening or in much more interpenetrated interactions later in the piece.

I opted for a modular interpretation. But I must confess that I stumbled upon it without realizing its implications. For me it was a simple matter. I didn't have a global plan for the piece so I began with drums for the opening music out of convenience and added instrumental groups from there as necessary. My tendency was to choose contrasting colors—usually using a different material for each new group—to create coherence within and differentiation among different groups at the same time. I elaborated the internal coherence within each group by means of a dual strategy. A single mallet type played the material of each group in order to sharpen its sonic personality. (Eventually I adopted the use of a single mallet type for most of the metal instruments.) Each group was further unified by a common intervallic profile. My choice of two bongos and tom-tom for the opening supplied an intervallic template for the rest of the piece. It was easy enough to follow the same model in the other groups: drums could be tuned and the wooden and metal instruments were easily chosen or cut to size to recreate the same intervallic structure.

Certain practical considerations were also a part of my decision-making process. I would later be grateful for an arrangement of small, ordinary instruments, considering the demanding logistics of either traveling with or borrowing instruments on tour. However, simple availability was the issue at the beginning. At the University of Iowa in 1977 there were few exotic instruments—no *bonang* or quarter-tone marimbas—however, bongos, congas, and other drums were in plentiful supply, as were brake drums, bells, and other pieces of junk metal. (My childhood on the farm was largely spent tripping over things that I would later convert to use as instruments and transport all over the world.)

Inevitably every percussion set-up is a combination of conception and accident. My instrumentation for *Psappha* is no exception. I made my best guess on the basis of available materials and learned to live with the results. I also thought at the time that if I were unhappy with the sounds I could always change them. I was wrong. A nascent interpretation seeks to make sense of the sounds at its disposal. You begin by playing a certain way because the instruments sound right that way. Later the physical responses of interpretation harden and you need *those* instruments to make your interpretation sound right. In any event my instrumentation for *Psappha* has not changed substantially in more than twenty-five years:

Group A	Two high wood blocks; medium wooden *simantra*
Group B	Two high bongos; tom-tom
Group C	Two medium-low congas; pedal bass drum
Group D	Three small steel pipes
Group E	Frying pan
Group F	Three brake drums or *sixxen* bars

The metal pipes of group D produce quite pure pitches in opposition to the frying pan, which makes a flat noise. Group F, originally played on brake drums, is now played on extra bars from a set of *sixxen* that were built in San Diego to play Xenakis's sextet *Pléïades*.[2] They are midway between the tones of the pipes and the noise of the frying pan and are further distinguished from the other metal groups by register.

A careful balance of cohesion and tension between groups drives a dialectic of *fluid opposition* in the modular approach to *Psappha*. Distinctive sonic profiles among the groups make conflict inevitable. Yet together they comprise a compatible universe—relative similarities of duration and attack bind them together as players on the same stage. The logic of the work expresses equilibrium where opposition prompts conflict among groups and, conversely, fluidity enables sonically diverse materials to meld together as forward momentum in an otherwise static formal design. In my view, events in the first half of the piece are oppositional. For example, in the first full page of the score group B provides a consistent *parlando* line against which group A provokes increasingly frequent and potent confrontations (figure 6.8). The growing dissonance between the two voices eventually prompts the first major shift of expressive modality: the long crescendo/decrescendo figure in voice A at bar 380.

2. The San Diego instruments were designed and constructed by Brett Reed for the percussion group "red fish blue fish," which is in residence at the University of California, San Diego.

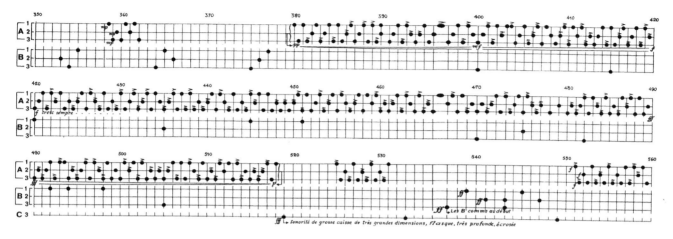

Figure 6.8. Iannis Xenakis, *Psappha*, crescendo/decrescendo figure, bars 350–560. Paris: Salabert, © 1976. Used by permission.

Change begets change. In figure 6.8 the potent contrast between the skin instruments of group B and the wooden instruments of group A, each articulated in time along two very different expressive medians, catalyzes the entrance of the powerful C group of instruments at bar 519. The shocking bass drum note at 519 generates an escalation of the interactions among the three groups. The music becomes more charged and the rapport among the groups more confrontational, first in the three-part polyphony at bar 631 and continuing in the complex five-part polyrhythm at bar 740. The piece is running out of room to maneuver: the acoustical space has been saturated, the conflicting forces are completely interpenetrated, and the energy of the performer has been depleted. Something must change.

The mounting chaos is terminated in a series of brutally articulated silences (refer to figure 6.7) creating one of the most potent moments in the entire percussion repertoire.

Fluidity marks the second half of the piece. Material is consistently interpenetrated in a multilevel strategy with flexible rules of engagement. Note the extent of sonic mixture in the passage at bar 1411, seen in figure 6.9, as the music circulates freely through five instrumental groups. Later, another five-part exchange is energized by repeating notes and highlighted by the rarest of dynamic markings in the music of Iannis Xenakis—*piano*. The extensive tremolo section at the end of the piece is the ultimate meeting

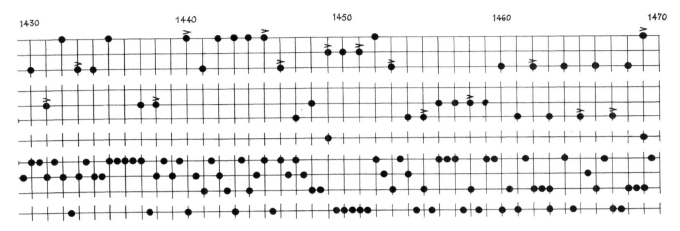

Figure 6.9. Iannis Xenakis, *Psappha*, sonic mixture, bars 1430–1470. Paris: Salabert, © 1976. Used by permission.

ground of opposition and flexibility. This moment might be clangorous and chaotic but it must also serve as a crucible in which diverse sonic materials are mixed and ultimately reconciled. Here fluid opposition reveals its central metaphor wherein the forces of opposition also contain the key to their redemption in common cause.

The very practical question for any performer of *Psappha* is simply how to survive the experience of playing the piece. The work is loud, long, and difficult. Any attempt to simply overpower it is doomed to failure—if you actually have the strength to do so, the music quickly degenerates into a slugfest that has more in common with a monster truck rally than it has with the poetry of Sappho. A performance of *Psappha* must be strong and convincing but it must be elegant also. Take the question of how to play the tremolos seen in figure 6.10. Xenakis provides the distinctly unhelpful indication that each note head should receive three strokes. Playing a single instrument at this speed is *just* barely possible (be sure to have a good breakfast that day), but a quick calculation reveals that a tremolo involving two or more notes simultaneously, each of which gets three strokes per note head, is physically impossible to play. How do you play something that is impossible to play? (There are similar "impossible" passages in most of Xenakis's solo music. Although the question does occur: if so much of Xenakis is truly impossible, then how is it that so many people are playing his music?)

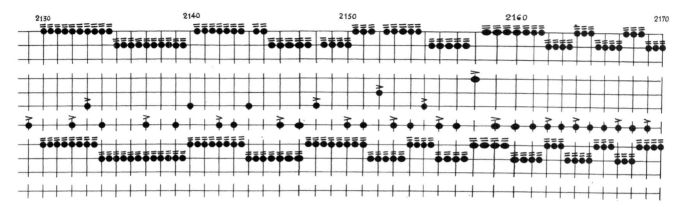

Figure 6.10. Iannis Xenakis, *Psappha*, bars 2130–2170. Paris: Salabert, © 1976. Used by permission.

The inclusion of an *unplayable* moment in *Psappha* has produced a number of innovative solutions. These range from elaborate constructions that allow the performer to double the rolling speed by playing between sandwiched sets of instruments,[3] to my solution, the eminently practical decision simply to ignore the indication in the score. In any event we have a problem, since all possible solutions are unsatisfactory in one way or another. I must confess that my decision to ignore Xenakis's indications in the score made me feel uneasy. There are certainly instances when an interpreter might have good reasons to make an editorial change in a score. However, inconvenience is not among those reasons. Nevertheless, I was ultimately convinced that a straightforward tremolo was the best solution. If the tremolos are played as fast as possible they devolve naturally from the preceding material and fully satisfy their purpose to mix the colors of groups A through E.

I found that playing with specially constructed or sandwiched instruments was unsatisfactory solution for several reasons. Even if a specially constructed instrument satisfies the indications in the score, it does so awkwardly. The tremolo section is the highpoint of *Psappha*: it should be the loudest and most persuasive music of the piece. Furthermore, to whatever extent a modular approach has set in motion the forces of opposition and resolution among the materials of the piece, this is also the moment of greatest metaphorical power. The

3. The most common construction consists of two sets of bongos, one mounted above another, thus allowing the player to strike one instrument on the upstroke and the other on the downstroke.

materials of construction have been heated by the energy of performance; they have been excited to the point of metamorphosis. Then precisely at this moment—the one that defines the emotional and formal axis of the piece—the player contorts him or herself and partially disappears behind a Rube Goldberg construction of sandwiched bongos or metal plates. The sudden dilution of the physical energy of performance at the most euphoric and liberating moment of the piece has ruined more than one performance. Balancing the physical energy of performance with the musical requirements of the score is in fact the secret to interpreting *Psappha*. An unbalanced version risks banality, either as a consequence of excessive force as a player seeks to dominate the piece, or in an overly meticulous and cautious reading of the score as "contemporary music." At its best *Psappha* exists in that rare state of grace where personal force is united with musical force and the vehicle of the score is synonymous with the vessel of a human being who seeks to embody and communicate it.

Rebonds (1989)

Iannis Xenakis

Rebonds was born into a very different world than was *Psappha*. Nearly fifteen years had passed. It was a period that saw rapid growth in the solo percussion repertoire with major new works by Vinko Globokar, Frederic Rzewski, and James Wood among many others. Furthermore the specialized art of solo marimba playing, and to a lesser extent solo vibraphone, had flourished. Xenakis himself had also changed considerably. His early ideas about composition for percussion—the often brutal opposition of blocks of sound and psychologically shattering silences of *Psappha* and *Persephassa*—had given way to the more continuous, rhythmically driven music of *Pléïades*, *Okho*, and finally *Rebonds*.

Rebonds is a work in two movements, called *Rebonds A* and *Rebonds B*. The order of the movements in performance is free and to be played without interruption. *Rebonds A* is scored for skin instruments only: two bongos, three tom-toms, and two bass drums. (Xenakis lists only two tom-toms in the legend of the manuscript, but three tom-toms are in fact required.) *Rebonds B* is scored for two bongos, *tumba* (an Afro-Cuban barrel drum), tom-tom, bass drum, and five wood blocks. The scale represented by skins and wood blocks should be as wide as possible. Although there are slight differences in instrumentation between *Rebonds A* and *Rebonds B*, most players now use a single set-up that can accommodate both movements, perhaps by replacing one of the tom-toms in *Rebonds A* with a *tumba*.

A quick analysis of *Rebonds* reveals a forthright rhythmic elaboration of homogeneous sonic materials. His *Okho*, composed around the same time for three *djembes* (African hand drums) provides an even more purified version of this model. The combination of straightforward drumming and use of "ethnic" instruments in both works prompted some discussion of the permeability of cultural boundaries in the new Xenakis percussion music. As if to head criticism off at the pass, Jacques Lonchampt wrote in the French daily *Le Monde* that *Rebonds* was utterly devoid of any sense of "*contamination folklorique.*" Even today, this phrase is routinely passed along in the form of the officially sanctioned program note for the piece and serves as an epigraph in the published version of the score. I have just one question. Who is he kidding?

Of course we know that Xenakis was not interested in African music in the way that, say, Steve Reich was in the years before he composed *Drumming*. Xenakis did not travel to Africa to study rhythm; he did not quote African rhythms or conceive of either *Rebonds* or *Okho* as a study in the cross-cultural musical idiom. Nevertheless, these pieces, *Rebonds* and *Okho, are* thoroughly "contaminated" by traditional African music, judged solely on the basis of their material. What Xenakis demonstrates so persuasively is that the choice of sonic material itself plays a considerable role in determining how it will be used. A composer who listens carefully to the *djembe*, for example—to the quality of attack and sustain, to the variety of tonalities available through various hand strokes, and to the visceral power of the instrument—will necessarily compose something that reflects its African heritage. If that composer is as sophisticated as Iannis Xenakis, this will clearly not involve a simpleminded cut-and-paste technique. But *anyone* who plays a *djembe* in whatever context inevitably also puts his or her hands directly on the sonic DNA of African music. *Rebonds* may use the less obviously "folkloric" instrumentation of bongos, congas, tom-toms, wood blocks, and bass drum, but a clear understanding of the piece must be rooted in an appropriately contaminated point of view. That means that a performance of the piece can and must reveal both the sources of its material and its structure. With *Rebonds* that means acknowledging the African and Latin roots of its sound world, as well as the largely European orientation of its structural idiom, parsed as Xenakis's lifelong interest in consolidating musical material, mathematics, architecture, and large-scale musical forms.

From the standpoint of sound and form *Rebonds* is a very different piece from *Psappha*. Absent in *Rebonds* are the grand clashes of sonority: those pivotal moments of articulation whereby new elements are born out of the heat of friction among sonic elements. The global arc in *Rebonds* is effectuated by smaller changes, nudges here and there to guide the work along its ultimate direction. But what is that direction? This question of form in *Rebonds* is certainly complicated by the fact that the order of the movements is free. Many performers have agonized over the order of movements. There is, however, one simple way to decide: just choose. My decision to play *Rebonds* as B/A was the result of a friendly wager with James Wood who, during the period when we were both learning the piece, claimed a preference for an A/B version.

Indeed the decision is not as important as it might seem at the outset. Both movements detail a progression from a simple and categorical exposition of material through a presentation that is increasingly fractured and alienated from its original form to a final phase consisting of new mutually dependent categories. In both *Rebonds A* and *Rebonds B*, initial materials are sufficiently reorganized by the end of each movement to create a new kind of unity. *Rebonds A* deals in this way with rhythm; *Rebonds B* with texture. As a result the piece functions as two sequential trajectories of statement, disintegration, and reassimilation, no matter which order is chosen.

What fuels rhythmic and coloristic metamorphosis in *Rebonds*? Recall in *Psappha* that sparks flew as polarized sound groups careened off one another. The interaction of at least two groups was necessary to create a release of musical energy potent enough to steer the piece. This implies that the source of power lies in the rapport among groups and is therefore external to any given group. On the contrary, each movement of *Rebonds* begins with structures that are preloaded with energy. The source of energy is therefore internal, produced by friction among forces within the music. The performer's job is to locate the triggering mechanism that allows this energy to be released in a way that pushes the piece in a forward direction.

A performer's analysis should start with an examination of the initial conditions—the preloaded energetic structures—within groups of percussive material.

Rebonds B begins with internally charged "rebound" material: a driving rhythmic line in the right hand is counterpoised against a looser loping melodic structure in the left hand. Both parts of this structure flirt with predictability but ultimately avoid dry repetition. In the right hand the steady reciting line on the high bongo itself consists of two primary features. Grace note rebounds appear on the first and third beats of every bar and are overlaid with a slightly eccentric accent structure. (The accent pattern seems as if it will repeat on the second sixteenth note of each second beat for example, but never continues the pattern for more than a few beats.) The left-hand part is an isorhythmic melodic cycle on the remaining drums. The order of notes and the accent structure remain the same, but variations of duration serve to reposition the sense of strong and weak beats in the line.

Examine the initial rebound material in figure 6.11. With its crosscurrent of accents, melodies, and rebounds, it forms a compactly structured linear complex, within which internal dynamic force depends on tension among opposing metrical and melodic structures. The formal arc of the piece consists of changes in the complex opening music triggered by a series of monophonic interruptions. Each interruption is successively more vivid and acts as a more powerful catalytic force. The first of these interruptions consists of two short passages on drums (see bars 8 and 9 in figure 6.11). Later Xenakis uses wood blocks

REBONDS

b

Figure 6.11. Iannis Xenakis, *Rebonds B*, bars 1–12. Paris: Salabert, © 1991. Used by permission.

Figure 6.12. Iannis Xenakis, *Rebonds B*, bars 29–34, showing wood block disruption at bar 31. Paris: Salabert, © 1991. Used by permission.

(bar 31, seen in figure 6.12) and later still rapid interactions among drums and woods (bar 75, seen in figure 6.13).

The goal of the interruptions is to dislodge the stability of the initial complex material so that it releases its constituent components as independently functioning elements. At first the initial material does not give way easily. After every interruption it returns to reassert its primacy. Only after repeated assaults does it begin to soften and allow the possibility of metamorphosis. After two vigorous drumming interludes, the rebound is cut loose. What was once a two-note grace note loses its structural attachment to the ongoing rhythmic line and begins to pile up as a chain of increasingly longer rebounds (see figure 6.13). By bar 65 these notes have finally become dense enough to sustain a lengthy tremolo passage between drums and wood blocks. Eventually, the increasingly frequent and potent monophonic interpolations mount an attack sufficient to atomize the original material. The piece becomes a centrifuge, flinging fragments of the opening complex into extreme associations with the now-dominant monophonic music. Tremolos, the ultimate version of the opening grace note figure, follow the melodic shape of the opening left-hand melody this time on wood blocks. A devilish unison figure unites two versions of the monophonic voice into a wood/skin complex. The charged materials, in a whirlwind, finally produce the only possible result: an arrival on "tonic" in the sustained tremolo between the top wood block and the lowest drum.

Figure 6.13. Iannis Xenakis, *Rebonds B*, grace notes and wood blocks, bars 64–74. Paris: Salabert, © 1991. Used by permission.

Metamorphosis in *Rebonds B* means that the two faces of the piece—complex/polyphonic and monophonic/intrusive—that at the outset seemed to stand in arch contradiction with one another start to sound and act more and more alike. The rebound material has lost its complexity and the monophonic incursions have lost their ability to stand apart; they tamely interweave themselves into a generalized texture. This process in interpretation requires a gradual turning up of the heat. My strategy is to play the opening a bit softer and very slightly faster than marked—I offer the softest possible dynamic that could still be considered *forte* (following the dictum: if you have something important to say, say it quietly). There are several very good reasons not to play the initial rebound material too strongly. An adequate representation of the complex opening music requires careful shading. The bongo should ideally get a different sound from the tom-toms; the rebounds should perhaps be colored differently than the accents. Loud playing is a problem because it tends to minimize the coloristic distinctiveness of the music, in effect flattening the sonic spectrum. This is especially true if one uses plastic-headed drums. The piece progresses as every monophonic interruption is played more vigorously than the one before and every reassertion of the rebound material is played a little louder and a little slower. In effect I redefine *forte* at an increasingly higher level over the course of the movement. As the battle for primacy between the two kinds of material turns towards an increasingly shared vocabulary in the realm of composition, increasingly loud playing also assures that the coloristic differences between the two are smaller and smaller. By the time one reaches extremely loud playing at the end of the movement, the dynamic and polarized engagement between two materials has replaced by common cause and underlined rhetorically in performance by increasingly similar coloration. The battle is essentially over by the time things get really loud (following the dictum: when you have nothing to lose, start yelling).

The physical gestures of performance follow the same path. It is convenient that the complex music in the initial rebound material is neatly separated between two hands. A two-part musical structure can therefore be articulated by a clearly distinguished two-part approach to the physical act of playing. My interpretation relies on a right-hand stroke that is short and fast, producing minimally distinguished dry sounds. The left hand is more voluble: its irregular terrain implies a flexible and melodic approach. A gestural polyphony occurs: the right half of the body looks almost immobile while the left half is highly engaged. With louder playing and an increasingly interleaved presentation between the opening two groups, the gestural vocabulary between the right and left sides of the body is slowly rhymed. Distinctions between left and right disappear and physical gesture is prompted from a deeper and more central part of the body.

Rebonds A follows a similar path. A clear statement of internally charged material is first challenged and finally disintegrates in the face of a disruptive triggering mechanism. This time the process revolves around rhythm. A simple rhythmic figure starts the movement: two consecutive sixteenth notes played on the high bongo and the low bass drum. The stability of this figure is quickly threatened by the addition of a third sixteenth note in a figure that gradually works its way up and down the scale of drums. The fate of *Rebonds A* is determined on the fourth beat of bar 1 (see figure 6.14). A small elaboration in the opening rhythm triggers change, and once effected, change itself is unstoppable. The paradigm for metamorphosis is simple: an empty rhythmic framework will be filled. The music will continue until the void between the high bongo and the low bass drum is saturated. It's simple.

The piece might be simple, but that does not make it easy. The density and difficulty of the polyrhythmic material that Xenakis uses to fill the empty space makes *Rebonds A* one of the most challenging pieces in the entire solo percussion repertoire. In particular the performer is faced with the daunting challenge of

Figure 6.14. Iannis Xenakis, *Rebonds A*, bars 1–12. Paris: Salabert, © 1991. Used by permission.

controlling the arc of change. How can gradual rhythmic change be parsed over the course of nearly six minutes of music? Will it be smooth or contoured? And what catalyzes the forces of change?

Rhythmic change in *Rebonds A* proceeds by quanta, since the granularity of transformation is not fine enough to allow a smoothly flowing transition from emptiness to saturation. When Xenakis adds an extra sixteenth note at the end of bar 1, for example, the music instantaneously becomes 30 percent denser. Likewise, with the first true polyrhythm, a 3:2 in bar 7, the density of strokes per eighth note more than doubles. Rapid linear music starting in bar 27 confounds the issue. The 32nd-note passages immediately make the music much faster, but the absence of polyrhythms makes it less dense at the same time. In the end, the piece does not then trace a continuous arc of change. Rather, change progresses as a series of stages, each denser or faster than the one before.

In my mind these points of articulation—the moments where a new rhythmic element triggers a new *phase*—are also the keys to interpretation. The music is about the saturation of space, but space extends in multiple directions. On the horizontal plane rhythmic change is a process of densification. Change also operates on the plane of depth by creating variations in the sense of fore- and background importance attached to the new material. Seen this way *Rebonds A* results as the elision of several smoothly evolving processes: each progresses in an arc of change defined by rhythmic content, relative saturation of register, depth of field, and in my view, depth of emotional effect.

No precise rendering of a formal plan in *Rebonds A* is possible. Interdependence among adjacent phases tends to obscure the boundaries. However, one might consider the architecture of the piece as follows:

Bar 1: *Declamation.* The first three beats outline the rhythmic and sonic void to be filled. In the same way that a Henry Moore sculpture consists largely of its negative space, the music here consists as much of what is not there as what is. Everything is in the foreground. Tension derives from the need to fill the void.

Bars 2–5: *Elaboration.* Sixteenth notes persist but cycle around the instruments. Accents rotate giving the sense of a shifting tonal center among the drums.

Bars 6–28: *Polyrhythm.* Polyrhythms of 3:2 and 4:3, as seen in figure 6.14, begin to fill the space. None of these rhythms involves both of the original instruments, the high bongo and low bass drum, at the same time. The music is being pulled towards the middle register. None of the polyrhythms is accented allowing the sixteenth-note patterns, vestigial remnants of the opening music, to retain their primacy. Polyrhythmic groupings begin to form a more distant middle ground layer of music.

Bars 29–35: *Linear.* Running 32nd notes (figure 6.15) blur the boundaries between fore- and middle ground. The accent structure is a remnant of earlier material. The music collects in knots of fast rhythms and disperses in slower ones.

Bars 36–50: *Density.* The knots of dense material such as those in figure 6.16 continue as polyrhythmic constructions. Accents remain in the foreground; polyrhythmic clusters occupy the middle- and background; linear music connects the two. The music pulses in clusters of varying density and proximity.

Bars 51–61: *Recollection* (figure 6.17). The first beat of bar 51 features the first polyrhythm to include both original instruments, the high bongo and the low bass drum, at the same time. This recalls the

Figure 6.15. Iannis Xenakis, *Rebonds A*, bar 27. Paris: Salabert, © 1991. Used by permission.

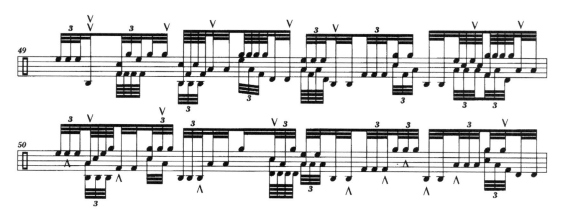

Figure 6.16. Iannis Xenakis, *Rebonds A*, bars 49–50. Paris: Salabert, © 1991. Used by permission.

outline of the original void. Middle and background music quickly falls away leaving a series of grace notes and a final figuration on the high bongo and low bass drum. The entirety of the music resides again in the foreground, but this time without the initial tension. Silence, at first dissonant and begging to be filled, has become home.

These sections are easy enough to demonstrate, yet the music does not sound sectional. In the end *Rebonds A* is a slow burn—a single long breath. It's the familiar model of gradual metamorphosis heard

Figure 6.17. Iannis Xenakis, *Rebonds A*, bars 54–60. Paris: Salabert, © 1991. Used by permission.

in pieces from *Bolero* to *White Rabbit*. But Xenakis invests us so heavily in his premise that change in *Rebonds A* is anything but simple. By the end much remains from the original music. Accents are still primary; the high bongo and the low bass drum retain their initial importance; "tonal centers" still cycle round the interior drums. The countenance of the music has not changed. The gap between two sixteenth notes has simply been filled—nothing more has happened. But, the mandate of the original void—its need to be filled and completed—overwrites old markers with new meaning, and with that, everything has been changed.

This is ultimately why I continue to play Xenakis. The lessons of *Rebonds* and *Psappha* seem clear enough: strength is not brutality; intelligence is not weak; change is inevitable, but if you do things just right you can still remember where you came from. Thank you, Mr. Xenakis.

Material as Metaphor

Rogosanti (1986)

James Wood

Any discussion of percussive material naturally draws on pieces of percussion music for illustration. But I don't wish to construe my comments above as musical analyses. They are much more personal responses to specific problems in performance. In fact, although I think a lot about percussion music, I would not characterize my interpretations in any of the above works as being cerebral or at times even rational. For me the most rewarding moments in performance have consisted of a complete range of qualities including the engagement of the intellect, the immediacy of physicality, and the union of music with emotion. The most important musical experiences, in short, resemble to a very large extent the most important experiences in the rest of life.

This has meant that in large measure I have looked to percussion music for its metaphorical rapport with the nonmusical parts of life. The idea is that if a single tool—in my case the performance of contemporary solo percussion music—can be sufficiently sharpened, it might be used to puncture layers of thoughtless habituation and potentially reveal something interesting or important about living. I have learned a lot from Alvin Lucier's *Silver Streetcar*, for example, about not rushing towards a goal, about the rewards of staying with a worthy process no matter where it might lead. I can think of lessons in the shaping energy of transformation that come directly out of *Ionisation*; of the catalytic forces of otherness that I learned in Xenakis; or of the value of silence that I took from Cage. I learned that, even after you have played a lot of contemporary music, you can still encounter something very new and reinvigorating: such was the revelatory experience I had when I first played Morton Feldman's *For Philip Guston* a few months ago. You are right to think that these are very personal, perhaps even naive comments. But music *is* personal and naïveté is an essential component of remaining open to new ideas and experiences. Metaphorical connections between music and life that serve to reflect a player's responsibility to him- or herself or inform a relationship to a broader community—even if these ideas are never expressed publicly—are the necessary difference between music as art and music as mere skill.

Nowhere has the value of metaphor been clearer to me than in James Wood's *Rogosanti*, the demanding and relentless solo he wrote for me in 1986. From 1982 to 1992 James Wood and I worked together in even-numbered summers at the Internationale Ferienkurse für Neue Musik in Darmstadt, Germany. James led the course and I assisted him. Together with ever-growing classes of young percussionists, we performed a very large part of the serious contemporary percussion repertoire. In 1988 we premiered James's own *Stoichiea*, a massive work for two solo percussionists, an accompanying percussion sextet, twelve auxiliary antiphonal percussionists and a bank of four synthesizer players. The work is scored for more than seven hundred percussion instruments; a fact that registered in a practical way when we subsequently began to tour it.

Rogosanti grew out of our close working relationship and mutual desire to create new percussion music together where vivid sonic materials could be used to make meaningful and emotionally powerful music. I was then only too pleased when James announced that the new piece he was writing for me would have an explicit emotional and metaphorical point of departure. *Rogosanti* is the Sanskrit word for healing, or more literally, the "quieting of disease." The piece is scored for two groups of instruments. Skin and wooden sounds consisting of an array of eleven drums, large timpano, large wooden *simantra*, tambourine, and bamboo clapper open the piece and represent an advancing disease. A metallic group—quarter-tone glockenspiel, large Javanese gong, triangle, temple bowl, chime, and two crotales—represents the healing process that dominates the second half of the piece. The fricative sounds of swirled maraca and thunder sheet, positioned midway between the noises of the skin/wood group and the purity of the metals, serve to bridge the gap and connect the two main sections of the piece.

At first glance *Rogosanti* has straightforward programmatic associations. The disease music is aggressive and implacable, as seen in figure 6.18. It consists of highly syncopated rhythms with distant ties to the rhythmic language of northern India that wheel around explosive punctuations in the bass drums and bamboo clapper. In four consecutive passages following an introductory duo for vocal and drum sounds, the music grows in vigor until at a moment of maximum strength and density it triggers the balm of the healing metallic instruments. With the first entrance of the metals (figure 6.19) the tenor of the music changes abruptly as the cooler sounds begin to extinguish the fire of disease.

The immediate temptation is to treat the two sections of the piece very differently—essentially to maximize the difference between the aggression of the disease and the peacefulness of health. However, a closer look at the material reveals a similarity of process that connects these two states in spite of their very different sounds and the emotional states they represent. Both sections are organized harmonically whereby slow articulations in the low instruments are elaborated by rapid tonal configurations of higher sounds. In effect the two sections of the piece are fueled by and derive forward momentum from the same source. In the drum sections, the harmonic basis is supplied by the marcato markings on low drums and bass drum and ornamented by congas and bongos; in the metals section a foundation consisting of the pedal tone of the low gong, chime, and temple bell anchors a floating quarter-tone line in the glockenspiel. How different can the two sections—and by extension the states of being they represent—really be if they *function* so similarly?

This similarity of musical function, especially as it relates to the strong programmatic elements of disease and healing, leads back to the role of metaphor in *Rogosanti*. In a perverse coincidence I was learning *Rogosanti* during the time my mother was battling and eventually died from lung cancer. My first performance of the piece took place in Los Angeles just a few weeks before she died. Believe me, at that time I really wanted to paint disease as hateful and evil, and by contrast, the healing process as the answer to prayers. But the disease music in *Rogosanti*, in spite of its pernicious advancement, is in fact quite beautiful.

Figure 6.18. James Wood, *Rogosanti*, drum passage, bars 85–118. Used by permission.

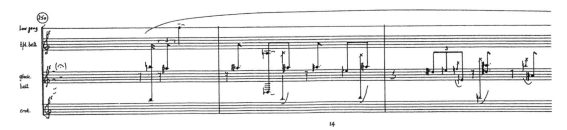

Figure 6.19. James Wood, *Rogosanti*, 3 bars from metals passage, bars 250–252. Used by permission.

It is sinuous, melodic, and ultimately seductive. Disease in *Rogosanti* (as well as in my experiences in real life) coaxes and invites until finally the temptation to surrender becomes greater than the will to resist.

I have heard many other percussionists—including James Wood himself—present the drum materials as incisive and aggressive with great musical success. But I cannot liberate myself from my own metaphors. I prefer to think of the drum passages in *Rogosanti* as hypnotic and beautiful, as a Salome who lures rather than drives us towards a terrible fate. For me fury and defiance do not work as interpretive postures. An aggressive performance may convey the strength of disease, but simple loud playing presents an unconflicted emotional state that lets us off the hook too easily. Programmatic complexity degrades to simple description. The goal in *Rogosanti* is not to paint a villain and hero, as a conventional morality play might do, but rather to show the tension and contradiction inherent in process.

As we translate these ideas to performance strategy, each of the four opening drum phases gathers energy from beginning to end. The growth of intensity within each phrase follows a pathway of tonality where vigor increases at moments of dissonance and abates in moments of consonance. Configurations of dissonance and consonance in the upper drums derive from the tuning of the drums and their pitch relationship to the harmonically grounding marcato tones of the lower instruments. In my interpretation, the drums are tuned so that maximum consonance can be heard in scales featuring even or odd numbered drums. That is to say playing down a scale of drums 1, 3, 5, and 7 (effectively the outer rank of the set-up of drums), or playing drums 2, 4, 6, and 8 (the inner rank) produces the most coherent and consonant intervals (see figure 6.20).[4] Dissonance is caused by figures that cross between the two scales or by

4. I cannot suggest to others what might constitute a consonant set of tones. For me this has meant tuning the drums a bit lower than usual to maximize their sense of pitch and adopting diatonic intervals within a scale of consonance.

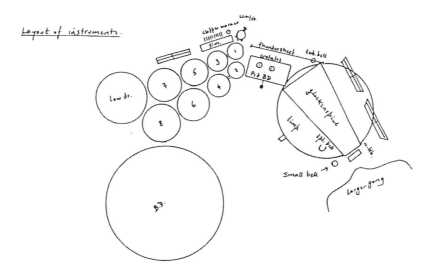

Figure 6.20. James Wood, *Rogosanti*, drawing of set-up. Used by permission.

moments where there is conflict between the tonalities of the rapid higher music and a harmonic marker in the instruments below. Swatches of consonance create brief moments of relative repose and recollection by means of euphonious tunings but also because consonant music focuses performance gestures over one of the two ranks of instruments. In these passages the player can face the instruments directly, allowing for greater ease and relaxation in performance. Dissonance torques the body and the music surges as the physical tension of performance abets the musical tension of disharmony to produce forward momentum. This alternation is very fast on the local level, but is reflected on a larger scale by the sense of cadence and repose at the end of each major section.

In global terms *Rogosanti* must always be in motion. The disease music is more *implication* than statement, constantly showing us what might happen, pathways it could take but will reserve for later. It teases with feints of growth and retreat, always in serpentine motion towards a goal, albeit a goal that we hope to avert. Nowhere, even at the tops of phrases, do I allow myself the expiatory release of real *fortissimo*. In my version, the single passage of all-out *fortississimo* playing comes just before the entrance of the healing

Figure 6.21. James Wood, *Rogosanti*, soft drum Passage, bars 124–133. Used by permission.

metals. It is the only point of stasis in the first part of the piece, and it signals that the disease has made its final play. This is the moment of truth and it can happen just once.

Even the succession of drum passages sketches an irregular path. One might expect each section to be louder and more forceful than the one before, but in fact the opposite occurs. The second section is steadier than the first (in my version the growth to *forte* also takes place later in this passage than it did in the first drumming passage) and the third is quite soft and spare. This third section, seen in figure 6.21, is the most beautiful and therefore the most emotionally serrated moment of the drum music. The unanswerable questions of false optimism surface here: Things are getting better, right? We've turned the corner, right? The *forte simantra* music that follows does not have to be played very loudly to achieve its sobering effect. Its very existence means that we are not finished.

When the healing music finally comes, the effect is almost rhetorical. The disease yields quickly and easily. (James told me that he had originally planned a protracted struggle between the metals and skins, but the performance difficulty of that many instrumental layers in different rhythms proved to be insurmountable.) After a quick revisitation of the opening vocal part and an ambiguous moment for maracas and thunder sheet, the metallic instruments assume primacy. But again, things are not simple. The quarter tones assure a sense of harmonic astringency that never really settles into the tonic of the gong/chime/temple bell cluster. The music is beautiful, but it is also distant, and the soft ticking of the wood block—the wooden sound is the sole vestigial remnant of the disease music—reminds us that the clock is running. We are safe . . . but perhaps only for the moment.

Is it necessary for a successful performance of *Rogosanti* to engage the programmatic aspects in such a literal and explicit way? Of course not. I have heard wonderful interpretations that seem to rely on a purely musical rationale. My claim here is simply for the value and strength of metaphor and how this can help cultivate emotional complexity in interpretation. The message of contemporary music has often been; *think,* don't feel. I avoided a purely "thoughtful" approach because I felt that *thinking* about *Rogosanti* would lead to straightforward virtuosity in performance. But thinking *and* feeling produces something much more improbable, contradictory, and inevitably more complex. How do we make sense of the dangerous disease music, even though it is beautiful and appealing? And what do we do with the repose of metal sounds that are laced with ominous sense of time running out? The answers to these questions outline the emotional relevance of this music and, beyond that, lead to issues of importance to any interpretation. They are the key to momentary vigor—in the form of passionate performances—and to musical longevity by developing the capacity to sustain a life's work.

Watershed (1995)

Roger Reynolds

My initial conversation with Roger Reynolds about a collaboration that would eventually become *Watershed* took place in 1991 at Chinary Ung's home in Tempe, Arizona, after a performance I gave of Reynolds' *Autumn Island* at Arizona State University. Talk turned to the emotional agency of gesture in percussion music; how meaning is conveyed by the way percussionists move while playing and even by the sculptural qualities of individualized percussion set-ups themselves. In this way percussion, with its focus on the visceral power of the body, seemed opposed to most current trends in contemporary music. The latest music technology in particular was not designed to respond to the physicality of performance.[5] Instead it had been largely geared towards the creation of new sounds either by synthesis or transformation. Percussionists, however, already having more sounds than they know what to do with, had remained largely outside the scope of investigation of new musical technologies.

Reynolds suggested that new technology involving spatialization might be able to re-create the internal space of a percussion set-up and by extension intimate at least part of the physical language of percussion.

5. At the time of this writing significant technology is being developed to read, capture, and respond to performance gesture and physicality.

To a performer the space inside of a set-up is important and palpable: to us the bongos are on the right, the gong behind, and the crotale up and to our left, for example. To a listener in a concert hall it all sounds like it come vaguely from "over there." *Watershed* became the testing ground for a technology that could spatialize percussion sounds and deploy them in five channels of loudspeakers surrounding the audience. Working with Peter Otto, Miller Puckette, and Tim Labor at the University of California, San Diego, Reynolds developed TRAnSiT, a computer-driven system that enables a sophisticated, real-time spatialization of live percussion sounds.

My role in the project was to design and develop a large, sculpturally vivid percussion set-up. See the composer's renderings of the set-up in figure 6.22. The notion of the piece was to place the audience "inside" a virtual instrument that would be mapped onto the loudspeakers. For this to succeed a viewer would have to make a connection between the configuration of instruments on stage and the way these sounds were tracked and manipulated in space. I proposed a strategy to Roger, which we later shaped, in a substantial and rewarding collaborative phase of refinement, to create a large arrangement of instruments that was purposely *not* optimized for physical efficiency. An efficient arrangement of instruments minimizes the amount of space between instruments. Efficiency makes any piece more easily playable, but it does so at the expense of reducing the visibility and emotional impact of the gestures of performance. Inefficiency as architectural variety in a set-up might then serve to amplify gesture. In percussion music there is always a struggle for primacy between the eyes and the ears. We are torn between looking and listening. In *Watershed* the goal was to unite the two by creating a strongly visual piece where the gestures of performance both supported the acoustical music of the piece and served to cue movements of sound in space.

There is a lot to contend with in *Watershed*: it is a piece with a large and varied instrumentation; it contains a sophisticated technological agenda; and, finally, it exists in multiple versions. The piece can be played as a chamber concerto for percussion solo with mini-orchestra and real-time spatialization or as a percussion solo alone with or without spatialization technology. In spite of these numerous performance options, the focus in *Watershed* from the outset was on the percussive material. The goal was to establish a nexus of vivid sounds that could germinate on the visual plane of performance as readable and provocative gesture and on the acoustical plane as the statement and transformation of emotionally charged music.

The set-up of *Watershed* consists of four groups of instruments, each presenting a strong sonic profile, a unique gestural trajectory and a defining emotional state.

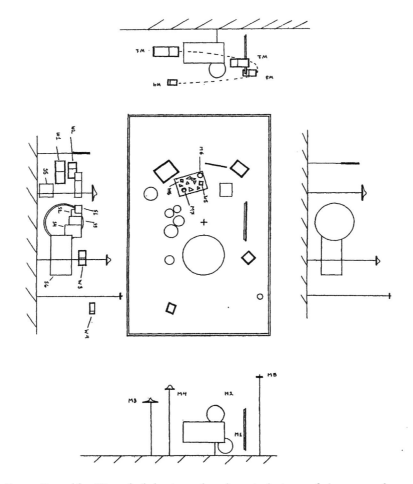

Figure 6.22. Roger Reynolds, *Watershed*, horizontal and vertical views of the set-up from score. Copyright © 1998 by C. F. Peters Corporation, Inc., New York. All rights reserved. Used by permission.

Drums: This group consists of a pair of bongos, a pair of "mini-congas," a pedal bass drum, and a concert bass drum. The drums are arranged in a tight formation with the high instruments on the right. They are positioned in typical fashion with stands placed at equal heights. The performer faces the audience directly while playing the drums and uses short and efficient gestures in performance. Especially at the beginning of the piece the drums are laconic and didactic, comprising a kind of philosopher's music.

Metals: The metal instruments are arranged in a loose rising spiral. The lowest instrument, a very large tam-tam, is placed on a low stand behind the performer. The rest of the instruments—a thin "wind gong," two cymbals, and a single crotale—move up on successively higher stands and to the left. This arrangement requires circular, sweeping movements. To fill in the large sonic gap between the gongs and the crotale, I piggyback two cymbals of slightly different sizes together using a hi-hat clutch to mount their domes back-to-back. This doubles the spectral density in the middle part of the metals scale. The metal instruments are resonant, enunciatory, and volatile.

Oddities: This is a heterogeneous scale of "odd" instruments small enough to be placed on a tray to the right of the player. The highest two are metallic sounds connecting to the scale of metal instruments; the lowest two are wooden sounds connecting to the group of wooden instruments described below. The oddities are the *id* of the set-up, by nature a group of quirky and unpredictable noises that perturb the otherwise unified sound fields of the other groups.

Woods: A set of four wooden snare drums—each consists of a simple wooden box mounted on a cymbal stand where several strands of wire have been affixed to the underside of the striking surface— is positioned in a spiral rising from right to left at the extreme periphery of the set-up. The lowest is located to the right of the player at about the level of the drums; the treble drum is positioned just within reach as high as possible and to the left. The wooden drums are sharp, irritating noises. They criticize and interrupt the efforts of the other instruments from afar.

The specific choice of sounds was the key to dealing with a broad range of related issues, especially the projection of form, a central concern in all of Roger Reynolds' music. In a Reynolds piece, ideas joust in a dense musical space. Each seeks room to grow and flourish. *Watershed* is certainly no exception, and consequently controlling the flow and focus of information became a critical problem for both the composer and performer. The composer was faced with the need to create a formal design large and resolute enough to frame and focus the plenitude of momentary possibilities. Too many sounds and ideas in a vessel that was not seaworthy would result in "leakage." Sounds would spill out, and since they were unaccounted for within a large-scale formal plan and robbed of purposefulness, they might easily become mere sound effects. On the performer's side of the equation, a robust and expansive formal scheme demands that material be vividly and energetically engaged. An overly polite approach in performance would fail to activate the sonic material sufficiently to fuel forward momentum. As a result *Watershed* became a long and intensely driven piece.

The length and intensity of *Watershed*—thirty minutes of nonstop action—became the topic of many conversations I had with Roger in the planning stages of the work. I expressed concern that the solo percussion repertoire consisted almost entirely of short pieces. There is a handful of works that last about six or seven minutes in length (Javier Alvarez' *Temazcal*, Morton Feldman's *The King of Denmark*, and Vinko Globokar's *?Corporel* among others). However, most pieces are between ten and twelve minutes in length. Why were there no percussion pieces equivalent in length and scope to the great works of tonal music, the late string quartets of Beethoven, for example? And by extension, what would it take in the world of percussion to construct a longer, more formally complex piece?

Extended pieces of tonal music function by channeling an unpredictable flow of information—the unique ideas and visions of a given composer—along a known pathway—the inherited and mutually understood grammar of tonal harmony. But in posttonal, postserial, essentially *postgenre* percussion music, a "mutually understood" compositional grammar simply does not exist. Many composers solve this problem by adopting preexisting compositional or cultural models. This method has produced a lot of good music. Among the finer examples are Kevin Volan's *She Who Sleeps with a Small Blanket*, which draws upon the composer's African heritage, and the Zen rituals of Toshio Hosokawa's *Sen VI* (1993). Even Cage's indeterminate *27'10.554"* relies on the familiar model of the ultimate randomness of nature. With many other pieces that lack an external point of reference, brevity itself often becomes a formal strategy. The secret to the twelve-minute piece is that it is long enough to define its own world of ideas, but short enough to be fueled by momentary interactions among materials.

However, *Watershed*'s thirty minutes of bongos, gongs, scrapers, and boxes—no matter how interesting the music may be at any moment—demands a sophisticated strategy of organization. Reynolds quotes neither tonality nor world music. Instead he offers an interlocking two-part global strategy. One part is musical: Reynolds maps an interleaved formal plan that evolves by means of the statement and contraposition of the four instrument groups. The other is metaphorical: each group is laced with emotional inclinations that are revealed to the listener through sound and related physical gestures. Instrumental groups therefore function as a cast of characters with the dual roles of creating a fluidly evolving musical sense that is firmly anchored to the universalizing terrain of human emotion.

Sonically *Watershed* accumulates around a primary spiral of massive metallic "clock events," indicated by boxes in the score. The player interrupts the flow of time to play the clock events: they are the mammoth, weight-bearing pylons of the formal architecture of the piece. The clock events start with the low tam-tam and work upwards through the scale of metal instruments to the critical "watershed" point of the piece where the direction of the clock events reverses. (Note that in the score the lowest metal instrument is found at the top of the staff to maintain the convention of a keyboard notation where instruments to the player's right are at the top of the staff. This notational decision underscores the critical concern of the location of instruments in space.)

As a consequence of the very slow pacing of the spiraling clock events over the course of the piece, rising from the lowest metal through the scale and back, *Watershed* is a piece in slow but constant motion. The opening passages of the piece show how this constant sense of circular movement is reinforced on the local level by smaller spirals in three of the four instrument groups. On page 1 of the score (figure 6.23), the metals rise quickly through their scale and are immediately imitated by the drums. A longer downward scale of metals in bar 4 is echoed by a quick descent in the drums. At the end of the first page the oddities join the fray as they outline the descending metals phrase. Instrument groups feature shared behavior here, but are clearly differentiated by phrase and color: musical lines do not cross the boundaries among groups and differences of color neatly articulate the acoustical capacities and expressive intent of one group from another.

Clearly the instrument group is central to the development of *Watershed*. Equally clearly, each group attempts to imitate the spiraling shapes of the clock events. The shared spiral shapes confer a unity of design and urge common cause among groups in spite of their dissimilar sounds. Common cause is easily derailed however, as we shall soon see, and the opposing sound worlds of the groups quickly begin to chafe. Soon the rhetoric of each group—its particular set of colors, performance techniques, and aesthetic disposition—begins to create a vocabulary that is increasingly specialized and idiomatic to each. Uncommon cause, in other words. The drums begin by exploring the same terrain as the other groups do, but they become increasingly "drum-like" as the piece progresses through its opening stages. The same goes for the metals, which are pushed by their intrinsic sonic qualities towards spectral complexity and musical volatility. In the same way the wooden instruments sharpen their voice as critics and the oddities become

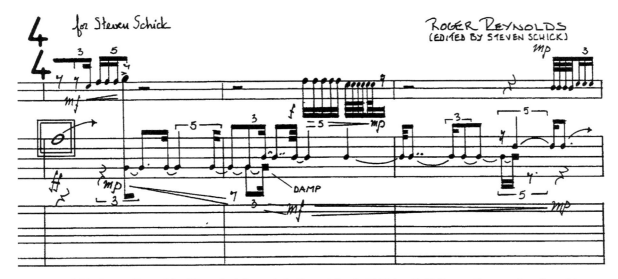

Figure 6.23. Roger Reynolds, *Watershed*, bars 4–6. Copyright © 1998 by C. F. Peters Corporation, Inc., New York. All rights reserved. Used by permission.

increasingly odd. This is the force of percussive material at work: medium determines message, and as a result the voice of an instrument develops in response to its sound. The sense of sharpened opposition among the groups is critical to the compositional intent of the first part of *Watershed*. The process of rapprochement, which dominates the second half of the piece and creates both sonic and emotional common ground among the groups, would certainly lose its impact as metaphor if the groups were not sufficiently polarized at the beginning.

The opposition of groups also creates a collage of physical gestures. *Watershed* embodies a basic truth of percussion playing: it is the shape and disposition of the instruments and not the nature of their music that determines gesture. A simple scale on a series of tightly arranged drums looks very different from the same scale on a dispersed arrangement of large gongs and cymbals. In *Watershed* these oppositions are telegraphed vividly. Performing the drum music means that the percussionist faces the audience and plays small instruments mounted at waist height. This music produces almost no readable gestures. The same

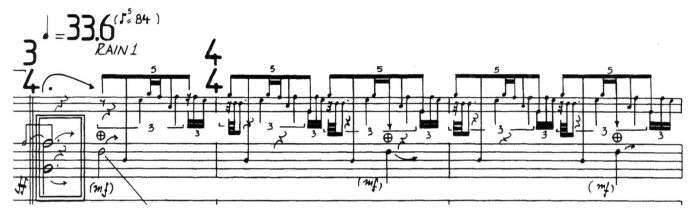

Figure 6.24. Roger Reynolds, *Watershed*, Rain I, opening. Copyright © 1998 by C. F. Peters Corporation, Inc., New York. All rights reserved. Used by permission.

phrase played on metals involves the whole body in large swinging motions. The forward momentum of the piece—as it results from the opposition of instrument groups—is mirrored exactly by a unique repertory of gestures. The shape of the piece is clear even with the sound turned down.

As the piece drives towards its watershed moment and the inevitable combat among oppositional forces, three curiously static and poignant sections interrupt forward motion. The composer calls these sections Rain I, Rain II, and Rain III. (These sections will be mirrored in much more turbulent form by sections in the second half of the piece that Reynolds refers to as "storms.") Part of the beauty of real rain is the depth of its sound and by consequence the diminished importance of any fixed point of perception: when you stand in the rain you are neither closer to it nor farther away from it than another person standing in the rain. Another great beauty of rain is that it is in fact not the rain that we hear at all; it is the object that the rain strikes. If we say we love the sound of rain on our rooftop, it is really the sound of the roof that we love. In an unexpected meteorological confirmation of my mother's dictum, rain is not an instrument, but a mallet. And like all sticks it focuses our attention on the act of playing rather than the sounds of playing. The three rain sections in *Watershed*, Rain I on page 5 (seen in figure 6.24), Rain II on page 9, and Rain III on page 16, as models of sonic integration, therefore tend to flatten the sense of depth in the world of sonority. The performer's gestures follow suit, and a sense of choreographic weightlessness ensues as the gestural imperatives of any given instrumental group are suspended in favor of coexistence among all groups.

As if to recover from the embarrassment of their momentary complicity, the groups attack each other with renewed intensity after each "Rain." The drums become increasingly percussive, the metals more mercurial. The friendly opposition of the opening yields to open conflict as the piece approaches its critical pivotal moment. This pivotal moment is the "watershed" of the piece: it is the point of no return, where spirals spin downwards rather than up; group identity begins to soften, sonic materials commingle, and nothing will ever be the same again.

This is the moment in the piece that I live for. It is the moment that poses questions of the greatest personal importance to me. What happens to a secure identity in the face of ratcheting pressure from the outside? What happens to memory after profound change? (I sometimes wonder if the instruments remember the repose and communion of the rain music after they have been whipped into a renewed fury of opposition.) It is largely the answers to these questions and their impact on the metaphor of the piece rather than the organization of sounds as pure music that drives my interpretation. I am fascinated by the interaction of the drum and metal music, for example. It describes a classic arc of personal transformation. At the beginning the drums are laconic and self-confident. Their brush with the more voluble metals group, especially in the intimate environment of the rains, challenges their academic smugness. Their reaction? At first, reassertion and reinvigoration of the innate rightness of their original point of view. Continued pressure by the increasingly volatile metal music yields a violent counterattack in the form of the drum cadenzas on pages 13 and 23. The metals mount their own response in the form of a series of single long screams (see figure 6.25).

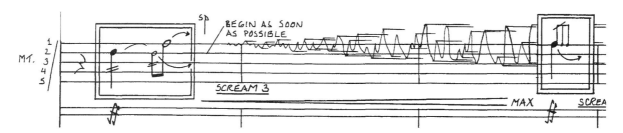

Figure 6.25. Roger Reynolds, *Watershed*, Scream. Copyright © 1998 by C. F. Peters Corporation, Inc., New York.

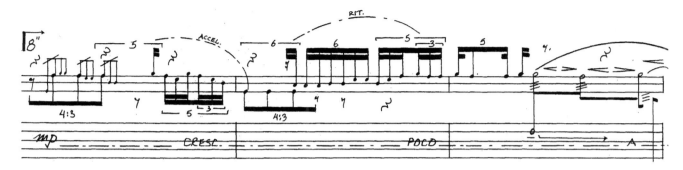

Figure 6.26. Roger Reynolds, *Watershed*, Lyrical drums, 3 bars near end of piece. Copyright © 1965 by C. F. Peters Corporation, Inc., New York. All rights reserved. Used by permission.

However, even as each increasingly vigorous drum moment is answered by escalating energy from the metals and each metal scream seems to redouble the efforts of the drums, the two groups begin to approach one another. By increments the drums extend their short repetitive phrases as though in imitation of the inherent qualities of resonance and decay of the metals. The large sweeping gestures associated with the metal instruments become smaller and more intense as the music imitates the short, focused strokes of drumming.

Combative energy is finally spent; the assertion of the self and resistance to the other has dissipated, and both groups find themselves fundamentally changed. The drums, once confident and rational, have entered the much less predictable world of intuition and lyricism (figure 6.26). The metals have become chaste. Their power comes from a quiet statement of their inherent beauty rather than from vigorous assertion. The heat of interaction has warped the divergent paths of the two groups towards each other. The drums have inherited poetry from the metals; the metals a new modesty from the drums. Each group has found something new by giving up something old.

This is ultimately what both produces and requires that *Watershed* be a piece of length and intensity. Profound change does not come quickly or without cost. It takes a long time. It's exhausting and requires, as my grandmother used to say, that you have to give to get.

I often tell my students that percussion is irrelevant. Admittedly this is something of a pedagogical provocation—I want my students to think carefully about what they are doing and why. But in many ways I also really mean it: percussion *is* irrelevant, which is not to say that it is unimportant. What I mean is that the material of percussion—the perfect gong or just the right marimba—is irrelevant until it is applied against just the right musical problem. And that musical problem is irrelevant until it is applied to an important part of life beyond music. Under some circumstances "just the right marimba" might be the out-of-tune instrument that nobody plays. Ask Tom Waits or Arnold Dreyblatt about that one. Instruments are not sacred in percussion; sounds and ideas in isolation aren't either. Real music played by real people is, though. And sometimes I feel that I can't hear the music or see the people because they are obscured by just the right sound.

A moment that I will never forget clarified this for me once and for all. It is a small and personal story. In May 2000 I played a concert in Israel with my duo partner, the extraordinary cellist Maya Beiser, to celebrate the fiftieth anniversary of the founding of the kibbutz she grew up on. Even after several visits to Israel, the Middle East is a pretty exotic place for me. We drove up from Tel Aviv, passed by the mosque in the nearby Arab village and were greeted at Kibbutz Gazit by members of the concert committee who were eager to show me the marimba that they had borrowed from a local school. I was also anxious to see it since our repertoire is centered largely on the marimba, often in combination with other instruments. They wheeled an instrument in and, with all eyes on me, said they hoped it would be satisfactory. It wasn't. I had traveled nearly ten thousand miles and the concert instrument I requested turned out to be a student model xylophone. But I nodded bravely and said it would all be fine. After all, these were good people who had gone to great trouble to find what they thought I wanted. It was a beautiful spring afternoon going on 6 P.M., and I sat at the stage end of the dining room where the concert was to be held and wondered just exactly how it would all be fine. I was still sitting there when some older people started to file in for the concert. A man sat next to me, looked up and smiled. When I saw the fading numbers tattooed on his arm, I realized, as though further realization was needed, that there are so many more important things in life than finding just the right marimba.

By the way, the concert was fine.

Same Bed, Different Dreams
A Personal Epilogue

When I turned fifty a few months ago I was struck by the thought that I was older than the oldest solo piece in my repertoire. Of course I was older than the oldest piece when I was ten too, but that fact didn't seem to have the same impact then as it has now. As a percussionist, I again found myself in the midst of a unique contradiction: percussion playing is an ancient art form, but notated music for solo percussion is very recent. Almost as soon as there was a piano or a cello or a violin, there was music for piano and cello and violin so that the history of those instruments and the history of music for those instruments is nearly indistinguishable. With percussion playing, the discrepancy between the history of the instrument and its first use in the practice of notated classical music is extreme. A *tabla* player draws on a tradition that is thousands of years old unless that player is playing the *tabla* music in Berio's *Circles*, in which case he or she is drawing on a tradition that can be measured in decades.

Imagine a pianist who is older than the oldest piece in his or her repertoire. Or imagine what it was like to play the first performance of the Brahms Violin Concerto or a Bach Cello Suite. Imagine in essence what it was like when the music we think of as classical—that is to say, established, revered, inalterable—was still new and unformed. You do not have to imagine. This is the current state of solo percussion, an instrumental art form that was born and has matured within the span of the lifetimes of many of us. The short history of notated percussion music also calls into question the matter of history itself. Percussion repertory that came of age in the historical period of Sputnik, Watergate, and Osama bin Laden functions very differently with respect to its position in history than does piano music, which reached early maturity with the French Revolution, the Napoleonic wars, and the cotton gin. To Mozart globalization meant an opera libretto in German rather than Italian. The world to him was Europe. Percussionists who live fully in the world at the beginning of the current millennium are thinking about the role of the Indonesian *bonang* in the music of the British composer James Wood or how *Snow in June*, Tan Dun's heart-wrenching piece for cello and four percussionists written as a response to the massacre at Tiananmen Square might play in Toledo (Spain or Ohio—take your pick). We must necessarily concern ourselves with places and contexts that would have been wholly foreign to music in the time of Bach or Mendelssohn.

Clearly we have changed. Beyond that, even the notion of "we" has changed. "We" has come to mean much more than composers and their pieces. "We" now also means performers, commissioning agencies, music critics, recording engineers, and listeners. As John Cage said, "Here comes everybody." Let's not forget that making and listening to percussion music is a group effort that involves foreground concerns like composition and performance, but also includes other essential activities like lighting design, mallet wrapping, arts management, and ticket sales. Try playing a concert in the dark the next time you think of yourself as a "solo artist."

Another realization caused no small amount of psychic discomfort as I turned fifty: I am a classical musician. After years of wishing that I were one of those highly adaptable creatures of the late twentieth century, equally at home in rock, jazz, World, improvised, and notated music, I see that I am actually quite limited. I perform my generation's version of classical music: that is to say that I almost always engage an objective reality—a musical score—with a range of skills that is rooted in subjectivity. In other words, I interpret.

There are considerable differences of opinion about what it means to "interpret" a work of notated music. There are also loud arguments about whether interpretation in any of its many forms is desirable at all. Interpretation has usually meant one kind of thing in the performance of late twentieth-century contemporary music: the interpreter was to be a dispassionate medium for the transmission of objectively coded musical material. The goal for a performer was to play the music as well as possible and, equally, to stay out of the way as much as possible. This approach was meant to depersonalize musical interpretation and at its best tended towards a universalizing performance practice. Many performers of recent contemporary music who underwrite this point of view believe that the purest musical experience is the one that most closely resembles the information in the score. These performers therefore tend to favor neutral interpretations designed to represent the point of view of the composer instead of personal or idiosyncratic ones that might be more about the views of the performer. There is no doubt that a strong sense of responsibility towards the wishes of the composer is a worthy stance, but what about those scores, several of which are discussed at length above, that posit multiple and mutually exclusive interpretative strategies—where a performer *must* make a personal and sometimes idiosyncratic choice among available interpretative options? The surest way to fail in *Bone Alphabet*, *The King of Denmark*, or *Watershed* is to try to do everything. By choosing among several possible interpretative strategies, an interpreter not only transmits, but also highlights, colors, and shades.

I admit that this implicit correlation between the fixed and flexible—the rapport between the score and any given interpretation of the score, between *the* world and *my* world—is what really interests me about performing. Each concert is not only a chance to reach a new audience; it is a chance to reach a new understanding of a piece of music. And, because "understanding the music" in the world of percussion invokes a web of issues that moves far beyond what may or may not happen onstage to embrace historical, cultural, intellectual, and emotional concerns of our time, the relationship between a piece and its interpretation is full of vivid and dynamic opportunities. We percussionists, whether we like it or not, are summoned to creative interpretative interventions that not only react to, but also serve to shape the world we inhabit.

The title of this book comes from an experience I had on a late-night flight home to San Diego. I had been on tour in Europe with the Bang on a Can All-Stars, and as usual, when the rest of the group disembarked in New York, I was left with another six or so hours in the air back to the West Coast. I was bored with the movie and was trying to read an article in the *Wall Street Journal* about western economic interests in Asia over the shoulder of a passenger in front of me. The headline read "Same Bed, Different Dreams." I couldn't really see the text of the article and was probably too tired to focus on the topic anyway, but the poetry of the headline intrigued me. To me the message was that different human beings confronting the same set of objective experiences would necessarily interpret those experiences differently as a reflection of their different cultural and personal views of the world. The fact that two people can sleep in the same bed and dream vividly different things means that the differences between the people override the sameness of the bed. The reverse also holds true: our differences of habit, culture, and appearance—no matter how significant these may seem—are only small variations on a profoundly shared common basis.

I quickly translated the two facets of this metaphor for coexistence into musical terms. Two musicians faced with the same score or the same instrument will necessarily make music that reflects the unique experiences of each. We celebrate the differences among percussive dreams, so to speak, by contrasting Sylvio Gualda's version of *Psappha* with Gert Mortenson's. Likewise we expect different music from the drummers of New Guinea than we do from the drummers of New Mexico. *Vive la différence!* But just as performing music diversifies us in important ways, it also communalizes us. The earliest stage of my friendship with the Polish percussionist Stanislav Skoczynski, for example, was based almost entirely on the fact that we both played *Psappha*. Stasek had spent his first years in communist-era Warsaw and I on a turkey farm in northern Iowa, but simply by confronting the galvanizing set of thorny problems and questions in *Psappha* we developed an important common bond.

Drumming (1971)

Steve Reich

From the fall of 1970 to the fall of 1971, the period during which Steve Reich wrote his percussion masterpiece, *Drumming*, he did many things. He created the first large-scale piece of percussion chamber music by an American composer in nearly thirty years. He established a working ensemble of percussionists who continue to play together to this day and who have performed this piece and many others throughout the world. And, importantly, under the heading of same beds and different dreams, he created an utterly ingenious dual model for musical coexistence within a discontinuous cultural environment. One part of the Reich model of coexistence regulates the relationship among a complex of musical cultures that influence this music, and the second part creates a unique rapport among no fewer than twelve musicians themselves as they rehearse and perform the piece.

Drumming lasts more than an hour, and, without exception, the entirety of the piece is based on a single rhythm in 3/2 meter (see figure 7.1). The piece consists of four parts: Part I for tuned bongos; Part II for marimbas and voices; Part III for glockenspiels and piccolo or whistling; and Part IV for all of the instruments playing together.

Four basic compositional treatments of the principal rhythm in *Drumming* provide variety and generate both localized material and large-scale form in the piece:

1. *Building up and down.* The principal rhythm builds up or builds down at least once in Parts I, III, and IV. Only Part II, for marimbas and female voices, does not feature a buildup or builddown. The process of building up starts with a single note. Gradually the performers add one note at a time, each time repeating the pattern several times in its partially constructed state, until the entire rhythm is present. Building down reverses the process by subtracting one note at a time until a single note is left.

2. *Phasing.* Rhythmic complexity is achieved when a performer phases forward or backward against a sounding rhythm. The most basic example of this comes at the beginning of the piece. Two bongo players play the principal rhythm in unison. One of them then speeds up very slightly so that the two

Figure 7.1. Steve Reich, *Drumming*, principal rhythm. Copyright © 1973 by Hendon Music, Inc., a Boosey & Hawkes company. Reprinted by permission.

rhythms come out of phase with each other. The phasing player continues to speed up until his or her rhythm locks into place one quarter note ahead of the basic rhythm. Although both players continue to play exactly the same rhythm, the first beats of their patterns now fall at different times and their combined patterns create a complex web of melodic and rhythmic interactions.

3. *Resultant patterns.* Brief sections of resultant patterns (see figure 7.2 for resultant patterns in Part II) underscore the new rhythmic combinations that result from phasing. Take the bongo phase above. After the phase has been completed, a third bongo player highlights the new composite rhythm by playing short patterns that combine material taken from both of the original players. This underscores the communal nature of the piece. The evolving rhythmic structures in the piece are composites and cannot be played by a single performer. In fact as a general rule the more complex and multifaceted the composite rhythm, the greater the number of performers needed to create it. Since the resultant patterns are not solos but rather reinforcements, an easily blended rather than a contrasting sound is used to articulate them. In Part I bongos or male voices are used to reinforce the resultant bongo rhythms; in Part II women's voices sing wordless syllables to underline resultant patterns from the marimba music; in Part III the piccolo and whistling imitate the sound of the glockenspiels; and in Part IV all of the above pairings are present in one final joyous moment where all instruments and their resultant partners play together.

4. *New material.* On occasion a player simply starts a new rhythmic or melodic version of the principal rhythm without building up or phasing into it. New material starts directly at full volume rather than fading in. The abruptness and relative rarity of these moments makes them especially memorable and therefore useful as demarcations of form. The sudden appearance of new material in each of the fours parts of the piece usually presages a passage of maximum ensemble engagement and energy.

Figure 7.2. Steve Reich, *Drumming*, last resultant of Part II. Copyright © 1973 by Hendon Music, Inc., a Boosey & Hawkes company. Reprinted by permission.

Drumming consists of 122 measures, each of which contains one of the four basic compositional actions of the piece: building the principal rhythm up or down, phasing forward or backward, presenting resultant patterns, or introducing new material. Each measure is to be repeated an undetermined number of times and is completed when the performer in charge of executing the action finishes his or her task. Thus the job of directing the forward motion of the piece is passed around the ensemble. At some point or another each of the twelve musicians has the chance (and responsibility) to control the pacing of the piece.

Each section of the piece differs slightly in the way it deploys the four basic compositional actions. The formal design of Part I establishes the paradigm for the entire piece as follows. The principal rhythm is first built up. A single player plays one note and is then joined, one by one, by the others. A second note is added, also joined player by player, then a third, and so on, until the entire rhythm is present. Once the principal rhythm has been established, it is then followed by a series of phases separated in each case by resultant patterns. This leads ultimately to a four-part polyphonic complex where each percussionist performs the principal rhythm starting on a different beat of the bar. The entire complex then phases to unison and builds down, player by player, as a single note of the rhythm is removed until the four bongo players arrive at a single note. Up until this point the bongo players have been using the hard side of double ended sticks. While the group continues to repeat a single note, the players change one by one to the soft end of the stick.

A second buildup produces the same principal rhythm. However this time the melodic profile is different and utilizes only three of the four bongos. A new round of phasing ensues until a rich three-part polyphonic structure is reached and, as before, each player begins his or her rhythm on a different beat of the bar. The remaining fourth player then "turns the sticks around." He or she doubles the rhythm of each of the players one at a time, allowing that player to drop out momentarily and change the sticks back to the hard side. The three-part polyphonic complex changes color before our ears. At this moment, the smallest drum pitched at C sharp, which has been missing since the midpoint of the movement, is added to the mix one player at a time. On a cue the players change suddenly to new material: an entirely new melody still using the principal rhythm creates a swirling moment of maximal polyphonic density. Then one by one the sticks are turned around again to the soft side. The three players hold this rhythm as three marimba players, playing exactly the same patterns and pitches fade up to replace the bongos. Part II begins. Variations on this formal paradigm of buildup, phasing, resultant patterns, color change, and new material ensue in each of the remaining three parts of the piece. A performance of *Drumming* then consists of an ordered series of tasks, each of which is led by one of the performers.

Drumming could not have come into my life at a better moment. In August of 1992 I was at the end of a ten-year period during which I assisted James Wood in the summers of even-numbered years in our percussion course at the Darmstadt Ferienkurse für Neue Musik. The preceding musical season of 1991–92 had been an especially productive and occasionally turbulent one for me: I had started a new teaching position at the University of California, San Diego, and over the first year or so of my new position I had premiered Brian Ferneyhough's *Bone Alphabet* and David Lang's *The Anvil Chorus*, and given the American premiere of Xenakis's *Rebonds*. It seemed as if learning these works brought me to an impasse in my development as a percussionist. If solo playing was about self-definition and accomplishment, as I believed at the time, then what came next? Did I try to find music that was more difficult then *Bone Alphabet* or more resolute than *The Anvil Chorus*, more heroic than *Rebonds*? I didn't know where to go or what to do next. In what was to be my final year on the Darmstadt faculty, I had just played the Lang and the Ferneyhough pieces on the regular concert I shared with pianist James Avery, my longtime friend and duo partner. As usual, when that concert was over, I joined James Wood and the rest of the percussion studio in a large-scale project. Next was Steve Reich's *Drumming*.

Years of playing complex music had prepared me for certain kinds of technical difficulties and a certain quality of joy in performance. I thought I had seen everything, but *Drumming* opened the doors to a completely new set of problems and experiences for me. On a technical level, none of the rhythmic patterns was difficult to learn, but holding a rhythm in a loop of repetition, sometimes for many minutes, while other players phased against it *was* difficult. Until I played *Drumming*, I am sure I had never performed anything with that many repeat signs—my mostly modernist repertoire placed greater value on nearly constant change rather than on verbatim repetition. That much repetition left me without a constant stream of varied problems to solve. And without a rapidly changing and highly differentiated set of problems, I literally did not know what to *think* as I played *Drumming*.

I was lost: the music seemed simple to me, yet I was not playing it very well. Following my usual practice method—one that had worked until then—I simply tried harder. I devised strategies to keep my mind engaged in the task of repeating the same rhythm: I imagined the music on the page; I observed the patterns on the drums; I focused on my right and then my left hand; I changed the feel of the 3/2 rhythm from three to two and back by concentrating on the half note then dotted half note pulse respectively. In short, I thought about what I was doing as intensely as I could. Nothing seemed to work. One of the early problems I confronted in *Drumming* rehearsals was that when my concentration failed, I simply stopped playing. Not a good idea. I had just come off a performance of *Bone Alphabet*, arguably the most difficult work in the entire solo percussion repertoire, and now I was routinely being defeated by eighth and quarter notes.

Then in an unforgettable moment—when the technical problem I had struggled with mutated into an expressive possibility I had not yet considered—*Drumming* hit me over the head. Hard. I saw that I had not understood the piece at all, nor the rest of Steve Reich's music for that matter. In a realization that was simultaneously one of awakening and conversion, I saw that the piece was not about repetition as I had thought, but about transformation. In other words it was not about tasks, or at least not only about tasks, but about fluidly evolving contexts. I realized, among many other things, that even when one player repeats a pattern, other players are changing their patterns. The global sense of the music is *never* static: the piece in other words is not about one of us; it is about all of us.

As I moved my focus away from my personal task to the communal task, I began to adopt a state of mind in performance that was more defined by "fluid" than by "solid." I began think of this state of mind as an *aware trance*, a condition which, among other things, redefined the notion of the *problem* of performance. I had thought of performing chamber music as the attentive stewardship of a small part of a larger whole. Information was to flow from small to large along the scale of detail whereby each individual playing his or her part well predictably created an effective and good-sounding performance. The final result was designed to reflect the sum of its parts. With *Drumming*, the problem in performance was reversed. I learned that the first goal was to assure the rightness of the community—if everybody sounds good together then that means that you are playing your part well.

I should like to take a moment to explain what I am doing here. My comments above are not an elaborated discussion of Steve Reich or his music. That is clearly not the case and would certainly lie beyond the scope of this book. Nor am I offering a theoretical or practical analysis of *Drumming*—this is, after all, a book about solo percussion music. What I am engaged in here is a simple appreciation of the enormous impact *Drumming* has had on me and on my playing, and of what I have learned from the music of Steve Reich as I have returned to it again and again in the years since my conversion on the road to Darmstadt. In August of 1992 I was wondering how to go forward—not just how to play better, but how to play in a way that deepened the relationship between the music I played and the life I was living. By articulating and elucidating questions of culture and of the rapport between the individual and group, *Drumming* in essence got me unstuck. The questions I found there might be broadly construed as: "Where do I come from?" "How did I get here?" And further, "What do I do with the other people I find here?" Such questions always lurked towards the background of my musical consciousness as seemingly less relevant to the performance of a piece of music than questions like "How do I learn this rhythm?" or "Where can I buy that mallet?" By reversing these fore- and background relationships, *Drumming* functioned, almost from the first moment I played it, as an allegory for culture and context.

Steve Reich visited Ghana on a study trip of the music of West Africa in the year before he composed *Drumming*. As a result he has repeatedly been asked about the role of African and other non-Western sources on his subsequent music. He answered these questions eloquently in his *Writing about Music*,[1] sections of which were reprinted as the notes for his recording of *Drumming*. Here he stated that for him the study of African music was *confirmation*. I can think of no more illuminating comment than this for a percussionist who seeks to disentangle issues of globalism and cultural homogeneity that surround current practices in contemporary percussion music. Yes, the use of drums in tightly cycling periodic patterns in *Drumming* is a quality found in African music, just as the heavily nested contrapuntal structures where several simple parts combine to create a complex whole is a characteristic of Indonesian gamelan. But the former is also part of every jazz drummer's vocabulary thanks to African American music, and the latter is a technique well known to anyone who loves the music of Bach. *Drumming* does not appropriate ideas from other cultures; it confirms them and resonates with them.

Any percussionist who worries that by borrowing an idea or a sound across cultural boundaries he or she may cross the line between healthy cross-fertilization and the hegemony of appropriation would do well to rephrase Steve Reich's observation as a question. To what extent does the idea or sound in question reinforce strands of connection among cultures and tap a mutually sustaining pool of musical wisdom? Is there resonance or is there only decoration? With the former something is created and with the latter something is lost. Evolutionary biologists measure the health of an ecosystem by its biodiversity: that is to say the extent to which an environment is creating or losing species and whether those species are viable and individualized. This is an important issue in the world of percussion as well. I once heard a performance by a well-known American university percussion ensemble of a piece in which a standard blues progression was meekly rendered on the instruments of a Balinese gamelan. The piece, while raising a few smiles among the mostly academic percussion audience, managed to diminish the blues, the tradition of the gamelan, and the worthy history of the percussion ensemble in western classical music all in one blow.

---

1. Steve Reich, *Writings about Music* (Halifax, NS: Press of Nova Scotia College of Art and Design; New York: New York University Press, 1974).

Beyond pointing to a model of cultural coexistence, *Drumming* also demonstrates a new way of musical interaction within a chamber ensemble. This is simple to describe: no one leads *Drumming*. In fact nowhere else in the entire chamber music repertoire for percussion is there an example of such a mutually dependent and communally reinforced musical structure. Stewardship of the piece is a group concern, progressing as one player after another completes his or her specific task(s) from building up to phasing to playing resultant patterns. For audiences who are accustomed to understanding chamber music in the model of the string quartet, where the first violinist plays the primary—read dominating—role of dictating the pacing of a piece and the nuances of interpretation as a conductor might do, *Drumming* seems to progress, leaderless, with very few visual cues and no real dominant voice. True, the opening bongo player has an especially visible role—and I can tell you from experience that the moment of breaking the silence with the first stroke of the first buildup of the piece is a heady one—but there will also be a moment when the ninth marimbist or the third glockenspiel player will hold the piece in his or her hands. Reich was right in making this an ensemble piece of live performers rather than one his "counterpoint pieces" where most of the parts are prerecorded. The great parable of this music—that the health and vitality of the whole is tied to the health and vitality of the smallest of its parts—requires the presence of human beings who need each other and who make space for each other.

This is the payoff for me—the way in which parable becomes practice. As Ghana was for Steve Reich, *Drumming* has been for me. Confirmation. The central premise of *Drumming* is that a dynamic rapport among individuals within a group can be amplified by common cause among the individuals and enlivened by diversity within the group. This notion confirms the relationship between the one and the many that I see in John Luther Adams's *The Mathematics of Resonant Bodies*, with its image of the individual as a singular "vertical zip" against the unmapped vastness of environmental space. *Drumming* confirms my sense that groups are identified by the deep alignments of shared values and behavior rather than by superficial resemblance. This idea, seen in the way individual sounds adopt a strong sense of group affiliation, now nourishes my views of *Psappha* and of *The Anvil Chorus*. In the same vein *Drumming* confirms my view of *Ionisation* as "an immigrant's music" where questions of belonging (or failing to belong) steer powerful trajectories of transformation that shape the ways in which identity is created and guarded.

There is a dynamic harmony to be found among manifold competing and often oppositional forces within *Drumming*—oppositions parsed as the rapport between the individual and the group, between the simplicity of components and the complexity of the whole, between the need to repeat and the inevitability of change. Harmony here is then not defined by the absence of conflict but by the presence of a poetry born of frictions. This "harmony of opposition" confirms my understanding of George Lewis's *North Star Boogaloo* as fundamentally melancholy in spite of its raucous surface, and of Roger Reynolds' architecturally rigorous *Watershed* as mostly about the incandescence of intuition. The way I see oppositions in the solo music of Vinko Globokar is also there. Look to his twinned fables of *Toucher* and *?Corporel*: the former is a vision of the outsider looking in and the latter of the insider looking out.

I started my life as a musician by wanting to be a solo percussionist (as indeed I started this book by wanting to write about solo percussion). But in the end *Drumming* reminds us that "solo" does not mean "alone." *Drumming* confirms the communal nature of every aspect of music-making, regardless of whether one person or many people happen to be standing on stage. In a fitting bit of irony, the most important message for a solo percussionist can be found in a piece written for twelve musicians: you cannot go it alone.

I participated in a recent performance of *Drumming* in Perth with members of Defying Gravity, the percussion group of young students that Tim White founded at the Western Australia Academy for the Performing Arts. It was the gracefulness of passing the flame of responsibility around the ensemble that was, again as always, so moving. And again, as always, arriving at the final moment of the piece after the last phase of Part IV reminded me *why* this is the most joyous moment I ever experience on stage. At that very moment of the performance in Perth, after an hour of passing the responsibility and focus from one person to another, when we were finally locked in as one to the rhythm of blissfully spinning eighth notes, all of the members of the ensemble looked up spontaneously from their instruments and smiled at each other: we had arrived.

Together.

Bibliography

Baddeley, Alan. *Your Memory: A User's Guide*. New York: Macmillan, 1982.

Beckett, Samuel. *That Time*. In Beckett, *Collected Shorter Plays*, 226–35. New York: Grove Press, 1984.

Borges, Jorge Luis. "Funes, the Memorious." In Borges, *Fictions*, edited with an introduction by Anthony Kerrigan. London: Calder & Boyars, 1974.

Ebbinghaus, Hermann. *Über das Gedächtnis: Untersuchungen zur experimentallen Psychologie*. Leipzig: Duncker & Humblot, 1885. Translated by Henry A. Ruger and Clara E. Bussenius as *Memory: A Contribution to Experimental Psychology*, with a new introduction by Ernest R. Hilgard. New York: Dover [1964].

Ferneyhough, Brian. Unpublished interview by Arun Bharali (November 1992).

Ferneyhough, Brian, and James Boros. "Shattering the Vessels of Received Wisdom." *Perspectives of New Music* 28, no. 2 (1990): 6–50.

François, Jean-Charles. *Percussion et musique contemporaine*. Paris: Klincksieck, 1991.

Gould, Stephen Jay. *Ever Since Darwin: Reflections in Natural History*. New York: Norton, 1977.

Griffiths, Paul. Review in *The New York Times*, November 6, 1998.

Philip Guston, Peintures 1947–79. Exhibition Catalogue, Centre Georges Pompidou, October, 2000. Paris: Centre Pompidou, 2000.

Reich, Steve. *Writings about Music*. Halifax, NS: Press of Nova Scotia College of Art and Design; New York: New York University Press, 1974.

———. *Writings on Music, 1965–2000*. Edited with an introduction by Paul Hillier. Oxford University Press, 2002.

Rich, Alan. *American Pioneers: Ives to Cage and Beyond*. London: Phaidon, 1995.

Rose, Steven. *The Making of Memory*. New York: Anchor Books, 1993.

Stockhausen, Karlheinz. *Texte zur Musik*. Edited by Dieter Schnebel. Vol. 2, *Aufsätze 1952–1962 zur musikalischen Praxis* (1964). Cologne: M. DuMont Schauberg, 1963–98.

Whitman, Walt. "I Saw in Louisiana a Live Oak Growing." In *Leaves of Grass*. Boston: Small, Maynard & Company, 1907.

Wright, Frank Lloyd. *In the Cause of Architecture*. Edited by F. Gultheim. Reprinted from *Architectural Record*. New York: McGraw-Hill, 1975.

Yates, Frances A. *The Art of Memory*. New York and London: Routledge, 1999.

Index

In the beginning there was noise. Drumming, the world's most ancient instrumental tradition, re-emerged explosively in the concert music of the twentieth century as music for percussion, involving drums and many other kinds of noisemakers. In the explorations of John Cage, Edgard Varèse, and others, percussion became the *lingua franca* of mid-century modernism. But how does one construct a coherent instrumental tradition when the instrument in question is not an object but a family of thousands of highly individuated objects? How does one apply an inherited musical discourse defined by the limits of the mind and imagination to instruments firmly bedded in the visceral, physical, and bodily? How can a performer embrace the growing range and complexity of percussion music in the early twenty-first century without losing touch with its inherent simplicity, directness, and universality? How can a music built upon a foundation of noise be capable of expressing subtle and diverse emotional states?

The Percussionist's Art: Same Bed, Different Dreams addresses these questions by examining major works from the solo and chamber repertoire for percussion, from Edgard Varèse's *Ionisation* (1931) and Cage's *First Construction (in Metal)* (1939) to Morton Feldman's *The King of Denmark* (1964), Steve Reich's *Drumming* (1971), *Bone Alphabet* by Brian Ferneyhough (1991), and *?Corporel* (1985), a piece by Vinko Globokar for percussionist performing on his or her amplified body. Percussionists demand attention—by the imprudence of hitting, choking, brushing, smashing, and rubbing any and nearly every available sound-producing object—and by echoing those sounds through a vivid world of gesture. This unique semaphore both enacts the music and resonates with the many gestures of real life. Percussion is the mother ship of noise: a righteous place where the bracing sounds that come from "hitting stuff" are the audible manifestations of a sophisticated and vital music.

Steven Schick is the world's leading exponent of solo percussion music involving multiple instruments. He has commissioned more than one hundred pieces from renowned composers including David Lang, Brian Ferneyhough, and Roger Reynolds. He was a founding member of the Bang on a Can All-Stars (1992–2002) and artistic director of the Centre International de Percussion de Genève (Switzerland, 2002–4). He teaches at the University of California, San Diego, where he directs the percussion group "red fish blue fish."

"A thoroughly impressive endeavour by master percussionist Steven Schick, *The Percussionist's Art: Same Bed, Different Dreams* is hugely informative and entertaining. Based entirely on Schick's first-hand experiences as a musician, this book encompasses great insight into some of the great music written for solo percussion. A 'must read' for every breathing musician, *The Percussionist's Art* will also fascinate those curious to know more about the current explosion of interest in the percussion world."

—Dr. Evelyn Glennie, OBE, world-renowned solo percussionist

"This is a really well-written, extremely knowledgeable, and thoroughly enjoyable book. . . . Incredible insights into and analysis of a huge array of important percussion music by one of our finest players. Highly recommended!"

—Steve Reich, innovative composer and author of *Writings on Music (1965–2000)*

"Insightful, informative, imaginative, and inspirational. Steven Schick is the world's master of multiple percussion, and *The Percussionist's Art: Same Bed, Different Dreams* is the definitive source of information on that medium. It is sure to interest percussionists, scholars, and lovers of new music and to become the measurement by which multiple-percussion performance is judged."

—John H. Beck, professor of percussion, Eastman School of Music,
University of Rochester